The Best
FREE
THINGS
for
SENIORS

by Linda & Bob Kalian

Library of Congress Cataloging-in-Publication Data
Kalian, Robert
Kalian, Linda

The Best Free Things For Seniors

ISBN 0-934968-22-5

1. Consumer Reference   2. Catalog Free Things

This book is intended as general consumer information only and does not contain professional advice. The reader is urged to seek out and consult with a lawyer, financial advisor, health care and other professionals.

Quantity discounts are available. Teachers, fund raisers, premium users, write to us at the address below regarding the quantities needed.

Publisher: Roblin Press, P. O. Box 125, Hartsdale, NY 10530   Fax: 914-372-1028
Be sure to visit our web site at: www.freethingsusa.com

Contents

A Few Words Before You Start

When 77 year old astronaut John Glenn made his historic return to space it proved once and for all what Satchel Paige said years ago: *"Age is a question of mind over matter…if you don't mind, it doesn't matter."*

This book is dedicated to the concept that your journey through life can be a ball at any age and especially during your senior years if you maintain a positive attitude and keep your mind and body active, healthy and involved.

We've discovered that no matter what your age, no matter what your financial situation, there are all kinds of special government and private programs to help you enjoy all the best life has to offer. And once you become a senior, it gets better…*much better!* It's true…the best is yet to come!

But to take advantage of all the terrific benefits, you must first know about them. That's why we researched and wrote this book. In it you are about to discover that you are floating in an ocean of free things, exciting programs and amazing discounts that you never knew existed. Simply keep your eyes and ears open and follow these few tips:

1. Use this book as your first and most valuable resource. It is chuck full of great stuff of every kind. Some are in this book to save you money, others will solve problems or bring you benefits. But there are also a ton of fascinating freebies that are here mostly for fun.

2. Always ask one simple question… *"do you offer senior citizen discounts?"* You'll be amazed at how often just by saying those 6 words you will save 10%, sometimes a

lot more, on whatever you are buying. But you must first ask.

3. If you're not a member already, join AARP. It's called the American Association For Retired Persons but it is open to anyone 50 years of age or older, retired or not. By joining you will immediately qualify for special discounts on everything from prescription drugs to car rentals and hotel reservations. The cost? Just $12.50 a year and that even includes your spouse! For that small amount you will be joining the over 32 million members who get all the special membership benefits including a subscription to their magazine, *Modern Maturity*. To join or to get more information, call them toll-free at: **1-800-424-3410**.

4. Keep it simple. No need to write if you can pick up the phone and call. We've included the phone numbers (many are toll-free) throughout the book along with web sites wherever they're available.

5. We've added hundreds of interesting web sites for your use (most but not all start with *www.* standing for World Wide Web). If you have a computer, you now have instant access to the entire world by *'surfing the net'*. The number is growing daily but today an estimated 50% of seniors have a computer. But if you don't yet have one, visit your local library which is almost certain to have computers you can use. You'll be amazed at how easy it is to use and just how much valuable information you can get off of the Internet in no time. It is extremely important to type in the web address correctly and with no spaces. Even a small error will cause the seach to fail.

6. Near the back of the book (in the sections with shaded page edges) we've included a number of important directories you'll find useful in getting answers, solving problems and getting benefits that are coming to you.

So if you need legal help, or dental care or if you have a consumer complaint, or need medications you can't afford, keep in mind that help is often just a phone call away. And if you need assistance and aren't sure exactly who to call for help, start by checking the directory and calling your local *"Office of The Aging"*. It is a great resource for an instant referral to the right agency or department.

7. If a listing calls for a 'SASE' that means that when you write in for your free item, include a long (#10) Self-Addressed Stamped Envelope that you've written your return address on.

8. While we've done our best to put together the most complete and up-to-date information possible, once the book is in print addresses and phone numbers can and will change. Offers may be withdrawn (although in our experience the offers are generally replaced with a new one.) But if you do come across a change or deletion that should be made in the next edition, we would genuinely appreciate it if you would let us know by writing:
   Revisions Editor
   Roblin Press - 06
   P.O. Box 125
   Hartsdale, NY 10530

9. Hope you enjoy the book. If you can think of anything that would make the next edition of the book better or if you have any freebie you think should go in this book, please let us know at the address above. If we use your suggestion or freebie, we'll send you a copy of our next edition...free of course. We want to make this guide better and we appreciate your help.

10. Remember, you worked your tail off all your life. Now it's your turn to enjoy all the very best your golden years have in store for you.

An Ocean Of free Things

Help For Seniors Is Just A Phone Call Away

Imagine how great it would be to be able to pick up the phone and get dozens of services delivered right to your front door! Well guess what? You really can. It's called *Eldercare Locator* and calling this one toll-free phone number will connect you to a wide range of services for seniors no matter where you live in the U.S. These services include Meals-On-Wheels (for home delivered meals), legal assistance, help with housing problems, recreation, adult daycare, home health care services, nursing home ombudsman (to help you get the treatment you deserve) and a whole lot more. Calling this one number allows you to tap into a nationwide network of organizations for seniors in all areas of the country.

Getting the right help at the right time is worth a fortune but it costs you nothing. If you are calling for someone else, just be sure to have the name, address and zip code of the person needing assistance plus a description of the type of service they need. Contact:

ELDERCARE LOCATOR
NATIONAL ASSOCIATION OF AREA
AGENCIES ON AGING
1730 RHODE ISLAND AVE. NW SUITE 1200
WASHINGTON, DC 20036
Call between 9 am and 5 pm Monday through Friday:
1-800-677-1116
If you would like you can also check out the Eldercare Locator on the Internet atat either of these two internet addresses:
www.aoa.dhhs.gov
n4a.org

Free For The Asking Right In Your Back Yard

In your search for the best that life has to offer for free or practically free, the first thing to remember is that there are lots of things all around you that are free for the asking that you might never have thought of. All you have to do is be aware of them and to *ASK*. Here are just a few examples:

Free Long Distance Phone Calls

Because of all the intense competition between phone companies, if you are willing to switch companies they will offer you all kinds of deals from $100.00 checks to several hours of free calls with no obligation to stay with them after you have used up your free long distance calls.

5¢ A Minute On All Long Distance Calls

After you've used your free calls, shop around for the best deal before you sign up with another phone company. Companies like IDT now offer long distance service for as little as 5¢ a minute, 24 hours a day, 7 days a week. Companies like IDT are called 'resellers' since they buy time from long distance companies and resell this time to you at low prices. For more information on their 5¢ a minute plan call IDT at: **1-800-CALL-IDT (THAT'S 1-800-225-5438)**

Free For Using Your Credit Card

The credit card war is heating up...and you stand to benefit. Today more and more banks and companies are offering credit cards that come with added bonuses for using them. For example, some banks offer credit cards that give you one frequent flyer mile for each dollar you charge on their card. You can use the miles to get free airline tickets. Also, many larger chain stores offer you free dollars to spend in their store just for opening a charge account with them. There is no obligation to use the card once you have it and you can cut it up if you don't plan to use it.

Also, remember you really can negotiate with your credit card company to lower the interest they charge and to waive the annual fee. Just be careful of the 'low introductory rate' offered by many banks. They may offer a finance charge of 4.9% for the first 6 months but then the rate could jump up to 15% to 20%. Don't be fooled by the introductory rate. If you shop around you will find rates of 10% or less year round (not just for a limited time.)

Free Haircuts

Did you know that free haircuts are available through many of your local beauty and barber schools? Check your phone book and give them a call. Some may ask a small fee or a tip for the trainee. Some of your larger hair designers may offer free style and cuts certain months or certain times of the year. Call your favorite salon and find out when they are training their students. You benefit by getting the designer him/herself for free. (In their salon they may charge anywhere from $50.00 and up.) Companies like Clairol often offer free hair coloring styling when they are testing new products. Don't hesitate to give any of them a call. Remember, if you don't ask you'll never know.

Want to try free perfume or have a makeover? Try any one of your larger department stores. You are never obligated to buy and some of the companies will even give you free product samples. You could have a ball going from store to store. Next time you need a new look, try your local department store.

Free For Consumers

Supermarket bulletin boards offer free items that neighbors may want to get rid of or trade.

Credit card companies offer free month trials on discount shopping clubs, travel, insurance and offer all kinds of specials. The one thing you have to remember is if you don't want it, after the month is up, cancel it.

You can even get free magazine subscriptions, tapes and CD's just for asking. Always remember to look in your local paper for deals at the supermarkets for *"buy one item, get one free."* On nonperishable items that you will use (like paper towels, soft drinks, canned soups, etc.), stock up when they are on sale.

'Grand' Magnet For 'Grand'parents

"My Grandchild Did This" refrigerator magnet is a perfect addition to include when sending along a child's art work to a grandparent. This will really show off those delightful creations of your grandchildren. Send $1.00 with a long SASE with 2 stamps to:

PRACTICAL PARENTING
DEPT MG BEST
15245 MINNETONKA BLVD.
MINNETONKA, MN 55343
Visit them on the internet at: www.practicalparenting.com

Free Top Soil and Fire Wood

When they excavate a building site, contractors frequently have a problem of what to do with the dirt they remove. Often they will offer free land fill and free top soil to anyone who wants it. The only catch might be that you have to remove it (or pay a nominal delivery charge.) If you have a piece of property that needs top soil or landfill, check out construction sites. Also, you can often get free fire wood when they are clearing the land.

Free Birthday Dinner

Don't forget that there are quite a few restaurants that offer you a free dinner on your birthday. All you have to show is a license or some proof of your birthdate. Check with your favorite restaurants to see if they offer this courtesy.

Also check the ads for local restaurants that offer those great coupons for buy-one dinner get-one free.

Enjoy A Free Concert

Don't overlook all the free concerts and theatre productions in all community parks outdoors especially during the summer months. Check with your local parks and recreation department or your local newspaper.

Many local movie theatres have deals on slow nights. For example, a local movie theatre offers a special on Tuesday nights: Buy one ticket, get one free. Check it out.
If you like concerts and drama some theatre and opera companies offer volunteer ushers free tickets in exchange for their work.

These are just a small handful of the tons of free and practically free offers all around you all the time. The important thing is to keep an eye out for them and take advantage of them where they are of interest to you.

Life Advice

Met Life has a series of educational brochures called *Life Advice*. There are more than 70 topics from doing your taxes, to starting a business or planning for retirement. They all offer you valuable advice. For a specific brochure or for a

listing of all of the topics available, call them at:
1-800-638-5433
Or visit their web site:
http://www.lifeadvice.com.

Trace Your Family Tree

Many diseases run in families. One of the first things a doctor might ask you is for a family tree to see if you may have a predisposition for a particular disease. If you are interested in tracing your family history, the first place to start might be asking your relatives. Next, your local library often has a family history center where you can track your lineage. The family history library of the Church of Latter-day Saints has the largest collection of genealogical records in the world. For the free booklet, *Discovering Your Family Tree,* write to:

FAMILY HISTORY LIBRARY
35 NORTHWEST TEMPLE ST.
SALT LAKE CITY, UT 84150

Another resource for genealogical research is the National Genealogical Society. You can call them toll-free at:
1-800-346-6044

Gifts For Your Grandchildren

If you are a grandparent, just wait until you see the delight on your grandchild's face when he or she opens this package with a surprise gift with a personal note from you. The Grandparents Surprise Gift of the Month Club does all the work. They will send a different gift each month like... books, toys, puzzles, stickers and craft kits. To send the current month's gift, send $3.00 postage & handling and include their name, address, age, gender and your relationship (grandma, grandpa, Nana, Pa Pa, etc). The gift will be sent immediately and you will receive more information on the club. Send to:

SURPRISE GIFT OF THE MONTH CLUB
P.O. BOX 11-S
GARNERVILLE, NY 10923

Consumer Complaints

We've all had this happen to us. You buy a product that turns out to be of inferior quality. When you return it to the store, they refuse to give you a refund or exchange. You leave in frustration and wonder what to do about this problem. Next time you have a serious complaint about a product or service you purchased and aren't sure where to write or who to complain to, get this free brochure and learn more about complaining effectively. For a free copy of *How to Resolve Your Consumer Complaint*, send a long SASE to:

COMPLAINT RESOLUTION
CONSUMER FEDERATION OF AMERICA
1424 16TH ST. N.W.
WASHINGTON, DC 20036

Help For Consumers

For more help in resolving your complaint be sure to get a copy of *The Consumer's Handbook*. It includes a directory of government, nonprofit and corporate consumer complaint assistance sources you can contact. This is something no one should be without. For a copy, include $2.00 for handling and write to:

CONSUMER ACTION HANDBOOK
CONSUMER INFORMATION CENTER
PUEBLO, CO 91009
www.pueblo.gsa.gov

Don't forget that you can also check the *Directory of Consumer Protection Agencies* at the back of this book. In it you will find the phone numbers of your local consumer protection agency. Call the office closest to you and explain your complaint to them.

Consumer Action

If you ever wanted to complain to a company about one of their products but didn't know how to go about it, this is for you. *How To Talk To A Company And Get Action* should help you get your problem solved—fast. You'll also receive the *Story of Coca Cola*. Write to:

CONSUMER INFORMATION CENTER
COCA-COLA CO.
DEPT. FR, P.O. DRAWER 1734
ATLANTA, GA 30301

Consumer Complaint Tip...
Go Right To The Top

Whenever you have a complaint with a larger company, get their phone number and call them directly. If the person you speak to tries to give you the brush off, ask to speak to their supervisor and if you still don't get satisfaction, ask to speak to the supervisor's supervisor all the way up to the top. If none of that works, ask for the name and mailing address of the president of the company, and write him/her a polite letter explaining your complaint in detail. You'll be amazed. Nine times out of ten the president will hand the matter over to someone who will contact you with an offer to resolve the complaint to your satisfaction. Try it...it works!

Book Bargains

Catalog of Book Bargains is for all book lovers that want to save 90% or more off original prices. Some recent best sellers are sold in this 50 page catalog at very sharp discounts. The catalog is free from:

P. DAEDALUS BOOKS INC.
9645 GERWIG LANE
COLUMBIA, MD 21046
OR CALL: 1-800-395-2665
www.salebooks.com

Get Rich At Home

Have you ever dreamed of starting your own business from your home? If so you will want to get the *Mail Order Success*

Secrets report. Learn how to start your own successful business in your spare time with little money and grow rich in the most exciting business in the world. Send a SASE to:
ROBLIN-BSR03
PO BOX 125
HARTSDALE, NY 10530

"The Good Life Catalog"

If you're a cigar smoker or know someone who is, this catalog is a must. Not only will you find every cigar you can think of, but all the accessories that go with them. There is a *Cigar Hall of Fame* and even some unusual and interesting gifts for people who don't smoke. Drop a postcard to:
THE THOMPSON COMPANY
5401 HANGAR COURT
P.O. BOX 30303
TAMPA, FL 33630-3303
1-800-216-7107
www.thompsoncigar.com

Surprise Gift Club

We've all faced the problem of what to give someone as a gift. Finally there's help. The Surprise Gift of the Month Club has developed an innovative solution. They offer you a broad selection of items from kites, iron-ons, coasters, stickers, and records to crewel and needlepoint kits plus many more items to select from. Anyone young or old will be delighted to receive a surprise gift each month. It's a beautiful way to say "I'm thinking of you" to someone special. For a sample of the assorted crewel and needlepoint kits, send $1.00 for postage and handling to:
SURPRISE GIFT OF THE MONTH CLUB
PO BOX 11
GARNERVILLE, NY 10923
www.myfree.com

Go On A Learning Vacation With Elderhostel

Elderhostel offers moderately priced learning vacations across the United States and Canada as well as 70 nations abroad for senior citizens who enjoy adventure and travel but who have a limited amount of money to spend. The subjects taught on these vacations range from astronomy, to zoology. For a catalog of courses and travel itineraries, or to be added to their mailing list, contact:

ELDERHOSTEL
11 AVENUE de LAFAYETTE
BOSTON, MA. 02111
OR CALL TOLL-FREE: 1-877-426-8056
WWW.ELDERHOSTEL.ORG

House Of Onyx

If you like gems and gemstones...whether in the rough or finished into fine jewelry or artifacts, this catalog is for you. You will find some fabulous closeout buys on some fantastic gemstones, geodes even Mexican onyx and malachite carvings. If you are just a collector or need some great gifts, send for this catalog. Write to:

HOUSE OF ONYX
THE AARON BUILDING
120 MAIN ST.
GREENVILLE, KY 42345
1-800-844-3100
www.houseofonyx.com

What To Look For In A Gem

Buying a valuable gem can be a tricky affair unless you are prepared. Have you ever wondered what makes one diamond more valuable than another that may look the same to the naked eye? Before buying any gemstone it is essential to learn exactly what to look for. For example do you know the 4 'C's' that determine a diamond's value? They are... Cut...

Color... Clarity... Carat (weight). To learn more about what to look for when buying a diamond, send for a free consumer kit from the American Gem Society. Send a long SASE to:
THE AMERICAN GEM SOCIETY
8881 W. SAHARA AVE.
LAS VEGAS, NV 89117
www.ags.org

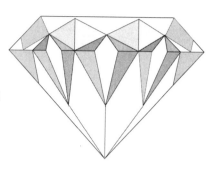

Sleep Tight

A healthful good night's sleep makes for a very productive, pleasant person. Learn all the facts on how to get a healthful sleep, by selecting the right bedding pillows and positions. The makers of Simmons will send you this free book, *Consumer Guide To Better Sleep,* plus several others including *It's Never Too Early To Start Caring For Your Back* and tips for shopping for the right bed. To get your copy, send a business-sized SASE to:
SIMMONS BEAUTYREST
ONE CONCOURSE CENTER, SUITE 600
BOX C-93
ATLANTA, GA 30328
www.simmonsco.com

Planning To Buy A Home?

If you are thinking of buying a home any time in the near future, there are certain things you should do to protect yourself. For example, before buying a home, it is a good idea to hire a trained inspector to check for defects you might not see such as termites or a roof in need of repair. But first be sure to get a free copy of *Top Ten Home Inspection and Buying Tips* from the American Homeowners Foundation. Call them toll-free at:
1-800-489-7776
www.americanhomeowners.org

Money Saving Tips

The publishers of *Frulgal Mom* newsletter would like to send a sample issue. It's loaded with information in the form of a newsletter with handy, easy-to-understand tips, on the all important topics of saving both time and money. You'll also find an assortment of quick and easy recipe ideas. For your free newsletter visit *Frugal Mom Weekly Newsletter* on the internet at:

WWW.THEFAMILYCORNER.COM

Love Letter Newsletter

Love guru, Greg Godek, author of the bestselling book, *1001 Ways To Be More Romantic*, would like to give you a free one year subscription to *LoveLetter Newsletter*, chuck full of great romantic ideas. Put the spark back in your love life. Call Casablanca Press at:

1-800-43-BRIGHT
Or visit their web site: www.sourcebooks.com

Before You Buy A Wig

For the best prices on the finest wigs, send for your *free catalog*. You will be amazed at the beautiful selection of wigs from Revlon, Adolfo and many more. So if you are in the market for a wig, write to:

BEAUTY TREND
PO BOX 9323, DEPT. 44002
HIALEAH, FL 33014.

Easy Reading

This freebie is for adults whose reading levels is grade 4 to 6, and is a great way to help improve their reading skills.

Each issue contains articles covering important international news as well as features on education, health, leisure, law, and more in a format that is easy to read and understand. To get a free sample, ask for a sample copy of *News For You.* Write to:

**NEW READERS PRESS
PO BOX 35888
SYRACUSE, NY 13235
1-800-448-8878**
WWW.NEWREADERSPRESS.COM

Keeping Your Home Healthy

To help make housework easier and less time consuming, Bounty has developed their new Rinse & Reuse paper towel that keeps its strength when wet allowing you to reuse the towel. You'll receive a sample plus the booklet, *The New Rules of Cleaning* with cleaning tips. Just call:

1-800-9-BOUNTY
WWW.BOUNTY.COM

Shop Easy

Do you like to relax and shop at home? If so, be sure to get a copy of Lillian Vernon's *free catalog.* You'll find that it's full of affordable treasures from around the world. Drop a post-card to:

**LILLIAN VERNON
1-800-545-5426**
OR VISIT THEM ON THE WEB AT:
www.lillianvernon.com

CLASSIC GIFTS

Harriet Carter has provided distinctive gifts since 1958. This fun-filled catalog is chuck-full of unique gifts you will find fascinating. Write to:

**HARRIET CARTER
425 STUMP RD
NORTH WALES, PA 19454
Or visit thgem on the web at: www.harrietcarter.com**

GET THAT BUG

The makers of Raid bug sprays would like you to have a highly informative chart, *Raid Insecticides - What to Use For Effective Control.* Learn how to deal with crawling, flying and biting pests both inside and outside your home (including plant pests). You'll also receive a money-saving coupon. Send a postcard to:

"INSECT CONTROL"
S C JOHNSON
1525 HOWE STREET
RACINE, WI 53403-5011
1-800-494-4855
www.johnsonwax.com

Free Art Films

To help bring art appreciation to a wider audience, The National Gallery of Art would like to send you a video without charge. They have dozens of videos and slide programs to lend to individuals, community groups and schools. Your only obligation is to pay the postage when sending the video back. For a complete *catalog and reservation card* send a card to:

NATIONAL GALLERY OF ART
EXTENSION PROGRAM
WASHINGTON, DC 20565
www.nga.gov

Free Tickets To TV Shows

The TV networks will provide you with free tickets to any of their shows that have audiences. If you plan to be in Los Angeles or New York and would like to see a TV show write to the network (care of their 'Ticket Department') before your visit. Generally you will get a letter you can exchange for tickets for any show open at the time of your visit. Write to:

ABC, 320 WEST 66 ST.
NEW YORK, NY 10023.
IN LOS ANGELES: CALL 818-753-3470 EXT. 214.
PARAMOUNT GUEST RELATIONS 323-956-1777, OR ON THE WEB:

www.paramount.com Then Click on "studio."

CBS Ticket Div.
Television City
7800 Beverly Blvd.
Los Angeles, CA 90036
In New York
524 W. 57 St.
New York, NY 10019

NBC
3000 West Alameda Ave.
Burbank, CA 91523
(or 30 Rockefeller Plaza, New York, NY 10112)
Or go to their web site at: **www.nbc.com**

Oprah
In Chicago: call **312-591-9222** or visit them on the
web at: WWW.OPRAH.COM
Check out these useful
websites:
WWW.ABC.GO.COM
WWW.NBCI.COM
WWW.NYTIX.COM

Ships And The Sea

This 100 page *catalog is* full of decorative nautical ideas for the home. If you're looking for a ship model, marine painting or ship's wheel you'll find it here. Drop a postcard to:
S. T. Preston & Son
Main St. Wharf
Greenport, NY 11944
1-800-836-1165
www.prestons.com

Free For Chapped Lip Sufferers

If you suffer from dry chapped lips or mouth sores, this is especially for you. You will receive sample packets of *Blistex*

Lip Ointment plus two informative brochures and a *money-off* coupon too. Visit them on the web at:
www.blistex.com

For The Larger-Sized Or Taller Woman

Lane Bryant offers a stunning collection of dresses, coats, jeans, sportswear, lingerie and shoes for the woman who wears half size or large size apparel. You'll find name brands and designer fashions in their free *catalog*. If you are 5'7" or taller also ask for their *Woman Within catalog. Call* Lane Bryant at:
1-800-677-0216
Or visit their web site:
www.LBcatalog.com

Are You Milk Sensitive?

If you are allergic to milk you will want to get a copy of 'Ross's Materials Catalog' designed specifically for those with a lactose intolerance. Write to:
Ross Products
625 Cleveland Ave.
Columbus, OH 43215
1-800-986-8510
www.similac.com

Your Own Flag Flying Over The U.S. Capitol

Your Congressman will provide a unique service for you free of charge. If you'd like to have your own flag flown over the U.S. Capitol Building write to your congressman. The flag itself is not free (prices range from $16.00 to $31.00 depending upon size and material) but the service of having the flag purchased, flown and sent to you is free. This also makes a unique gift for someone special. Write to your own Congressman at:

U. S. HOUSE OF REPRESENTITIVES
WASHINGTON, DC 20515

or

U.S. SENATE
WASHINGTON, DC 20510

Pay A Visit to Congress ... Online

If you would like to find out more about how your country is run, be sure to visit the U.S. Congress... on the internet. The Senate and The House of Representitives each has a web site that is chuck full of both historical and current information. For example, you can find a summary of debates in progress on the floor of the House. On these sites you will find a directory of all congressmen listed both by state and by name and discover which congressman voted "yea" or "nay" on any bill of interest to you.

Go to: www.senate.gov or to: **www.house.gov**

How To Buy Life Insurance

Buying the right amount and the right type of life insurance is one of the important decisions you must make. Before you make any decision, be sure to get your copy of *How To Choose A Life Insurance Company*. To get your copy of this informative booklet, simply send a postcard to:

OCCIDENTAL LIFE
BOX 2101 TERMINAL ANNEX
LOS ANGELES, CA 90051

You'll Save A Lot Of Dollars With These Great Scents

If you love all those expensive perfumes and colognes advertised on TV, radio and magazines but hate those high prices, this is a must for you. This company makes an affordable

line of perfumes and colognes that are almost identical to brands costing as much as ten times as much money. For your free list and scented cards, send a postcard to:
ESSENTIAL PRODUCTS CO. INC.
90 WATER ST.
NEW YORK, NY 10005

Soft And Warm

You know how terrific it feels to have something super soft gently touching your body. If this sounds appealing to you, check this one out. The Company Store offers a superior blend of hand selected white goose and duck down feather comforters, pillows or outerwear. Send a postcard and ask for their *free catalog* to:
THE COMPANY STORE
500 COMPANY STORE ROAD
LA GROSSE, WI 54601
1-800-285-DOWN
www.thecompanystore.com

Words of Wisdom

If you need words of encouragement to keep going in the face of adversity and failure (and who doesn't), *Portrait of An Achiever* will make an inspirational addition to your home. It tells of how one famous man (we'll keep his name a secret) turned a lifetime of failures into one overwhelming success. This beautiful parchment reproduction is suitable for framing and makes an excellent gift. Send $1.00 s&h to:
ROBLIN PRESS
PO BOX 125 - POA
HARTSDALE, NY 10530

Preserve Our History

If you'd like to participate in the preservation of sites, buildings and objects that are important to American history and culture, there is something you can do. Drop a card asking

for the *Historic Preservation package* to:
NATIONAL TRUST FOR HISTORIC PRESERVATION
1785 MASSACHUSETTS AVE. N.W.
WASHINGTON, DC 20036
www.nationaltrust.org

Cure For Bad Breath Is Here

If you are plagued with bad breath these great *Fresh Breath Capsules* will help you cure your bad breath right where it actually starts...in your stomach. Don't worry...the next time you eat garlic or spicy food, pop one of these Breath Fresh capsules. They also have other great products like Retinol A, Ultramins plus Vitamins and Thigh Cream. To try the Breath Freshener, send $1.00 to cover postage and handling to:
21ST CENTURY GROUP
10 CHESTNUT STREET
SPRING VALLEY, NY 10877

Mail Order Buying

When you buy by mail do you know your rights? Here's a practical and informative guide detailing the protection you have under the F.T.C.'s Mail Order Merchandise Rule. A free copy of *Shopping By Phone & Mail* is yours by writing to:
CONSUMER RESPONSE CENTER
FEDERAL TRADE COMMISSION
600 PENNSYLVANIA AVE NW ROOM H-130
WASHINGTON, DC 20580
WWW.FTC.ORG

Flags Of All Kinds

If you are looking for a U.S. or state flag, poles and accessories, custom designs, historic, patriotic or nautical, this company has them all. Visit their web site:
www.qualityflags.com

Free Gift From The President

Can you imagine how exciting it would be to get a letter from the President of the United States! The President will send a signed letter embossed with the Presidential seal to any couple celebrating their 50th anniversary (or beyond) or to any citizen celebrating their 80th (or subsequent) birthday. At the other end of the spectrum, the President will also send a congratulatory card to any newborn child. If you'd like, you can also have the card sent to you so you can frame it and give it as a great one-of-a-kind gift! Send or fax your requests at least 6 weeks in advance to:

THE GREETINGS OFFICE
THE WHITE HOUSE
1600 PENNSYLVANIA AVE. NW
WASHINGTON, DC 20502
FAX: 1-202-395-1232
www.whitehouse.gov/greeting

Free Photo Of The President

How would you like a full color autographed photo of the President and First Lady? To get your photo simply request it by mail or fax from:

WHITE HOUSE GREETING OFFICE
THE WHITE HOUSE
1600 PENNSYLVANIA AVE. NW
WASHINGTON, DC 20502
FAX: 1-202-395-1232

Free From The White House

The President would like you to have a beautiful full color book, *The White House, The House of The People*. It features a room-by-room photo tour and history of the White House. For your free copy write to:

THE WHITE HOUSE
1600 PENNSYLVANIA AVE. NW
WASHINGTON, DC 20502
FAX #: 1-202-395-1232

The President Requests Your Opinion

Yes, your opinion really does count. That's one of the great things about our country. And whether you agree or disagree with his policies, the President would like to hear what you have to say. In fact there's a phone number you can call that will connects right into the White House where you you will be asked to express your opinion on the subject that concerns you most. So if you always wanted to give them a piece of your mind, now you can just be calling...
1-202-456-1111

Are You Planning A Move?

If you are planning to move soon, be sure all of your important mail gets to your new home. To do that you will need to send out a notification to everyone you want to have your new address. To help you do that be sure to get your free *Address Express Kit* from State Farm Insurance. Call them toll-free at:
1-800-MOVE-299

Once You've Decided To Move

How To Stretch Your Moving Budget - The Interstate Moving Guide is a useful pamphlet that will help you make your interstate move run smoothly. It tells you how to prepare for moving day, how moving costs are calculated, a glossary of moving terms and lots more. It's yours free from:

ATLAS VAN LINES
1212 ST. GEORGE RD.
EVANSVILLE, IN 47711
1-800-252-8885
www.atlasworldgroup.com

A Moving Experience

To help you with your next move United Van Lines has set up a toll free number you can call. Their local offices are set up to answer any specific questions you may have. For example, your local office can find answers to your questions about employment, educational facilities, housing, and more, in 7,000 cities and towns throughout the 50 states (and foreign countries too). They can also provide you with guides which make preplanning a lot easier and they'll give you the local phone number of the United Van Lines nearest you. Call:

1-877-317-4636
OR VISIT UNITED VAN LINES' WEB SITE:
WWW.UNITEDVANLINES.COM

Free Moving Kit

Mayflower has a nice packet of moving materials free for the asking. It includes labels to mark your boxes with plus tips to make your move run smoother and faster. Ask for your *Moving Kit* from your local Mayflower mover or send a postcard to:

MAYFLOWER TRANSIT
1 MAYFLOWER DR
FENTON, MO 63026
www.mayflowertransit.com

Free Trout To Stock Your Lake

If you would like to restock your lake or pond, contact the Federal Hatcheries first. They offer free assistance in your restocking plans. If their production is sufficient, they may be able to supply the trout you need. They also have an interesting booklet you might want, *Endangered & Threatened Wildlife and Plants*. Write to:
U.S. DEPARTMENT OF THE INTERIOR
FISH & WILDLIFE SERVICE
WASHINGTON, DC 20240

Getting Rid Of Facial Hair

If you're a woman bothered by unsightly facial hair, you'll want to call the Nudit Hotline. Nudit allows women to discuss with experts the sensitive issue of hair removal treatments. Visit their web site at:
www.nudit.com

Free Home Economics Classes And Lots More

You may not even be aware of it but your local cooperative extension office offers an amazing range of free information and services to all who request them. Free cooking classes, home and garden seminars, soil analysis, 4-H information, home economics classes and money-management workshops are just a few of the services available. To find your local Cooperative Extension Service or Agricultural Extension Office, just check the Blue pages of your local phone book. Call the one in your state and they will tell you exactly what services they offer and will give you the address and phone number of their office closest to you.

Free Help Writing A Will

Another little known service offered by many Extension offices is free help in writing your will. Often they will have will forms and pamphlets as well as an instructor to help you write that will. Check the Extension offices in the blue pages of your phone book.

Raising Your Grandkids

If you are in the position of raising your grandchilden, you will want to get this free newsletter. Called *Parenting Grandchildren, A Voice For Grandparents* it is chuck full of useful information. Write to:

AARP GRANDPARENT INFO CENTER
601 EAST STREET NW
WASHINGTON, DC 20049
www.igrandparents.com

Free Medical Care & Health Information

Free Prescription Drugs

Yes it's true there are actually free prescription drugs available to those who can not afford them. Most people are not aware of the fact that drug manufacturers have programs that provide drugs to those who need them but do not have the money or insurance coverage to pay for them.

You may be suffering from cancer, a heart ailment or some other disease that requires a medication that's an essential part of your treatment, but one you cannot afford to pay for. Through these special indigent programs, drug companies will supply the medication free of charge directly to your pharmacy or to your doctor (if he must administer it).

Your first step is to tell your doctor that you will not be able to afford the medicines needed. Next ask him if he has any information on the *'indigent patient drug program'* for the medication you need. Suprisingly a lot of doctors don't even know these programs exist.

Since the majority of doctors will not have information on the program you need, in the back of this book you will find a *Directory of Free Prescription Programs* with full information on the drugs covered, who is eligible for the program and how to contact the pharmaceutical company.

Also, many states have programs that will provide prescripton drugs to you for as little as $1.00 or even free. Check the *State Pharmaceutical Pro-*

grams Directory in the back of this book.

Another place to check is the Pharmaceutical Manufacturers Association. They have up-to-date information on the various drug manufacturer's patient programs. Contact PMA at:

1-800-PMA-INFO (THAT'S 1-800-762-4636)
OR YOU CAN ACCESS THIS INFORMATION ON THE INTERNET AT
www.phrma.org

Striking Back At Strokes

There's great news in the battle against strokes! Modern medical treatments have reduced the death rate from strokes by 50% in the last 25 years.

Many doctors now feel that by taking a small dose of aspirin daily, controlling high blood pressure and practicing more healthy nutrition and exercise programs, we can reduce the health threat from stokes even more. To find out what you can do to avoid a stroke, Preventing Strokes is a one publication you will want to get. To get your free copy contact:

NATIONAL INSTITUTE OF NEUROLOGICAL DISORDERS & STROKES
PO Box 5801
BETHESDA, MD 20824
OR CALL TOLL-FREE: **1-800-352-9424**
Or visit them on the Internet at:
www.ninds.nih.gov

Free Hospital Care

If you don't have insurance coverage, even a very brief hospital stay can easily cost you tens of thousands of dollars and put you on the edge of bankruptcy. Fortunately now there is something you can do. If you need hospital care but can not afford it and have no insurance or if you already been in the hospital and can't afford to pay the bill, try calling the Hill-Burton Hotline. With this program over 1,000 participating hospitals and other health facilities provide free or low-cost medical care to patients who can't afford to pay.

You can qualify for this program even if your income is double the poverty income guidelines and even if the bill has already been turned over to a collection agency. For more information, call the Hill-Burton Hotline at: **1-800-638-0742** and leave your name and phone number. Or visit them on the internet: **www.hrsa.gov/osp/dfcr/about/aboutdiv.htm**

Controlling Chronic Headaches

If you suffer from migraine or chronic headaches, you'll definitely want to get this *Headache Information Package.* You will learn about the latest research, new drug treatments, biofeedback and lots more. In the package you will find articles, reports and resources for headache suffers. To get your free package, contact:

NATIONAL HEADACHE FOUNDATION
PO Box 5801
BETHESDA, **MD 20824**
OR CALL TOLL-FREE: **1-800-352-9424**
Or visit them on the Internet at:
www.headaches.org

Free Medical Care

How would you like to have the finest medical care money can buy...and not spend a cent for it? That's exactly what thousands of people are doing every year thanks to the National Institutes of Health Clinical Center. The NIH is funded by the federal government and is one of the nation's leading medical research centers.

At any one time they have as many as 900 programs under way in dozens of hospitals throughout the country studying the newest procedures in the treatment of every imaginable disease including all types of cancer, heart disease, and Alzheimer's to mention just a few.

And if your condition is one that is being studied you may qualify for free medical care at their 540 bed hospital in

Bethesda, Maryland. To find out about their ongoing research projects and clinical trials and whether you qualify for treatment, call their toll-free hotline:
1-800-411-1222
NATIONAL INSTITUTES OF HEALTH CLINICAL CENTER
6100 EXECUTIVE BLVD. SUITE 3C01, MSC7511
BETHESDA, **MD 20892**
www.cc.nih.gov

Free Eye Care

One of the key ingredients to enjoying a good quality of life is having good eye sight. This means taking care of eye problems like cataracts and glaucoma before they ruin your eye sight.

Your first step is to find out just what you can do to keep your eyes healthy. The National Eye Institute has a number of informative publications you will want to have. They will tell you about various eye diseases and what you can do about them. For a complete list of booklets available, contact:
NATIONAL EYE INSTITUTE
INFORMATION OFFICE
31 CENTER DRIVE, MSC-2510
BETHESDA, **MD 20892**
301-496-5248
www.nei.nih.gov

Next, check the community service pages of your local newspaper for announcements that organizations such as the Kiwanis or Lions Clubs are offering free eye glasses and eye exams to elderly people who can not easily afford to pay for them.

Finally, check with your local Office of the Aging (see the directory in the back of this book). There are a wide variety of eye care programs that are offered that include free eye exams and free eye glasses.

Choosing the Right Nursing Home

What should you do if a loved one needs the continuing care they can only get in a nursing home? What can you do to insure they get the proper care? How do you know how good a particular nursing home is? Your first step would be to get *A Guide To Choosing A Nursing Home*. In this great guide you'll find a step-by-step approach to evaluating and choosing the right nursing home. It's available free from the Medicare Hotline:

1-800-638-6833
www.medicare.gov

Free Health Care For Both You And Your Pet

Remember, if you live near a university that has a medical, dental and even veterinary school, they very often offer all kinds of medical, dental or veterinary services for free or for just a nominal charge. Just give them a call and ask.

Extend Your Life

The Life Extension Foundation is committed to helping people who are well, live longer and healthier lives. They publish an excellent magazine, *Life Extension,* that will keep you informed and up-to-date on all the new advances in how certain vitamins and nutrients keep our minds alert and our bodies healthy and strong.

Life Extension is a magazine that carries 'insider' reports on revolutionary research projects that might one day extend the healthy human life-span to 150 and beyond! They will send you a copy of *Life Extension* magazine along with information on how to become a member. So if you think it might be fun to live for a century and a half, write to:

LIFE EXTENSION FOUNDATION
1100 WEST COMMERCIAL BLVD.
FT. LAUDERDALE, FL 33309
1-800-544-4440
www.lef.org

Healthy Golden Years

Being a senior can sometimes bring with it special problems that can be easily solved if you have the right kind of information. And to bring this important information to you, The National Institute on Aging can help you in several ways. First, they act as a referral agency which means that if you have a problem they don't handle, they will refer you to the agency that can provide you with the help you need (usually with a toll-free phone number.) Next, their Internet 'Age Pages' offers valuable information on diseases, disorders and conditions. They also have a series of booklets you will find extremely useful. Some of the most popular ones are: *Aging and Alcohol Abuse, Dealing with Diabetes, Forgetfulness: It's Not What You Think, Osteoporosis: the Silent Bone Thinner, Stroke: Prevention and Treatment, Urinary Incontinence.* Their brochures will help you with questions you may have regarding medical care, medications, safety, even health promotion and disease prevention...all the topics that are important to every senior. They also have a long list of free booklets available in print or online. To get a copy of any booklet that interest you, contact them at:

NATIONAL INSTITUTE ON AGING
BUILDING 31 ROOM 5C27
31 CENTER DRIVE MSC2292

BETHESDA, **MD 20892**
Or call their toll-free order line:
1-800-222-2225
Or you can visit their Web site at:
www.nih.gov/nia
and click 'Health Information.'

Here's a partial list of the booklets and reports you can get:
• *Alcohol Abuse*

- *Aging and Your Eyes*
- *Arthritis Advice*
- *Crime and the Elderly*
- *Constipation*
- *Don't Take It-Exercise!*
- *Foot Care*
- *Health Quackery*
- *Hearing and Older People*
- *High Blood Pressure: A Common But Controllable Disorder*
- *Hypothermia: A Hot Weather Hazard for Older People*
- *Life Extension: Science or Science Fiction?*
- *Medicines: Use Them Safely*
- *Pills, Patches, and Shots: Can Hormones Prevent Aging?*
- *Pneumonia Prevention: It's Worth A Shot*
- *Sexuality in Later Life*
- *Shots for Safety*
- *Skin Care and Aging*
- *Taking Care of Your Teeth and Mouth*
- *What To Do About Flu*

Alzheimer's Disease Helpline

If someone you love has been diagnosed with Alzheimer's disease, there is a toll-free hotline you can call for information. It's called the Alzheimer's Disease Education and Referral Center and they will be happy to send you a several helpful publications such as the *Forgetfulness* booklet and the *Alzheimer's Disease Fact Sheet*. Call them at:
1-800-438-4380
Or visit them on the Internet at:
www.alzheimers.org

Healthy Smiles

Colgate Total wants you to have shiny healthy teeth and

gums. They'd like to send you information on how their formula works even after you stop brushing... fighting plaque, gingivitis, and cavities. You can call them toll free at:
1-800-763-0246
You can also visit Colgate's World of Healthy Smiles Website:
www.colgate.com.

Seniors Health Care & More

The *Education Center: Well-Being Newsletter* is an enjoyable and informative online guide from Cigna Health Care. At this site you'll find a variety of useful health and wellness articles from the Cigna's Well-Being online newsletter. Recent articles deal with proper nutrition, talk about retirement issues, physical and mental fitness, medical conditions and what to do when accidents happen....to mention just a few. Also discover the effects volunteering, working and playing has on seniors and their communities. To check out this site, just visit Cigna's web site at:
http://www.cigna.com/consumer/education/newsletter

How To Check Yourself For Thyroid Disease

The American Association of Clinical Endocrinologists would like you to stick your neck out a little. They've developed a new self-test for thyroid diseases, including cancer. It's as easy as drinking a glass of water, if you know what to look for. If you should notice a bulge or lumpiness below your Adam's apple as you swallow, it's a warning sign to see your doctor. Just be sure you're not confusing your Adam's apple with a bulge. For a free copy of *The Thyroid Neck Check*, send a SASE to:

THE AMERICAN ASSOCIATION OF ENDOCRINOLOGISTS
1000 RIVERSIDE AVE. SUITE 205
JACKSONVILLE, FL 32204
www.aace.com

Medicare Supplemental Insurance

Health insurance today is an absolute must for everyone, no matter what age they are. It becomes more confusing when you have to deal with all the questions involved with HMO's and their coverage. If that wasn't enough, you reach retirement age and realize that Medicare doesn't cover all your needs. You discover that you must supplement your Medicare insurance and the options become overwhelming. Every company has a different idea about how you should supplement your health plan. To help you decide what is best for you, the Health Insurance of America puts out a very informative 29 page book that answers questions regarding Medicare Supplemental insurance. It even includes an extensive list of where to find more information in your area. Ask for your free *Medicare Supplemental Insurance Guide.* Call:

1-800-MEDICARE

Do You Have Trouble Sleeping?

Did you know that 88% of all Americans suffer from some form of sleep disruption. To learn more about sleep, sleep disorders, and drowsy driving, visit the National Sleep Foundation Web site at:

www.sleepfoundation.org.

Or send long self addressed envelope with 2 stamps to:

THE NATIONAL SLEEP FOUNDATION
1522 K STREET NW SUITE 500
WASHINGTON, DC 20005

Dry Mouth Relief

If you suffer from dry mouth due to radiation therapy or age related problems, you'll want to try Salivart. Salivart is an easy spray application of synthetic saliva that will quickly add moisture to your mouth. For a spray can of Salivart, order online at:

www.gebauerco.com
Or call: **800-321-9348**

Nasal Moist Gel

Do you suffer from dry crusted inflamed nasal membranes, and have trouble breathing freely every day and every night? Now there may be a solution to your discomfort...Nasal Moist Gel from Blairex. For samples of this gel, send $1.00 postage and handling to:

Blairex Labs
PO Box 2127
Columbus, IN 47202-2127
1-800-252-4739
www.blairex.com

Daily's Food Supplement Sample

Many health professionals feel that taking antioxidants food supplements may help you avoid certain diseases. Now you can receive an informative chart of the antioxidants considered to be most important, their benefits and their natural dietary sources. You'll also receive a sample of Daily's One-A-Day tablets. Write to:

Daily's Food Supplement
4360 View Ridge
San Diego, CA 92123

Lower Your Cholesterol

Cholesterol is a natural fat-like substance that the body needs to function properly. Unfortunately some people's bodies produce too much of the wrong type of cholesterol. This can lead to clogging of the arteries and can put you at risk of a heart attack. To find out what you can do to bring your 'bad' cholesterol to more moderate levels, write for the booklet, *High Blood Cholesterol*. It's yours free from:

National Cholesterol Education Program

NHLBI Information Center
PO Box 30105
Bethesda, MD 20824
www.nhlbi.nih.gov

Cholesterol & High Blood Pressure Help

The National Heart, Lung and Blood Institute has a toll-free number you can call for helpful tips on lowering your cholesterol level and reducing your high blood pressure. In addition to recorded tips, you can also leave your name and address for printed booklets on these important life extending subjects. Call:
1-800-575-WELL

Taking Care of Your Feet

How many times have you ignored an ingrown toenail until you couldn't stand the pain anymore? Did you ever stub or injure your toe and find that it swells up like a balloon? Do you wear the wrong kind of shoes just because they look good? The American Orthopedic Foot and Ankle Society has some great information for you that will turn your sore feet into dancing feet. To get your free copy of *The Adult Foot*, just send a long SASE to:
American Orthopedic Foot and Ankle Society
2517 East Lake Ave. East
Seattle, **WA 98102**
www.aofas.org

Put Your Best Foot Forward

When your feet ache and you are looking for some kind of relief, what can you do? For answers to that question and for help with your aching feet, The Podiatric Association of America has a toll-free number you can call to get assis-

tance. Call them at:
1-800-FOOT-CARE
www.apma.org

Free Health Guide

If you are concerned about nonprescription drugs and what effect they may be having upon you, be sure to get a copy of *Nonprescription Medicines: What's Right For You?* It's yours free from:
CONSUMER INFORMATION
DEPT 556D
PUEBLO, **CO 81009**
1-800-688-9889
www.pueblo.gsa.gov

Family Emergency Handbook

Did you ever wonder what you would do if an emergency suddenly arose? The best way to deal with an unexpected emergency is to be prepared. And to help you and your family be prepared for a wide range of emergency situations, there's a terrific 200 page handbook. In it you will find all kinds of life saving procedures and ways of dealing with emergency situations. This handbook is a must for every household. To get your copy, send $1.00 for shipping and handling to:
THE SURPRISE GIFT OF THE MONTH CLUB
EMERGENCY HANDBOOK
PO BOX 11 SRS
GARNERVILLE, **NY 10923**

"Glide Floss"

How many times have you started to floss your teeth when the floss sticks between your teeth and half of it shreds and the rest is stuck there. The makers of *Glide Floss* have made flossing easier with their new patented fiber technology. It's

easy to use, slides easily between teeth without shredding and is clinically proven to remove plaque. Call for your free sample:
1-800-645-4337
Or check them out on the web:
www.glidefloss.com.

Keeping Your Lungs Healthy

Do you know what the warning signs of lung disease are or what to do if you have emphysema? Are you aware of the common hazards around us in our everyday environment that affect our lungs? Would you like helpful hints on quitting smoking? For answers to these questions and lots more, The American Lung Association has a number of booklets you will find useful. To find out more about lung related problems and solutions, call The American Lung Association at:
1-800-LUNG-USA
WWW.LUNGUSA.ORG

Help For Stutterers

If you stutter or know anyone who has a stuttering problem, you are not alone. The Internet has some excellent sites you might want to check out.
National Stuttering Project at:
www.nsastutter.org
The site includes essays about stuttering, contacts for local support groups, information on upcoming workshops and links to related sites.

The Stuttering Foundation of America at;
www.stuttersfa.org
Helpful information on stuttering, lists of upcoming workshops and referrals to speech pathologists and clinics. The nonprofit group can also be reached at:
1-800-364-1677

Free Remedy Magazine

With the rapid breakthroughs in medicine today, it's hard to stay on top of it all. One way of doing that is to get a free two year subscription to *Remedy Magazine, Prescriptions For A Healthy Life*. In each issue you will find useful information like medically proven ways to lower your blood pressure, what the lowdown on salt really is, are there really vaccines that can keep you from getting cancer, arthritis, diabetes and multiple sclerosis? To get your free subscription all you need to do is fill out and return a simple health survey. Write to
REMEDY MAGAZINE
SUBSCRIPTION DEPT.
120 POST ROAD WEST
WESTPORT, CT 06880
Also visit their web site at:
www.remedyonline.com

Keep Yourself Cancer Free

The American Institute For Cancer Research has tons of valuable information available for those suffering from cancer and for those who want to keep themselves cancer-free. If you already have cancer, you'll want to learn more about how to maintain a healthy diet while fighting your illness. You'll also want to receive information on how you can help prevent certain cancers by living a healthy lifestyle, through exercise and by following a well balanced diet. These booklets are free, but if you want to help further the research and education on the link between diet and cancer, a small donation would be greatly appreciated. Write to:
AMERICAN INSTITUTE FOR CANCER
RESEARCH
1759 R STREET N.W.
PO BOX 97167
WASHINGTON, DC 20090-7167
www.aicr.org

Breast Cancer Support

Y-ME Breast Cancer Support Program was created in 1978 by Ann Marcou and Mimi Kaplan, who turned their own difficult experience into a positive network of volunteers that provides counseling and information to thousands of women suffering from breast cancer. For a free copy of *Y-ME Hotline* newsletter write to:

Y-ME
212 W. Van Buren
Chicago IL 60607
You may also call their 24 hour support hotline:
1-800-221-2141
Or visit their Internet site at:
www.y-me.org

Get Rid Of Heartburn Before It Starts

Do you suffer from the agony of heartburn or other acid distress because of the acid in the foods you eat? Now you can enjoy all those spicy foods without having to worry about chewing antacids. *Prelief* is not a drug but a dietary supplement. It works on the food, not on you. It's tasteless and doesn't change the taste of your food in any way. They will gladly send you a free trial coupon. It comes in tablet or granule form and you'll even receive a money saving coupon. Call:
1-800-994-4711
Or visit their web site at: www.prelief.com

Free Dental Care For Seniors

You know just how expensive dental care can be especially if you need dentures, tooth implants or gum surgery. Fortunately if you need expensive dental work but can not afford it, help is close at hand. Top quality dental care is available at little or no cost at local dental clinics and at dental colleges nationwide. Also, the dental societies in each state have a list of dentists who volunteer their services to help those who can not afford proper dental care. (See the *Directory of Free & Low Cost Dental Programs* at the back of this book).

Kick That Fungus

If you suffer from discomfort or embarrassment stemming from a fungal growth under your finger or toe nails there is something you can do to get rid of this problem. Your first step is to check out the helpful information on Sporanox's web site. On the internet go to:
www.sporanox.com/consumer/fninfection/index.jsp

HERE ARE SOME IMPORTANT TOLL FREE NUMBERS FOR INFORMATION ON MEN'S AND WOMEN'S HEALTH.

FOR MORE INFORMATION ABOUT MEN HEALTH ISSUES:

Call *Men's Health Consulting* for information on men's health reform and what you can do to help.
1-800-WELL-MEN

Men's Maintenance Manual. A free booklet by the founders of Men's Health Week and the Association of American Family Physicians that deals with stress management, sexual health and weight control and lists health hotlines for 23 helpful organizations that will provide information on topics ranging from aging allergies to sports medicine and stress. Contact them at:
MEN'S MAINTENANCE MANUAL
154-182 EAST MINOR ST.
EMMAUS, PA 18098
1-800-955-2002
Or you can reach them at their web site:
www.menshealth.com

FOR MORE INFORMATION ABOUT WOMEN'S HEALTH ISSUES:
Call the National Women's Health Network Information Clearinghouse. They can provide you with free information

packets on women's health issues including fibroids, contraception and estrogen replacement therapy. Call them at:
202-628-7814
Or visit their web site: www.nwhn.org

Also, for more information on women's health issues, The Office of Research on Women's Health, National Institutes of Health has a list of useful publications you'll want to get.
301-402-1770

What Are Your Pension Rights?

If you have questions about your pension and your rights, the Pension and Welfare Benefits Administration has a toll-free number you can call to order free publications about pensions and health coverage. They have over 30 free booklets you can request including:

• *What You Should Know About Your Pension Rights.*
• *Protect Your Pension- A Quick Reference Guide.*
• *Women and Pensions-What Women Need to Know and Do.*
• *How to File A Claim for Your Benefits; Health Benefits under COBRA*
• *Pension and Welfare Brief.*
• *Can the Retiree Health Benefits Provided By Your Employer Be Cut?*

There are also free guides for small business owners that outline *Simplified Employee Pensions* (called: 'SEPS') and *Savings Incentive Match Plans for Employees of Small Employers* (called: 'SIMPLE'). For your free information, call them 9am-8pm Monday-Friday toll-free at:
1-800-998-7542
You can also visit them on the web at: **www.dol.gov**

Controlling Your Cholesterol & Blood Pressure

We all know how critically important it is to keep our cholesterol and blood pressure at safe levels. To find out what you can do, call the National Heart, Lung and Blood Institute for recorded information on cholesterol and high blood pressure. When you call, you can also leave your name and address for written information. Call:

1-800-575-WELL
www.nhlbi.nih.gov

Taking Care Of Your Heart

When you call The American Heart Association's toll-free hotline, your call will be routed to your local AHA office for the latest information on heart disease, strokes, high blood pressure and diet. Many offices can tell you about local support groups or low-cost or even free screenings for blood pressure and cholesterol in your area. Call:

1-800-AHA-USA-1
www.americanheart.org

Staying Young At Heart

The National Institute on Aging would like you to have a copy of *For Hearts and Arteries: What Scientists are Learning About Age and the Cardiovascular System.* Learn how the latest research can help keep your heart running younger no matter what your age.

NIA INFORMATION CENTER
PO BOX 8057
GAITHERSBURG, **MD. 20898-8057**
OR CALL **1-800-222-2225**
www.nih.gov/nia

Free Holistic Herbal Healthcare Guide

This herbal guide will give you basic information about herbs, herbal combinations and homeopathic medicines. You'll learn the five main benefits of herbs, why people use herbs, what herbs are sources of vitamins, minerals and trace minerals and important points that should be considered when pur-

chasing herbs for personal consumption. If you would like a copy of *The Holistic Herbal Healthcare Guide,* send your name, address and 4 first class stamps to cover postage to:
DEBORAH COBLE
1420-E3 STEEPLE CHASE DRIVE
DOVER, PA 17315-3784

Discover the World of Natural Medicine

If you are interested in learning about natural remedies and natural products and their effect on your body, send for this *catalog of homeopathic remedies.* Enzymatic Therapy and Learning offers you some of their natural methods of feeling better. They will even send you a $3.00 coupon to try *Herpilyn*, a cold sore remedy. To get answers to your questions, you can call their consumer information line.
1-800-681-7099
www.enzy.com

Cold Sore Tip

Incidentaly, if you are prone to cold sores, ask your doctor about *Denavir* which is a new prescription medication. Research shows that applying the cream immediately after a cold sore first appears and then reapplying it every two hours helps cold sores disappear a full day earlier.
www.denavir.com

Using Biofeedback To Stay Healthy

Did you ever wonder how the process of reward gratification works? (When you accomplish something you're given a reward). Today's alternative methods of treating people include 'biofeedback' where your body learns to detect and control various functions. Learn more about these techniques and how they can make us healthy and happier. For infor-

mation about certified biofeedback professionals, send a long
SASE to:

BIOFEEDBACK CERTIFICATION INSTITUTE OF AMERICA
10200 W. 44TH AVE., SUITE 310
WHEAT RIDGE, CO 80033
www.bcia.org

Help For Back Troubles

The BackSaver catalog has a wonderful assortment of all
types of products for your back, including chairs, seat and
back support cushions, sleeping supports, reading tables and
more. It's free from:

BACKSAVER PRODUCTS CO.
53 JEFFREY AVE.
HOLLISTON, MA 01746
1-800-251-2225
www.backsavercorp.com

Dealing With Bladder Problems

Did you know that nearly half a million people suffer from
interstitial cystitis an often misdiagnosed chronic bladder
disorder. The National Institutes of Health has published a
free booklet that gives basic information in easy-to-understand layman's terms on the disease. Ask for *Interstitial
Cystitis* when you contact:

IC BOOKLET
NATIONAL INSTITUTE OF DIABETES & DIGESTIVE & KIDNEY DISEASES
3 INFORMATION WAY
BETHESDA, MD. 20892
301-654-4415
WWW.NIDDK.NIH.GOV/HEALTH/HEALTH.HTM

How to Curb Teen Smoking

If you have a teenager, you know that one of the most harmful things peer pressure may cause them to do is to start
smoking. Without the proper guidance, they may begin a life-
long battle with this dangerous habit. The Centers for Dis-

ease Control's Offices on Smoking and Health will help you tackle questions on what you can do to curb teen smoking. For specific advice, call them at:
1-800-CDC-1311
Visit their web site at: **www.cdc.gov/tobacco**

Keeping Your Heart Healthy

The American Heart Association has a valuable toll-free helpline you can call. By calling that helpline, you can get free copies of a host of booklets dealing with your heart. Topics include blood pressure, CPR, cholesterol, diet, exercise, heart disease and strokes to mention just a few. Learn the best ways to eat smart and healthy by reducing fat in your diet. You can also learn you how to read the new food labels to help you shop for healthier foods. Ask for *How to Read the New Food Label,* and *Save Food Dollars and Help Your Heart* and any other heart-related topics you are interested in. Write to:

THE AMERICAN HEART ASSOCIATION NATIONAL CENTER
7272 GREENVILLE AVE.
DALLAS, TX 75231
OR CALL TOLL-FREE: 1-800-AHA-USA-1
www.americanheart.org

Before Having A Joint Replacement

If you or anyone you know ever needs joint replacement, you will want to read this valuable information. You will learn why and when it is necessary... how it is performed, benefits versus risks and lots more. Ask for *Total Joint Replacement.* Send a SASE to:

AMERICAN ACADEMY OF ORTHOPEDIC SURGEONS
6300 NORTH RIVER RD.
ROSEMONT, IL 60018
1-800-346-AAOS
www.aaos.org

Sleep Hotline

The American Society of Travel Agents and Searle are happy to provide you with tips on how to feel your best while traveling. Request a free booklet called *Sleep Well... Stay Fit - Tips for Travelers.* Call toll-free:
1-800-SHUTEYE
www.astanet.com

Now Hear This

If you are experiencing hearing loss and your doctor has recommended a hearing aid, you may need help in determining what kind of device you need. The American Speech -Language-Hearing Association, offers general information about hearing aids and their costs, insurance coverage, proper fit and care. For your free copy of *How to Buy a Hearing Aid,* call toll-free:
 1-800-638-8255
www.asha.org

The Latest Information On Cancer

To help you keep informed about the most up-to-date information about cancer, the National Cancer Institute has a toll-free number you can call. When you call you can ask for free publications, ask for help locating FDA-approved mammography facilities or talk with cancer specialists.
 1-800-422-6237
www.nci.nih.gov

What You Can Do About Prostate Cancer

Did you know that next to lung cancer prostate cancer is the #2 cancer killer of men? Almost all men will have some kind of prostate problem if he lives long enough. Fortunately, with the modern advances in medicine and drug therapies, help is close at hand. Your first step is to inform yourself about this problem and the newest treatments for it. To get a copy of the free *Prostate Information Package* or for answers to specific questions you may have contact:

NATIONAL KIDNEY AND UROLOGIC DISEASE INFORMATION CLEARINGHOUSE
3 INFORMATION WAY
BETHESDA, MD 20892
301-654-4415
Or check out their web site at: www.niddk.nig.gov

The Facts About Prostate Cancer

Early Detection of Prostate Cancer answers the most often-asked questions about prostate cancer. Although the disease is of prime concern to men over 55, it explains that the disease can often exist without symptoms and that men over 40 should be tested annually. The National Cancer Institute also includes a list of problems that might indicate prostate cancer. It also covers the specifics of diagnosis, treatment, and prognosis. Incidentally the prognosis is excellent if the condition is caught early enough. For your free copy or to speak with a specialist, call:

1-800-422-6237 Or visit them on the web at: www.NCI.NIH.GOV

Essential Cancer Hotline

If you had been diagnosed with an advanced cancer, imagine how great it would be to find out there was a clinical trial program with new and promising treatments for the type of cancer you had. The good news is that there *is* a toll-free number you can call for help. The National Cancer Institute's Information Service provides the latest information about cancer, including causes and medical referral to low-cost clinics, medical consultation, referral to patient support groups and publications on request. They can provide you with literature and answer questions concerning various types of cancer and the standard treatment. Contact them at:

NCI, CANCER COMMUNICATIONS OFFICE
31 CENTER DRIVE MSC 2580
BUILDING 31, ROOM 10A31
BETHESDA, MD 20892
OR CALL **1-800-4-CANCER** (THAT'S **1-800-422-6237**)

You can also visit their web site at:

www.nci.nih.gov
At their web site for information on clinical trials, click on the *"Clinical Trial"* option

For Allergy and Asthma Sufferers

If you have questions about allergies or asthma, here's how you can find answers. The Asthma and Allergy Foundation will answer any questions you have regarding the symptoms of allergies to different substances, foods and how all these can be related to asthma. Visit their web site at: www.aafa.org Or CALL: **1-800-7-ASTHMA** (THAT'S 800-727-8462)

www.aafa.org

Parent Resource Guide

It's important for children to develop good eating habits when they are young so that they can grow up to be healthier, more active adults. The American Academy of Pediatrics has some important nutrition information just for the asking. Send a business sized SASE to:

NUTRITION BROCHURES DEPT. C
AMERICAN ACADEMY OF PEDIATRICS
141 NW POINT BLVD.
ELK GROVE VILLAGE, IL 60007
www.aap.org

"A Healthier You"

Research shows that eating fresh fruits and vegetables puts more fiber in your diet and helps you stay healthy. Finding out more about the vitamins, minerals and fiber in fruits and vegetables is essential to a healthier you. The booklet, *A Healthier You*, from the American Institute for Cancer Research also includes healthy recipes. Send a SASE to:

THE AMERICAN INSTITUTE FOR CANCER RESEARCH
1759 R STREET NW
WASHINGTON, **DC 20009**
1-800-843-8114
www.aicr.org

ABC'S Of Eyecare

The Better Vision Institute has some important information about your eyes and how to take the best care of them. Topics include everything from the proper selection of eyeglass frames, to eye care for children & adults, tips on correct lighting, correct type of sunglasses and more. Send a business-sized SASE to:

BETTER VISION INSTITUTE
1700 DIAGONAL ROAD SUITE 500
ALEXANDRIA, **VA 22314**
OR CALL **1-800-424-8422**
www.visionsite.org

There Is Something You Can Do About Depression

Today even when we are very aware of everything around us we sometimes blot out or deny the signs of depression in ourselves and those around us. There is some highly informative information on depression published by the National Institute of Mental Health. Learn all the facts and become aware. Send a business-sized SASE and reques the *Depression Awareness information package*:

NIMH PUBLIC INQUIRIES
6001 EXECUTIVE BLVD. ROOM 8184
MSC 9663
BETHESDA, MD 20892
www.nimh.nih.gov
OR CALL: 1-800-421-4211

Tips On Handling Tension & Depression

Chronic tension and depression are two emotionally debilitating illnesses that you can do something about. The National Mental Health Association has a ton of information on how to handle the problems of both tension and depression. If you have any questions about these conditions, they have a toll-free number you can call for help. They will also send you helpful information you can use. Call them at:
THE NATIONAL MENTAL HEALTH ASSOCIATION,
ALEXANDRIA, VA
1-800-969-6642
www.nmha.org

Healthy Teeth

Teeth - we only get one set of permanent healthy adult teeth so it's essential to learn how to keep them strong and cavity free. Dental care is also a very important career opportunity that also allows you to help others take care of their teeth. If you know someone who may be interested in finding out more about career options, ask for a copy of *Dental Hygiene - A Profession of Opportunities* and also *Facts About Dental Hygiene*. Send a long SASE to:
AMERICAN DENTAL HYGIENISTS' ASSOCIATION
444 N. MICHIGAN AVE.
CHICAGO, IL 60611
www.adha.org

Free Oil of Olay Samples

If you like to pamper your skin, you will want to try Oil of

Olay Complete Body Wash. It comes in four varieties and they will send you samples of all four if you complete a request form at their web site. When you visi their web site, click on "Join Club Olay and then on "News and Samples." **www.oilofolay.com**

Drink Tea...Live Long

Green tea has been valued for thousands of years in China for its wonderful medicinal powers. Now scientific research is showing that that folklore is based on fact and that really does promote good health. To learn more about the benefits of green tea and the art of brewing it, check out this very informative web site:
www.worldconsortium.com/tea/htm

Using Your Mind To Heal Your Body

When used properly the mind is a powerful instument you can use to stay well. To learn just how powerful your mind can be in controlling your body and how your mind can help you heal yourself, be sure to get the free *Resource Directory* which comes to you from The Institute Of Noetic Sciences.
VISIT THEIR WEB SITE: **WWW.NOETIC.ORG**

Do You Really Need A Hysterectomy?

The American College of Obstetricians and Gynecologists has published a free brochure, *Understanding Hysterectomy* which outlines what constitutes a medically necessary hysterectomy and describes what the surgery involves. Before having this operaton, request a free copy by calling:
1-202-863-2518 OR VISIT THEIR WEB SITE: **WWW.ACOG.COM**

Hiking Safety

Whether you are walking to lose weight, exploring a tourist attraction, or hiking to enjoy scenic trails, there are a num-

ber of guideline you should follow. Send a SASE and ask for *Hiking Safety* from:
AMERICAN HIKING SOCIETY
1422 FENWICK LANE
SILVER SPRING, MD 20910
www.americanhiking.org

"Megabrain"

Now you can actually improve your creativity, enhance mental functioning, induce deep relaxation and reduce stress. Sounds to good to be true but the people from Comptronic Devices say it can be done through the use of a product called 'DAVID' Light and Sound devices. There's even a special application to improve sports performance. To get your free information on this amazing device write:
COMPTRONIC DEVICES LIMITED
9008 51AVENUE
EDMONTON, ALBERTA, CANADA, T6E 5X4
1-800-661-6463
www.comptronic.com

Massage Therapy

Stress got you down? Maybe you need a good massage. The *Massage Therapy* booklet will give you detailed information about different methods of massage and the benefits of each type. It will also answer many of your questions about stress and the reasons massage therapy works. Write to:
AMERICAN MASSAGE THERAPY ASSOCIATION
820 DAVIS ST., SUITE 100
EVANSTON, IL 60201
www.amtamassage.org

Asthma Relief

Asthma patients who use inhalers may be masking the physical cause for their symptoms. Doctors have come up with a checklist for asthma patients who rely on those inhalers to open their airways. If you use your inhaler more than three times a week, if you go through more than one canister a month, and if your asthma awakens you at night…you may be suffering from an inflammation of the airways that is the real cause of your symptoms and may need drug treatment to clear it up. To receive a copy of the list, write to:

ASTHMA INFORMATION CENTER
BOX 790
SPRINGHOUSE, PA 19477

Speak To A Dietician On The Toll-Free Nutrition Hotline

Find out how your diet is affecting your health. Call the American Institute for Cancer Research, Nutrition Hotline and ask a registered dietician your personal questions on diet, nutrition and cancer. When you call you can leave your question with an operator and a dietician will call you back within 48 hours with answers to your questions.

CALL BETWEEN 9AM-5PM, EST MONDAY-FRIDAY:
1-800-843-8114

Free Health Publications

The AICR also has a variety of free publications designed to help you live a healthier lifestyle. A small contribution gets you a very informative newsletter and you can ask for the following booklets by name: *Get Fit, Trim Down* - how to lose weight sensibly. *Alcohol and Cancer Risk: Make The Choice For Health.* - find out how alcohol affects your cancer risk. *Diet & Cancer* - are you eating enough fiber, something that's been linked to lower cancer risk? *Reducing Your Risk of Colon Cancer* - learn steps you can take that may reduce your risk of one of the most common cancers in the United States. Also ask for *Everything Doesn't Cause Cancer* which will calm many of the concerns you may have about what causes cancer. You can ask for one of these or all. Write to:

AMERICAN INSTITUTE FOR CANCER RESEARCH
WASHINGTON, DC 20069

Free Child Care Information

Met Life offers a wide range of child care information every parent will find useful. Ask for the "Life Advice Program on Family" and also their booklets: "About Becoming A Parent and "About Choosing Child Care" and"About Litle Miracles". You can call them at

1-800-MET-LIFE (THAT'S) **1-800-638-5433** (PRESS **3**)

or visit them on the web at:

www.metlife.com

Does Your Child Have An Iron Deficiency?

To understand the effect that iron and iron deficiency has on health development of your child, be sure to get this free brochure on iron from Carnation, makers of Good Start Infant Formula, and Follow-Up Formula. Ask for the *Iron Brochure*. You'll also learn that although iron is essential for your baby, it is just as essential to a mature adult. Send a long SASE to:

NESTLE INFANT NUTRITION
IRON BROCHURE OFFER
PO Box **AW**
WILKES BARRE, **PA 18703**
1-800-782-7776
www.nestleusa.com

Health At Home

This Home Health catalog is the official supplier of Edgar Cayce products for health, beauty and wellness. You'll find over 50 products to help you feel and look your best. There is everything from juices, vitamins, even minerals and salts from the Dead Sea. Write to:

HOME HEALTH
BAAR PRODUCTS
PO Box 60

Downingtown, PA 19335
1-800-269-2502
WWW.EDGARCAYCE.ORG

Your Family Health Record

Every member of the family should keep a written medical record. The family's medical record will be useful to you in filling out insurance forms, as well as school and travel records. It can also be vital in helping a physician diagnose a medical problem a family member might have. If you would like, they will also send you information on prenatal and natal care, guide to healthy pregnancy and information on how your baby grows. They also have informative brochures for teens about drugs and sexually transmitted disease. Write to:
MARCH OF DIMES
1275 MAMARONECK AVE.
WHITE PLAINS, NY 10605
1-888-663-4637
www.modimes.org

Help For The Visually Handicapped

A great series of publications are free to those with impaired vision. Printed in very large type are instructions for knitting, crocheting, and gardening plus children's books and more. Also available are guides for the partially sighted including a dial operator personal directory. There are also 2 free newsletters...*IN FOCUS for youths* and *SEEING CLEARLY* for adults. For a complete listing write:
NATIONAL ASSOCIATION FOR VISUALLY HANDICAPPED
22 WEST 21ST STREET
NEW YORK, NY 10010
(IN CALIF. ONLY—3201 BALBOA ST., SAN FRANCISCO, CA 94121).
www.navh.org

Johnson & Johnson Hotline

Who can you turn to for answers to your questions concerning hygiene, personal care and baby care? To help you with answers to these questions, Johnson & Johnson has set up a toll-free consumer information hotline you can call. Call them with your questions Monday thru Friday between the hours of from 8:00am to 6:00pm EST.

THEIR TOLL-FREE HOTLINE IS:

1-800-526-3967
www.jnj.com

Help For The Deaf

Every year over 200,000 children are born deaf or suffer hearing loss in their first years of life. *Speech and Hearing Checklist* tells parents how to detect possible deafness in their children. Another nice booklet, *Listen! Hear!* is for parents of children who may be deaf or hard of hearing. Both are free from:

ALEXANDER GRAHAM BELL
ASSOCIATION FOR THE DEAF
3417 VOLTA PL. N.W.
WASHINGTON, DC 20007
www.agbell.org

How To Keep Your Bones Strong

Supplements can help replace the calcium in your bones that age takes away. Just two of these soft chewy, vanilla-flavored squares give you 1200 mg. of calcium daily. For more information on keeping your bones healthy and staying fit, call toll free weekdays between 9:00 am and 5:00 pm EST:

1-800-STAY-FIT

Free Medical Supply Catalog

If you have a disability or illness that requires you to use medical equipment or supplies, now you can order your medi-

cal supplies from your home by phone and save up to 60%. Send for this free catalog from America's leading mail order medical supply catalog. Call Bruce Medical Supply at:
1-800-225-8446
DEPARTMENT 712
411 WAVERLY OAKS RD.
WALTHAM. MA 02154
www.brucemedical.com
ALSO, BE SURE TO GET A COPY OF THE DISCOUNT HEALTHCARE CATALOG FREE FROM:
DR. LEONARDS HEALTH CARE PRODUCTS
1-800-785-0880
www.drleonards.com

Questions About Medicare? Call This Toll-Free Hotline

If you have questions or problems regarding Medicare, now there's a toll-free number you can call for help. When you call you can get additional information regarding a Medicare claim you may have, general information about Medicare and the services it provides. They can also help you with information regarding insurance supplements to Medicare, mammograms and lots more. Call:
1-800-MEDICARE
www.medicare.gov

Physical Fitness For Seniors

It's always a great idea to get in shape and stay in shape. Just remember that if you take better care of your body, it will take better care of you. The President's Council on Physical Fitness & Sports has useful information that can help add years to your life. You'll get an introduction to exercise, weight control, physical fitness, sports, running and lots more. Here are a few titles you will want to ask for
• *Pep up Your Life*—fitness for seniors

- *Older American Fact Sheet* - what to do to stay in great shape
- *Exercise & Weight Control*-they go hand in hand.
- *Fitness Fundamentals* - how to develop a personal fitness program

Drop a card to:
THE PRESIDENT'S COUNCIL ON PHYSICAL FITNESS & SPORTS
200 INDEPENDENCE AVE. SW ROOM 738H
WASHINGTON, D.C. 20201
202-690-9000
www.fitness.gov

What To Ask Your Doctor Before You Have Surgery

If you are considering having any type of non-emergency surgery, be sure to get your free copy of *Questions to Ask Your Doctor Before Surgery*. It will help you be informed about the options and risks involved. Call toll-free:
1-800-358-9295
www.ahrq.gov

Sexually Transmitted Diseases Hotline

If you suspect you may have contracted a sexually transmitted disease, there's a toll free hotline you can call for help and for information. Their specialists will answer your questions concerning STDs and tell you the symptoms that are the warning signs of disease and how to get help. You'll be referred to free or low-cost public health clinics or doctors in your area. They will also send you free brochures concerning STDs. Call Monday thru Friday between the hours of 8 am and 8 pm at:
1-800-227-8922
www.cdc.gov

Eat Your Way To A Healthy Heart

If you would like a copy of the American Heart Association's recommendations for a healthy heart including lists of good and bad foods, plus practical suggestions for cutting out the bad stuff. Ask for *Exercise Your Heart, An Eating Plan For Healthy Americans; Cholesterol & Your Heart* and *Recipes For Low-Fat, Low Cholesterol Meals.* Just send a SASE to:

AMERICAN HEART ASSOCIATION
7272 GREENVILLE AVE.
DALLAS, TX 75231
1-800-242-8721
www.americanheart.org

Avoiding Skin Cancer

Prevention is always far better than a cure. And one of the most preventable diseases is skin cancer. To find out what you can do to prevent this disease, be sure to get a copy of the free booklet *Skin Cancer: If You Can Spot It You Can Stop It.* Send a long SASE to:

THE SKIN CANCER FOUNDATION
245 FIFTH AVE. SUITE 1403
NEW YORK, NY 10016
1-800-SKIN-490
www.skincancer.org

Free Guide To Strokes

For up-to-date information on strokes and the most effective treatment and therapy for those who fall victim to a stroke, ask for your free copy of *Guide To Strokes.* Write to:

STROKE
NINCDS-W
9000 ROCKVILLE PIKE, BLDG 31, RM 8A16
BETHESDA, MD 20892

Headache Hotline

If you are plagued with headaches and don't know where to turn, The American Council for Headache Education may be able to offer you a solution on how to lessen your pain and discomfort. Call them toll-free:

1-800-255-ACHE
www.achenet.org

For Asthma Relief

If you suffer from asthma, you'll want to get a free copy of *Making The Most of Your Next Doctor Visit.* In it you'll discover what you can do to assist your doctor in helping you relieve your asthma suffering. Call toll-free:

1-800-456-2784
www.aafa.org

Allergies Be Gone

If you suffer from allergies, you may need some help to make your allergies easier to handle. Call the American Allergy Supply and get answers to your allergy questions.

1-8 00-321-1096
www.americanallergy.com

Free Contact Lenses

If you wear contact lenses or are thinking of getting them, Johnson & Johnson would like you to try their Acuvue contacts. They have made arrangements with local optometrist throughout the country to supply you with a your first pair. Just ask an optometrist in your area who carries *Acuvue* contacts for a free pair or visit:

www.acuvue.com

Free Focus Contacts

If you always wanted to try soft contact lenses but weren't sure you'd like them, here's your chance to try a free pair. For a certificate you can take to your local eye care store for a free trial pair of O2Optix breathable disposable contact lenses, visit their web site at:

WWW.O2OPTIX.COM

Save 50% On Contact Lenses

To save up to 50% on your contact lenses, consider buying them by mail order from a company called 1-800-CON-TACTS. They carry a full line of first quality contact lenses in all prescriptions from all manufacturers. Their toll-free order line is easy to remember since it's the same as their company name...

1-800-CONTACTS (THAT'S **1-800-266-8228**)
www.contacts.com

Important Health Hotlines

To help answer various health questions you may have there are a number of toll-free hotlines you can call:

CALCIUM INFORMATION CENTER:
1-800-321-2681

MILK CONSUMER HOTLINE:
1-800-WHY-MILK

NATIONAL CENTER FOR NUTRITION & DIURETICS
1-800-366-1655

NATIONAL OSTEOPEROSIS FOUNDATION
1-800-223-9994

FOOD ALLERGY NETWORK
1-800-929-4040

CONSUMER NUTRITION HOTLINE
1-800-366-1655

If You Have Cancer, Call This Hotline First

If you've been diagnosed with any type of cancer, be sure to call the *Cancer Toll-free Hotline.* They will put you in touch with someone who has had the same type of cancer and will help you deal with the initial fear. Speaking with another person who's had to deal with the same life-threatening disease that you have can be highly informative and enormously comforting. Call:
1-800-433-0464

Lifeline Pilots

If you live in the mid-west and need medical attention in a distant city and can not easily afford to travel to the medical facility, there is a wonderful non-profit volunteer organization that will fly you free of charge. To find out more, call their office at **800-822-7972.**

Or visit their web site at:
www.lifelinepilots.org

Health Web Sites

There is so much material on the World Wide Web that people new to the Internet often find searching for information a bit overwhelming at first. To help make your search simple and successful there are a number of useful search resources you can use to locate a wide range of information.

For example, if you would like to explore the area of health Lycos, Excite and Yahoo are three of the best 'search engines'. Just by typing in their web address and following the directions below, you will instantly be able to find the latest health related news, information and answers to health questions you may have.

EXCITE
www.excite.com
They have what they refer to as their *Health Channel*. Click on that and you'll find listings for Mayo Health Oasis, Healthy Ideas and New England Journal of Medicine Online.

LYCOS
www.lycos.com
Click on *Health* and you'll get a general web page on Health plus another page with options like Health News, Eating & Exercise and Health Care.

YAHOO
www.yahoo.com
This may be your best bet. Yahoo Health, offers a breakdown of about 50 categories ranging from alternative medicine to hospitals to transplant resources.

HERE ARE SPECIFIC HEALTH SITES YOU MAY
WANT TO VISIT ON THE INTERNET:

HEALTH A TO Z
www.healthatoz.com
This is designed to be a health navigational tool. Health A to Z is useful both for medical professionals and consumers. To locate information, you can either enter your own search words or click on one of 30 categories for a listing of related sites.

HEALTHFINDER
www.healthfinder.gov
This is a consumer health and human services information Web site from the U.S. government. It leads you to online publications, clearinghouses, databases, Web sites and support groups, including government agencies.

MEDSITE
www.medsite.com
Enter a medical or health key word and click on the search button and you're on your way.

MEDSURF
www.medsurf.com
You can do a word search for specific health questions or sift through the categories under General Information, Practitioners' Information or Researchers' Information.

IF YOU SUBSCRIBE TO AMERICA ONLINE:
AOL has a Health and Fitness "channel" (key word: *'Health'*). You'll find a health library, the Better Health and Medical network, plus health resources, support groups and the Medline database you will find useful.

IF YOU SUBSCRIBE TO COMPUSERVE:
CompuServe has a useful health database (go: *'Health'*) and Health-Net. They also use information provided by John's Hopkins and include resources on alternative medicine, women's health and specific ailments.

NATIONAL INSTITUTES OF HEALTH INFORMATION
www.nih.gov/health.com
This includes Medline, Medscape, patient information and journals. Very well organized.

MAYO HEALTH OASIS:
www.mayo.ivi.com
You get the Oasis Library, The Cancer Center, Heart Center, Women's Health and medicine Center. The Library has great resources and links to other sites.

ASK DR. WEIL:
www.drweil.com
Dr. Andrew Weil's site is for those who are interested in finding an alternative to traditional medicine.

FAMILY CAREGIVER ALLIANCE
www.caregiver.prg
This site combines a clearinghouse for publications, newsletters, diagnoses and research with a resource center for care services, public policy and links.

ATLANTA REPRODUCTIVE HEALTH CENTRE
www.ivf.com/home.shtm
One of the oldest Web sites, it has a host of information on women's health.

WEEKEND MAGAZINE
www.usaweekend.com
For helpful information on men's and women's health, visit *Weekend* magazine's website

THE BLACK HEALTH NET
www.blackhealthnet.com
This site provides information and resources on topics such as AIDS and African Americans, sickle cell and other diseases.

ARTHRITIS FOUNDATION
www.arthritis.org

For comprehensive information on arthritis call the Arthritis Foundation toll-free at **1-800-283-7800** or for a brochure on rheumatoid arthritis, call toll free **1-877-467-3472** or visit their web site.

For more information on on the latest research on arthritis, you will also want to visit the following web sites:
www.rheumatology.org
www.nih.gov/niams

NEW CANCER DRUG
www.entremed.com

Entremed, the new cancer drug that cures cancer in mice will begin clinical trials on humans by the middle of 1999. A toll free number will be posted on the company Internet site at that time to recruit participants. It's too soon to say, but this could be a major breakthrough for those suffering from cancer and certainly adds hope to all those afflicted with that disease. Log onto their web site for the latest on their clinical trials.

Health Tips

What You Can Do To Help Your Doctor Help You

Next time you are suffering from pain and discomfort and can't easily pinpoint exactly what hurts, follow this checklist. It will not only help you identify the problem but will help the doctor diagnose the ailment .

* When did the pain or symptoms start?
* Did it follow an accident?
* Does it happen before meals or after meals?
* Did symptoms develop gradually or suddenly?
* Are the symptoms intermittent or constant?
* Are symptoms worse in certain positions, such as sitting or lying down, or at certain times such as morning or evening, or during certain activities?
* How have the symptoms affected your normal activities?
* Make a list of prescription and nonprescription drugs you are taking.
* Describe your pain. Words like cramping, sharp, throbbing, aching, all give different information to your doctor.

This is the best way to assist your doctor by providing accurate information about your medical concerns.

Can Apples Reduce Your Cancer Risk?

In a Finnish study of 10,000 adults, eating three apples a week appears to have shown a reduction in lung-cancer risk by 58%. It seems apples are high in quercetin, an antioxidant that appears to be protective against lung cancer.

Everyday Exercise

Looking for a great exercise routine, well no need to look any further. Here are a few tips to get you going!
• Do some spring cleaning around the house and scrub the floor a little harder
• Do some gardening and yardwork
Clean out that attic and garage
• Walk, don't drive !
• Looking for a fun aerobic workout…dance. Try learning one of those new funky dance steps.

Caesar's Garlic Wars?

Many claims have been made in recent years about the important medicinal value of garlic. But did you know that the Greeks favored garlic to ward off evil, while the Romans ate whole cloves for strength and courage, preparing themselves for battle with doses of it. Could it be that their breath sent their enemies into retreat?

Why Doctors Use Vitamin E

In a recent survey of medical doctors as to what vitamins they took on a regular basis, it was found that 40% of the doctors took vitamin E. A study of men aged 50 to 69 found that those who took 50mg of vitamin E daily for five to eight years lowered their risk of prostate cancer by 32%. Even among those who did get cancer, vitamin E reduced their chances of dying from it by 41%.

No one is quite certain just how vitamin E protects us against this cancer but it is said that its antioxidant powers prevent cell damage that sets the stage for cancer. Other studies suggest that vitamin E may reduce the risk of heart attacks too. If taken as a supplement, you may want to consider taking one with 400 IUs of E for maximum protection.

Make sure to buy the natural vitamin E with is better absorbed than the synthetic form.

Chew Away Your Heartburn

If you're prone to getting heartburn after eating a hearty meal, try chewing gum for a half hour after meals. It seems chewing gum boosts saliva production which neutralizes stomach acid and washes it away from the esophagus where it can irritate tender tissues.

Now Hear This: Another Reason To Stop Smoking

Along with all of the serious health risks that have been linked to smoking, there is now a new risk. A study shows that smokers are twice as likely to suffer age-related hearing loss as nonsmokers. Researchers speculate that smoking reduces blood flow to the ear.

To Cut Your Risk Of Heart Attack

In a new study of 80,000 women, Harvard researchers found that there was a greater risk of having a heart attack among women who eat lots of *partially hydrogenated vegetable oils* also known as *'trans fats'* (found in margarine and thousands of other processed foods) than in those who eat lots of saturated fats (found in butter, steak and other animal foods). Check the food packages and cut back on those that list hydogenated vegetable oils as an ingredient. If you use margarine, remember that the harder the spread the more trans fats it contains. Use soft or liquid margarines instead.

Sit and Be Fit

Sit and Be fit is committed to improving the quality of life of older adults and/or physically limited individuals. You can watch the program on most public television channels. They will also answer you health and exercise questions and give you free advice and information.

SIT AND BE FIT
PO Box 8033
SPOKANE, WA 99203
www.sitandbefit.com

Get Help Losing Weight

Are you in a constant battle to lose weight and keep it off? If so you may need a clearer idea of how your body works. At freeweightloss.com you will find tools that will help you lose weight including a free e-newsletter, a weight calculator, a calorie counter and lots more. Knowledge is power so use this web site to get control of your body and maintain your good health. Visit them at:
www.freeweightloss.com

Volunteer Just For The Health Of It

We all know that *"it's better to give than to receive"* but did you know that studies have shown that people who volunteer actually live longer, happier, healthier lives? Volunteering has been shown to reduce anxiety plus it provides you with a renewed sense of purpose and a feeling of fulfillment.

Besides seniors (folks 50+ years young) have a lot to give. They have a wealth of knowledge, talent and experience (not to mention a wealth of wisdom) that they can now share with others. Remember, giving of your time to help someone else, helps you as well. Plus one day you may be on the receiving end of this aid.

If you have a little time and would like to make a difference in your life and in the life of someone else or if you currently need help, here are a few places to start.

The National Senior Service Corps for National Service

This is a network of more than a half million seniors who are making a difference through the following programs:

FOSTER GRANDPARENTS

In this program seniors are caring for kids. They help children who have been abused or neglected; they mentor troubled teenagers and young mothers and care for premature infants or children with physical disabilities.

SENIOR COMPANION PROGRAM (SCP)

Isn't it wonderful to help a friend in need? With this program there's help for seniors who have difficulty with day-to-day tasks or who have lost family and friends and need help getting things done. Senior Companions not only provide assistance and friendship but help with chores like paying bills, grocery shopping, providing a ride to a medical appointment and more. Senior Companions also receive training in Alzheimers, strokes, diabetes and mental health, so they are able to alert doctors and family members to potential problems.

RETIRED SENIOR VOLUNTEER PROGRAM (RSVP)

This program has helped those 55 and older put their skills and life experience to work for others. As an RSVP volunteer, you might teach English to immigrants, organize a neighborhood watch, or help people recover from natural disasters. The number of hours you serve is flexible. You will receive appropriate on-the-job training from the agency or organization where you are placed.

FOR ALL OF THE ABOVE, CALL THE NATIONAL SENIOR SERVICE CORPS AT: **1-800-424-8867**

Or contact them at their Internet site:
www.seniorcorps.org

Service Corps Of Retired Executives (SCORE)

This program, sponsored by the U.S. Small Business Administration, matches volunteers with small businesses that need advice. So if you're thinking of joining the ranks of entrepreneurs - this is the place to get free advice from a seasoned pro. On the other hand, if you are a retired executive and would like to help other budding businessmen get started on the right foot, call them for information on how you can be of service at:
1-800-634-0245
www.score.org

Global Volunteers Make A World Of Difference.

If you've always thought about joining the Peace Corps but hesitated because you couldn't commit for two years, Global Volunteers may be for you.

For the last 14 years Global Volunteers has sent people to 18 countries around the world for a 2-3 week stay. You will be a part of a team of 10-20 volunteers plus host country participants, working on projects that include teaching English, improving health care, working on forest trails and teaching business practices. Since Global Volunteers is a private nonprofit organization, participants pay their own transportation as well as a land package and administration fee that averages $1,000-$2,000. But their entire outlay is tax deductible, including transportation to and from the country. What a great way to see the world and to help your fellow man at the same time. For more information about Global Volunteers, call:

1-800-487-1074
www.globalvolunteers.org

American Association Of Retired Persons (A.A.R.P.)

A.A.R.P. provides a variety of volunteer programs, services and activities that help older Americans. One example is the *'Widow Person'* referral program (for widows and widowers). With this program, a widowed person can meet with another widowed volunteer in their area for mutual friendship and support. Another service offered is a program that will refer you to organizations in your area either to volunteer your services or to be helped by a volunteer. For a full information package on all of the services offered, call the A.A.R.P. Volunteer Talent Bank.

CALL: 1-800-424-3410
www.aarp.org

Peace Corps

The Peace Corps can give you the chance to immerse yourself in a totally different culture while helping to make an important difference in other people's lives. If you like helping people and want to get involved, get the *Peace Corps information package.* Call toll-free:

1-800-424-8580
www.peacecorps.gov

ALSO, CONSIDER VOLUNTEER OPPORTUNITIES IN YOUR TOWN AND CHECK IN YOUR PHONE BOOK FOR YOUR LOCAL CHAPTER OF:
- American Cancer Society
- Chamber of Commerce
- Forest and Wildlife Service
- Forest Service Volunteers
- Hospice, Lions Club
- National Parks Service
- Red Cross
- Vista
- Respite
- Rotary Club
- The United Way

Also check out these web sites with volunteer opportunities:
SERVEnet:
www.servenet.org

Habitat For Humanity
www.habitat.org

AmeriCares
www.americares.org

Free Health & Beauty Aids

For many large companies the best way to promote their products is directly to the consumer. And what better way of doing it, than by giving you a free sample. You'll like it, pass it on to your friends and family and the company will have more loyal customers. Everyone comes out ahead!

Some of the free samples listed below may have limited availability, so call now!

10 Steps To Healthy White Teeth

The makers of Rembrandt toothpaste want you to be aware of how you can keep your teeth healthy and white and to show you how to do that they want you to have, *Top Ten Oral Care Problems Have One Solution- Rembrandt*. They also have valuable information they will send you on aging teeth. Along with your free sample of Rembrandt whitening toothpaste they will also send you coupons worth a total of $7.00 for all of their products. To get your free sample and money-off coupons call toll-free:
1-800-548-3663
www.rembrandt.com

Plus, if you have canker sores in your mouth, call this toll-free hotline for information on a toothpaste specifically designed to relieve your problem.
1-800-548-3663

Taking Care Of Your Skin

Alpha Hydroxy will be happy to send you information about all their skin products and how they will work for you. They

also have a consumer hotline updated monthly that tells about their products and where they are available. If you are interested in finding out about their facial, body care and foot care products, call:
1-800-55-ALPHA
www.alphahydrox.com

If You Suffer From Migraine Pain

For anyone who suffers from the excruciating pain of a migraine headache, *Chart Your Route To Relief,* is a personal migraine management program that actually helps you find relief. It includes a comprehensive chart that will help you and your doctor pinpoint the cause. To get your free chart simply visit the web site:
www.eatright.org

Migraine Relief

If you suffer from migrane headaches, you will want to get the *Excedrin Migraine Tablets and Relief Guide.* When you request it, you'll also receive a free sample of their new migraine tablets plus helpful information on dealing with migraine headaches. Call them toll-free:
1-800-392-3374
Or visit their web site at: www.excedrin.com

Milk Sensitive?—Now You Can Enjoy A Milk Shake

Do you have trouble digesting milk and milk products? Now for the first time you can enjoy a big glass of milk or even a delicious ice cream sundae with the help of Lactaid Ultra tablets. To have your questions answered and to receive a free sample plus a coupon to save money on your next purchase, call: **1-800-LACTAID (that's 1-800-522-8243)**

Free Earrings

Do your ears sting, turn black or just kill you when you put on your favorite gold earrings? Here's the answer to those sensitive ear woes. Once again you'll be able to wear those fashionable earrings you always dreaded to put on because you were allergic. Simply Whispers will not only send you a catalog of their quality earrings made of top-quality surgical steel with the look of silver or 24-karat electroplated for gold lovers, but a free pair to try as well. Best of all they are guaranteed for life. You have a choice of pierced or clip. Write to them at:

SIMPLY WHISPERS
430 COURT ST.
PLYMOUTH, MA 02360
OR CALL THEM TOLL-FREE AT: 1-800-451-5700
www.simplywispers.com

Pantyhose Problems?

The National Association of Hosiery Manufacturers would like to help you overcome your fear of stocking runs, snags and droops. They will provide you with valuable information and helpful tips on how to determine your correct size, stocking care and how to make your hosiery last. When you call them you can also ask them any specific questions you may have about stockings. Call:

1-704-365-0913
www.nahm.com

Leg Talk

Has this ever happened to you...you're down to your last pair of stockings and late for an important meeting when, for no apparent reason, the stockings 'run'? Would you like to find out why this happens and what you can do about it? Write for your free copy of *Sheer Facts About Hosiery*.

NATIONAL HOSIERY ASSN.

3623 LATROBE DRIVE SUITE 130
CHARLOTTE, NC 28211
www.nahm.com

Ask The Hair Coloring Experts

Are you thinking of changing your hair color? Having trouble finding the right shade? Can't cover that problem gray? The experts at Clairol have a toll-free hotline you can call for answers to all your hair coloring questions. Their color consultants will also provide you with helpful tips that will help you look your very best. Call them Monday-Friday 8:30am-8:30pm or Saturday 9am-6pm EST at:
1-800-252-4765
You can also visit the Clairol Women's Link site on the Internet at:
www.womenslink.com

Hair Care Guidance & More

If you would like advice on how to manage your hair, how to color it or just how to keep it looking good, L'Oreal has the answers for you. Next time you can't decide which shampoo or conditioner is best for your hair type, call the toll-free L'Oreal Guideline Monday-Friday, 10am-7pm EST at:
1-800-631-7358 or you can write to them at:
L'OREAL CONSUMER AFFAIRS
PO BOX 98
WESTFIELD, NJ 07091
Or visit them on the web at: **www.lorealparisusa.com**

Healthy Diet-Healthy Looks

We've all heard the expression, 'you are what you eat.' Well it's true, the basics of looking good and feeling good, start with healthy eating habits. The American Dietetic Association is making a concerted effort to get us back on a healthy eating track. They have a toll-free phone line you can call weekdays for more information on healthy eating and for a referral to a local dietician. Call the Consumer Nutrition Hotline at:

1-800-877-1600
www.eatright.org

Keep It Clean

The makers of Oil of Olay would like to show you just how well their skin cleansers and lotions work. Check out their web site where you will find all kinds of helpful information including makeup and cosmetic tips plus hints on face and body care. You can even fill out a form online and receive free product samples.

www.oilofolay.com

Free Pantyhose

As a way of introducing you to their fine line of pantyhose, the Silkies Company will send you a free pair of pantyhose. Along with the free pair will be two pairs that you will pay for if you decide you them. Otherwise you will return the two pair and they will pay the return postage.

Call them at:

877-745-5437

Or visit their web site at: **www.mysilkies.com**

NOTES:

Cooking Up A Storm

If you love to try new things, you're going to love the recipe collections we've found for you. The companies giving away these free cookbooks and recipe collections do so at great expense as their way of saying "thank you" to their loyal customers and also as a way of attracting new customers. They want to inspire you to even greater use of their products by showing you new and innovative ways of using them to create meals you and your family will LOVE.

Wonderful Cajun Style Cooking!

Get a free copy of Chef Paul Proudhomme's Magic Spice book and learn some of his cooking secrets. Imagine using the very same spices in your kitchen that he uses at his famous K-Paul's Louisiana Kitchen in New Orleans. You can receive his *Mail Order Sourcebook*, with 8 different recipes from Chef Paul himself. If you send $1.00 he'll send you a sample pack of his Magic Seasoning along with his catalog. Also, sign up for Chef Paul's Fan club and he will send you free recipes, tips, coupons and special promotional offers.

Visit his web site at
www.chefpaul.com
Or write to him at:
**Magic Seasoning Blends
PO Box 23342
New Orleans, LA 70183**

Delicious M&M Deserts

Everyone knows just how great M&M's are all by themselves. But did you know they also make a great ingredient in making deserts? The M&M's Recipe booklet tells you how to make delightful and fun deserts using M&M's. (That is if you don't eat them all first). For your free copy call them toll-free at: **1-800-627-7852.**

For a fun website with recipes, coupons, games and more, go to: **http://us.mms.com/us**

Yummy Cranberries

Ocean Spray would like to show you some of the great things you can do with cranberries. When you call, they will send you four different recipe collections of tasty things to do with cranberries. Just ask for *Cooking With Cranberries*. Call them toll-free at:
1-800-662-3263
www.oceanspray.com

Sample A Wonderful Gourmet Coffee

Peerless coffee has been providing the San Francisco area with the freshest and best quality coffee for years. The Peerless Colombian roast has been chosen number one by a panel of experts, and they will be happy to send you a free sample to try. You'll also receive a free catalog of all their delicious coffees and an equally distinctive selection of teas. Their catalog offers not only selected coffees and fine teas but a collection of coffee related gifts from around the world. Write to:
PEERLESS COFFEE CO.
260 OAK ST.
OAKLAND, CA 94607
OR YOU CAN CALL TOLL FREE:1-800-310-5662

Hints For A Healthier Diet

Today everyone is focusing on maintaining a healthy diet. Saco Foods will send you their excellent, *Hints For a Healthier Diet*, which discusses oils, fats, fiber, snacks, meats and dairy products, fish...even canned foods are best for you. You'll also receive a free sample of their low-fat cultured buttermilk powder (makes great pancakes) and also free recipes for their sinfully delicious cookies made with Saco's delicious chocolate chunks. They are really the best! Write to:

SACO FOODS
PO Box 620707
MIDDLETON, WI 53562
OR CALL TOLL-FREE: 1-800-373-SACO (7226)
www.sacofoods.com

Tons of Free Recipes

If you enjoy trying all kinds of new recipes, you are going to love this web site. At freerecipes.com you will find links that will take you to thousands of free recipes of every type and description. For example, you will find a link that will take you to free recipes for weight control and another that will take you to a web site offering unlimited access to over 30,000 recipes. And if sweets are your thing, another click of the mouse will take you to dozens of mouth-watering recipes like Strawberry Cheese Sweet Rolls or Chocolate Espresso Cake. Delicious! You'll find all this and much more when you visit the internet site at

www.freerecipes.com

Wonderful Low-Fat Meals

If you would like to improve your diet with more low fat meals, be sure to get *Simple Steps To Eating Smart* from Campbell low fat collection. You'll find a wide variety of healthy low-fat meals that are quick and easy to make. To get your collection, call them toll-free at:

1-800-442-7684
www.campbellsoup.com

It's Herbal Tea Time

If you really enjoy sampling all those wonderful herbal teas, this catalog is a must for you. Here's your chance to try Ginseng Power-Plus or one of their other popular teas. Along with their catalog, they'll also send you some free samples to try. Send an long SASE to:

SATORI FINE HERBALS
825 W. MARKET ST.
SALINAS, CA 93901

Low Salt Recipes

If you would like to cut down your salt intake without cutting down on taste, here's your chance. Try some of the tasty recipes using Nu-Salt, the salt substitute from the makers of Sweet 'N Low. In *Cooking With Nu-Salt* you will find a wide variety of sodium-reduced recipes ...everything from light and healthy Spinach & Pasta Soup to Trout Almondine and Coq au Vin. For your free copy, call Nu-Salt toll-free:
1-800-206-9454
www.nusalt.com

Eat More Grain

Near East Company, the makers of great tasty rice, wheat and grain products would like to send you their free recipe booklet with yummy new ways of using healthy grains in your next meal. Call them toll-free at:
1-800-822-7423
WWW.NEAREAST.COM

Vegetarian Delight

Have you been thinking of becoming a vegetarian? Well now is your chance to join the group of people who have decided they would rather be kind to animals and go vegetarian. It's easy to stay on a vegetarian diet while you are home, but when you go on vacation will you have to bring your own food? The Vegetarian Resource Group has a list of places throughout the U.S. and Canada where you can enjoy vegetarian dining in addition to your regular menus. To get your copy, send a long SASE to:

THE VEGETARIAN RESOURCE GROUP
BOX 1463
BALTIMORE, MD 21203
www.vrg.org/recipes

200 Treats Under 200 Calories.

Imagine trying some delicious low calorie treats for under 200 calories. This is a great low calorie guide to low calorie eating. This low calorie guide to low calorie eating gives you some great tips on calorie counting as well as tasty daily menus. They'll even give you a diet nutrition plan to follow and some yummy recipe collections including different baking ideas. Write:

ROMAN MEAL CO.
PO BOX 11126
TACOMA WA 98411
Or call them at: 800-426-3600
www.romanmeal.com

"The Little Book Of Secrets"

Did you know that soy sauce was first used as a vegetarian seasoning hundreds of years ago? Today millions of people now use it to intensify the natural flavor of meat. Kikkoman Soy Sauce, the big secret in the little bottle, is a great seasoning for all kinds of meats and vegetables. For more ideas, ask for *The Little Book of Big Secrets.* Call toll-free:

1-888-KIKKOMAN

"Clam Lover's Delight"

Gorton's Seafood is delighted to send you their great recipe

collection, *Clam Lover's Delight*. You'll be amazed at all the tasty ways you can use Gorton's chopped or minced clams. You will learn new ways to make tasty appetizers as well as stuffed seafood, or just delicious pasta recipes. Call them toll-free:
1-800-222-6846
Or visit their web site: www.gortons.com

The Art of Light Tortillas

Mission Light Tortillas has a wonderful recipe collection using their light tortillas. You can start with the delicious strawberry breakfast crepes or try meatless tortilla lasagna. You'll be amazed at all the tasty dishes you can make from appetizers to main meals. They will also send you some coupons to try their products free. Ask for, *The Art of Light Tortillas*. Write to:
MISSION FOODS CORPORATION
PO Box 2008
OLDSMARR, FL 34677
1-800-443-7994
www.missionfoods.com

"What's For Dinner"

The makers of Rice a Roni and Pasta Roni have some quick and delicious recipes to help make life easier for you. You'll want to try their Jazzy Jambalaya, lemon garlic chicken or quick taco salad. This collection of easy recipes all can be cooked in 30 minutes or less. These ten delicious recipes come to you on colorful cards which are easy to file with all your other recipes. Write to:
UNCLE BEN'S
PO Box 1752
HOUSTON, TX 77251
1-800-548-6253
www.unclebens.com

A-1 Sauce Recipe & Lots More

We all know that A-1 Sauce makes a terrific addition to your meat once it's on your plate but did you know that it also make a great seasoning for all kinds of foods while they are being cooked? Learn all of the great tasting meals you can make by using A-1 Steak sauce in new and innovative ways. Ask for *A-1 Steak Sauce Recipe Book* when you call:
800-323-0768.
Or better yet, visit Kraft's web site where you will find a host of wonderful recipes of all kinds:
www.kraftfoods.com

Meat & Poultry Hotline

The USDA has a meat and poultry hotline to help you with questions dealing with food safety. There are a full series of recorded answers to the most commonly asked questions or if you have specific questions, you can speak with a food safety expert. Call weekdays from 10:00am - 4:00pm EST to speak to a specialist. For recorded messages, you can call 24 hours a day.
1-800 535-4555
www.usda.gov

Simple And Tasty Recipes

The folks at College Inn Broth have a great recipe book to show you how to enhance all your dishes by using their chicken, beef & vegetable broths in new ways. To get your copy, call them toll-free:
1-800-55-BROTH
www.collegeinn.com

Flavorful Ways To Cut Back On Fat

Today we know just how important it is to cut back on our consumption of fat. But how do you do that without cutting back on flavor? For starters try using these great recipes using reduced fat sour cream. Just ask for the *Changing Courses Recipe Collection.* Call:
1-800-782-9602
www.landolakes.com

For Great Meals In Half The Time – Call this Helpline

Are you always in such a hurry that you never have the time to prepare a new nutritious main dish. Well now's the time to call the *Rice-A-Roni / Pasta-Roni Main Dish Helpline.* Calling this computerized phone service will help you put together a great meal in less than 30 minutes. You will receive a terrific selection of quick to prepare rice and pasta recipes. Call them toll-free at:
1-800-421-2444 Or write to:
Golden Grain Co.
PO Box 049003
Chicago, IL 60604
www.ricearoni.com

Great For Cookie Lovers

The ultimate cookie is here. Saco Foods will send you these *ten delicious recipes* plus a money-off coupon. Create a chocolate sensation today with these delicious chocolate chunks. Remember, it's the chocolate that makes the difference. Now it's easy to get more sweet satisfaction in each bite! They even have a *'Bake Your Best' hotline*:
1-800-373-SACO. Or send a **SASE** to:

SACO Foods
FREE COOKIE OFFER
PO Box 616
MIDDLETOWN, WI 53562
www.sacofoods.com

Prize-Winning Beef Recipes

If you would like to sample some of the best beef recipes in the nation, be sure to get a copy of the *National Beef Cook-Off Prize Winning Recipes*. You will find a host of delicious easy-to-prepare meals ranging from Chile Pizza to Gecian Skillet Ribeyes. Send a SASE to:

NATIONAL BEEF COOK-OFF RECIPES
BOX 3881
ENGLEWOOD, CO 80155
OR CALL TOLL-FREE: 800-848-9088
www.beefcookoff.org

Deli-Delicious

Easy Entertaining-Award -Winning Deli Meat Recipes contains 12 recipes for perfect party platters. Preparation times and even calorie counts accompany the recipes. This wonderful freebie comes to you from the National Live Stock and Meat Board. Ask for the *Easy Entertaining Brochure*. Just mail a SASE to:

NATIONAL LIVE STOCK AND MEAT BOARD
444 N. MICHIGAN AVE., DEPT. EE
CHICAGO, IL 60611

When In Rome

History shows that the Romans used clay cookware many centuries ago. Clay retains moisture which is released slowly during cooking resulting in savory self-basted food. For a terrific collection of recipes using clay Brique Ware, ask for *Brique Ware Recipes* and *Microwaving with Nordic Ware*.

Both come to you free from:
NORDIC WARE CUSTOMER SERVICE
HIGHWAY 7 AT 100
MINNEAPOLIS, MN 55416

Sizzlin' Hot Stuff

Red Devil Hot Sauce is a zesty hot sauce that has dozens of uses—in soups, stews, sandwiches and just about anywhere you want to add a lively taste to your food. For a compact collection of dozens of recipes, send a postcard asking for *Wright With Liquid Smoke and Regina Cooking Wine:*
B & G FOODS
PO BOX K
ROSELAND, NJ 07068
www.bgfoods.com (click on 'Red Devil')

Snap, Crackle &...Nutrition

When is a Rice Krispie more than a Rice Krispie? When it's part of a well-balanced nutrition program. The folks at Kellogg's would like to show you how to serve your family more nutritious meals using their outstanding line of food products. Send for *Kellogg's Favorite Recipes,* which is free from:
DEPARTMENT OF HOME ECONOMICS
KELLOGG CO.
BATTLE CREEK, MI 49016
www.kellogs.com

Fish Really Is Good For You

Research has proven that eating fish really is good for you. According to a study by the National Fisheries Institute, the average person eats a total of about 15 pounds of fish a year, or 4 1/2 ounces per week. Among the top 10 choices are salmon and catfish. The Catfish Institute has three recipe brochures waiting for you. In them you'll find a variety of ideas besides traditional high-fat frying. They can be ordered free just by writing to:

CATFISH INSTITURE
PO Box 924
INDIANOLA, MS 38751
www.catfishinstitute.com   On web site, click on **"Free Offers"**

Cooking Light

We all know that what we eat affects our health. But exactly what foods are the best for our health? How do you prepare foods that are good for you? Now there's a toll-free number you can call for answers to these and other questions you may have. This hotline sponsored by the *Healthy Cooking* magazine will put you in touch with registered dietitians who will answer your questions about cooking light. Call between 9 a.m. and 5:30 p.m. weekdays
1-800-231-3438

Bakers Hotline

The Fleishmann's Yeast Bakers Help Line, specializes in answering all your questions about yeast and bread-baking, including advice on using bread machines. Call weekdays between 10 am and 8pm.
1-800-777-4959

Tasty Sweet Nectar

Many people say that Golden Blossom Honey is the tastiest honey there is. To show you how to use their sweet and healthy necter in new ways, you will want to check out the *Golden Blosssom recipes collection.* To get these ecipes go to their web site at:
www.goldenblossom.com

The Perfect Grill-Out

If you love to barbecue, you're gonna love *A Barbecuer's Dozen Of Rib Ticklin' Recipes.* You can get yours just by calling the Weber Grill Hotline at **1-800-GRILL-OUT.** This toll-free phone number is in operation from April 1st to Labor Day each year. You can also call this same hotline to get answers to all your barbecue questions including cooking methods, fat trimming tips and proper methods of clean up and lots more.

Or visit their web site: www.weber.com

Fascinating Food Facts

The Department of Agriculture has a large package of fascinating and educational materials including a handy food pyramid guide waiting for you. Learn exactly what the USDA does in the areas of consumer services, food safety, nutrition and lots more. Excellent teaching and learning tool. Write to:

U.S. DEPARTMENT OF AGRICULTURE
PUBLICATIONS DIV.
WASHINGTON, DC 20250
www.usda.gov

Eating Healthy

AARP has a nutrition guide with information on dietary guidelines, the food pyramid, the new food labels and special diets for a better quality of life. To get a free copy of *Healthy Eating For a Healthy Life* (stock #D15565), send a postcard to:

AARP FULFILLMEMNT EE0924
601 E STREET N.W.
WASHINGTON, D.C. 20049

Fine Cheese Recipes

Six cheese recipes on file cards are available free from Marin French Cheese Company. Also included will be a mail order price list for their fine line of cheeses. Free from:

MARIN FRENCH CHEESE CO.
7500 RED HILL RD.
PETALUMA, CA 94952
1-800-292-6001
www.marinfrenchcheese.com

Poppin' Fresh Dough

In their new collection, Pillsbury brings you prize winning recipes including cakes from scratch, easy yeast baking and all kinds of new dough ideas. All this to help make your next dessert a sweet and tasty delight. It's yours free from:

GENERAL MILLS
ONE GENERAL MILLS BLVD.
MINNEAPOLIS, MN 55426
www.pillsbury.com

De-light Tortillas

To help you add a 'south of the border' touch to your next meal, the folks at Mission Foods would like to send you *The Art of Light Tortillas*. Learn how to make a delightful Spanish Pizza, Strawberry Breakfast Crepes, Fiesta Crab Crisps and lots more.

CALL TOLL FREE: 1-800-600-TACO

Just For Popcorn Lovers

If popcorn is a favorite of yours, the *Favorite Popcorn Recipes* collection is a must. It features mouth-watering popcorn balls, zesty treats and sweet 'n munchy snacks. Drop a postcard to:

AMERICAN POPCORN CO.
BOX 178
SIOUX CITY, IA 51102
www.jollytime.com

Do You Have A Sweet Tooth?

Looking for new dessert ideas your whole family will enjoy? You'll find lots of yummy dessert recipes and also learn how to cut the fat from sweets with *Plum Good Recipes.* For your free copy and discount coupon, write to:

SOKOL & CO.
5315 DANSHER RD.
COUNTRYSIDE, IL 60525
1-800-328-7656
www.solofoods.com

Pasta – A Food For All Times

Here are three excellent booklets for the health conscious. There are terrific recipes plus lots of things you can add to pasta to come up with a new meal. There are even quick microwave dishes you can make. Ask for *New World Pasta Recipes* from:

NEW WORLD PASTA
CONSUMER RELATIONS
PO BOX 126457
HARRISBURG, PA 17112
1-800-730- 5957
www.nwpasta.com

What's A Porcupine Meatball?

Roman Meal Company makes an excellent line of whole grain breads. *The Roman recipe collection* will show you how to make meals your family will love—like Porcupine Meatballs or Sloppy Joe's. You'll also receive budget stretcher ideas and low-fat diet menus. Free from:

ROMAN MEAL CO.
PO BOX 11126
TACOMA, WA 98411

Great Apple Sauce Recipes

This great cookbook has some of the most delightful recipes using Lucky Leaf Apple Sauce. You'll find recipes for everything from entrees to desserts to give your family new taste treats. It's yours free from:

KNOUSE FOODS
800 PEACH GLEN ROAD
PEACH GLEN, PA 17375
www.knouse.com

Do You Love Sausage?

Discover a host of tasty new ways of enjoying sausages with the *Hillshire Farm Sausage recipe collection.* For your free copy, send a postcard to:

HILLSHIRE FARMS
PO BOX 25111
CINCINATTI, OH 45225
www.hillshirefarm.com

Dinner Pancakes

From the makers of Mrs. Butterworth's buttered syrup, comes a nice collection of great budget recipes that will appeal to any palate. Send a postcard asking for *Mrs. Butterworth's Inflation Fighting Recipes,* to:

LEVER BROTHERS CO.
390 PARK AVE.
NEW YORK, NY 10022

Not For Dieters

Here's a yummy collection of *Hershey's Favorite Recipes* with selections like Chocolate Peppermint Whirlaway Pie. It makes your mouth water just thinking about it. Your diet can wait 'til next month. Also ask for *A Profile Of Hershey Foods.* Drop a card to:

CONSUMER INFORMATION
HERSHEY KITCHENS

100 CRYSTAL A DRIVE
PO BOX 815
HERSHEY, PA 17033
OR CALL: 1-800-468-1714
www.hersheys.com

Potatoes–A Heart's Good Friend

It's been known for many years that potatoes are one of the healthiest foods you can eat. Now with the *Heart Healthy recipe collection* you will learn how to enjoy this nutritious vegetable in new ways. In addition to tasty recipes you will discover some handy tips on buying and storing Idaho potatoes. Send a postcard to:
IDAHO POTATO COMMISSION
P.O. BOX 1068
BOISE, ID 83701
www.idahopotato.com

Enjoy A Georgia Peach

Like peaches? You're gonna love Georgia Peach Cobler, Peach Salsa, and other low fat recipes using peaches. Send a long SASE and ask for *Enjoy Georgia Peaches: A Southern Tradition,* to:
GEORGIA DEPARTMENT OF AGRICULTURE
COMMODITIES PROMOTION
19 MARTIN LUTHER KING JR DR. SW
ATLANTA, GA 30334
www.agr.state.ga.us

Super Suppers

If you are afraid to enjoy pasta meals just you're on a diet—this one's for you. With *Super Solutions For Super Suppers,* you will enjoy delicious Italian meals that are nutritionally balanced and still allow you to lose weight. You'll also receive a discount coupon. Send to:
RAGU FOODS, INC.
33 BENEDICT PL.
GREENWICH. CT 06830

Spice Up Your Life

Grey Poupon Dijon Mustard has a sixteen page recipe book that features over 35 different ways to spice up your menu with Grey Poupon Dijon Mustard. Here are tasty recipe ideas for red meat, chicken, pasta, fish and more. Check out this web site from Grey Poupon:

www.KraftFoods.com/greypoupon

Sweet As An...Onion?

An onion is probably the last thing you think of when you think of sweet foods. Vidalia Onion would like to change your mind. These special onions are mild and tasty. They're grown only in a small section of Georgia where weather and soil conditions blend to make the World's Sweetest Onion. Send today for the *Vidalia Onion recipe collection* which will also show you how to freeze and store these unique onions. Send a SASE to:

VIDALIA SWEET ONION
P.O. Box 1810
VIDALIA, GA 30474
1-800-892-3412
www.sweetvidalias.com

Salmon Delight

For a delightful collection of seafood recipe ideas check out this web site. On it you will find tasty delights that'll make your next barbecue more fun and gourmet delicacies that will liven up any meal. If you like fish and especially salmon check out this web site:

http://www.catchofthesea.com/

Why Fish For Kids

Learn why fish is an important food for kids as well as adults. Send for a free copy of *Why Fish For Kids.* Plus, for the youngsters there's a fun comic book called *Ricky & Debbie in SardineLand* that will entertain while it informs young people about the great benefits of eating fish. All are free from:

MAINE SARDINE COUNCIL
470 N. MAIN ST.
BREWER, ME 04412

Basket Of Fresh Ideas

Just about everyone loves fresh strawberries. Now this collection of yummy strawberry recipes will show you how to use this tasty fruit to make mouth watering desserts and drinks. Send a postcard to:

CALIFORNIA STRAWBERRY ADVISORY BOARD
P.O. BOX 269
WATSONVILLE, CA 95077
Check out their web site: www.calstrawberry.com

Cooking With Honey

Here's a double-barreled special. First, you'll find some fascinating facts about bees and honey plus a collection of taste tempting recipes using golden honey. Just ask for *Cook It Right With Honey.* Send a card to:

DADANT & SONS
HAMILTON, IL 62341

Top Hits From Frito Lays

This new recipe collection *Baked Low Fat - Taste The Fun Not The Fat* will provide you with a host of innovative new ways to enjoy Tostitos Tortilla Chips. Enjoy Chicken Curry Nachos or Italian Nachos. You'll also learn *The Story of Frito-*

Lay. Free from:
FRITO-LAY
PO BOX 660634
DALLAS, TX 75266
1-800-352-4477
Visit their web site: www.fritolay.com

Eat A Yam For Dessert

How would you like to enjoy a marshmallow yam dessert or yam orange cookies? These are just two of the tasty treats you'll find featured in the *Sweet Potato recipe collection* with dozens of prize winning yam recipes. Free from:
LOUISIANA SWEET POTATO COMMISSION
P.O. BOX 2550
BATON ROUGE, LA 70821
WWW.SWEETPOTATO.ORG

Birthday Party Planner

Before you plan your child's next birthday party, be sure to send for this freebie. Skippy has put together some great party ideas from invitations to decorations and activities. Ask for *Skippy Peanut Butter Party Planner* from:
SKIPPY PEANUT BUTTER
DEPT. SPP, BOX 307
COVENTRY, CT 06238

Spice It Up

Add a little zest to your next meal with these recipes using Tabasco sauce. Send a card asking for *From The Land of Tabasco Sauce.* This cookbook features dozens of tangy and tasty meal ideas and recipes for everything from Holiday Turkey to Cream Onion Dip. Put a little spice in your life and your meals. Write to:
MCILHENNY CO.
AVERY ISLAND, LA 70513
www.tabasco.com

New Adventures In Good Eating

Looking for new meal ideas your whole family will enjoy? Meals such as Stuffed Pork Chops and Tangy Chicken are among those you'll find in the *Heinz Recipe Collection*. Also ask for *Heinz Cooking With Beans*. All are free from:

H. J. HEINZ
PO BOX 57
PITTSBURGH, PA 15230
Visit them on the web at: www.heinz.com

Red Hot Stuff

If you like your food red hot, hot, hot...you'll definitely want to get this. *Tempting Recipes With Red Devil Hot Sauce* will show you some great ways to spice up your meals. So if you like it hot, you're gonna love like this compact collection of recipes"

B & G FOODS
PO BOX K
ROSELAND, NJ 07068
Or visit their web site: **www.bgfoods.com**

Fabulous Figs

The fig has been with us ever since Adam and Eve decided that fig leaves made nifty apparel. Now *Buyers Guide To Dietary Fiber* along with *Fabulous Figs - The Fitness Fruit* and *This Fig Can Teach You A Lot About Nutrition* will give you delicious new ways to use this delightful and nutritious fruit. Free from:

FIG ADVISORY BOARD
PO BOX 709
FRESNO, CA 93712
1-800-588-2344
Visit them on the web at: www.californiafigs.com

Being Creative With Olive Oil

When dinner's done you may receive a standing ovation from your family for the meal you just made with the help of this recipe collection. *How To Change Your Oil & Recipes* will give you a couple of dozen creative meal ideas using olive oil. You will also receive a store discount coupon. Send a postcard to:

POMPEIAN INC.
DEPT. W5
PO BOX 8863
BALTIMORE, MD 21224
1-800-POMPEIAN
WWW.POMPEIAN.COM

Millionaire Manhattan's & More

The makers of the original cream sherry - Harvey's Bristol Cream have a great recipe collection just for the asking. You'll find 'Peachy Cranberry Sauce' for pork, 'Millionaire's Manhattan' plus lots more. Send a long SASE and ask for *HBC's Recipes* to:

HBC RECIPE COLLECTION
PO BOX 767
HOLMDEL, NJ 07733
www.harveysbc.com

Cookouts Are Fun

How would you like a grill chef's hat or a new set of barbecue tools? Be sure to get a free copy of the *Grill Lovers Catalog*. In it you'll find something every barbecue chef will enjoy having. It's yours free from:

BRADLEY GRILL LOVER'S CATALOG
BOX 1300
COLUMBUS, GA 31902
1-800-241-7548
Also, visit their web site: **www.grilllover.com**

Ummm ... Good

Campbell has a special collection of recipes along with a discount coupon waiting for you. They feature their tasty line of soups. When you write, ask for the *Golden Corn Soup Chronology*. Write to:

CAMPBELL SOUP CO.
HOME ECONOMICS DEPT.
CAMPBELL PLACE
CAMDEN, NJ 08101

For over 1,500 great recipes go to their web site at:
www.campbellsoup.com

Wonderful Almonds

For a change of pace try using almonds to flavor your next meal. The *Fast & Fabulous collection* will show you how to use almonds in everything from chocolate-almond apricot bread, turkey tetrazzini almondine and almond-blueberry fruit cake. Free from:

ALMOND BOARD OF CALIFORNIA
12TH STREET, BOX 31307
MODESTO, CA 95354

For tons of great ideas and recipes, visit their web site at:
www.almondsarein.com

Saucy Recipes

The Light & Elegant Cookbook includes recipes of all kinds with everything from soups to nuts. All these exciting meals feature Lea & Perrins Sauce. There's even a nice index to help you easily find the recipe you want. Free from:

LEA & PERRINS SAUCE
CALL THEM AT: 1-800-987-4674
Or visit them on the web at: www.lea-perrins.com

Butter Recipe Of The Month

One call to the *Best of Butter Hotline* will reveal a world of ideas, recipes and tips on how to use Kellers Hotel Bar Butter in delightful new ways. When you call you will be taken step-by-step through the special recipe for that month. To find out more about their new recipes, cooking tips and product information, contact:

KELLER'S/HOTEL BAR FOODS
CALL THEM TOLL-FREE AT: 1-800-582-4382
www.butter1.com

"Cooking With Sweet Potatoes"

Here's a collection of over 70 tasty meals using sweet potatoes. You'll enjoy the main dishes and colorful casseroles featuring sweet potatoes in combination with other vegetables and meats. Visit the North Carolina Sweet Potato Commission on the web at:

www.ncsweetpotatoes.com

Free Sweet 'N Low Samples

For an envelope full of Sweet & Low samples plus a handy carry case, just send a SASE and request *"Sweet & Low Samples."* Send to:

SWEET 'N LOW
CUMBERLAND PACKING CORP
2 CUMBERLAND ST.
BROOKLYN, NY 11205

For tons of recipes using Sweet 'N Low, visit them on the web at:

www.sweetnlow.com

Fresh Ideas From Florida

What a wonderful package this is—an outstanding collection of recipes and information on seafood and aquaculture. Discover how to make a Seafare Saute & lots more. Send a long SASE to:

COMMISSIONER OF AGRICULTURE & CONSUMER SERVICES
BUREAU OF SEAFOOD & AQUACULTURE

2051 East Dirac Dr.
Tallahassee, FL 32310
WWW.FL-SEAFOOD.COM

Thomas' Promises..

If you like Thomas' English Muffins plain—you'll love 'em fancy. To get their *English Muffins Recipes* plus a discount coupon, call: S.B. Thomas, Inc. at:
1-800-356-3314
Also, check out thie web site at: **www.gwbakeries.com**

"Texasweet Citrus Recipes"

This collection of mouth-watering citrus recipes comes to you from TexaSweet. Their Ruby Red grapefruit has a sweet, juicy flavor. The recipes cover breakfast, dinner, dessert and drinks using this delectable citrus. Send a postcard to:
TexaSweet Citrus Marketing
901 Business Park Drive #100
Mission. TX 78572
www.texasweet.com

A Sweet Way To Cheat

If you love sweets (and who doesn't) but must watch your weight *26 Ways To Get Back To Nature* is for you. For your free copy of this booklet plus four others including *Cakes For All Occasions*, send a postcard to:
Sugar Foods Corp.
9500 El Dorado Ave.
Sun Valley CA 91353
In California call: **1-800-424-1919**
Outside California call: **1-800-732-8963**
www.sugarfoods.com

Spread The Nutrition

Oscar Mayer sandwich spreads are easy and versatile to use. Try the spreads on crackers, breads and in other recipes. For a nice collection of recipe ideas called *Nutrition Facts,* send a postcard to:

OSCAR MAYER CONSUMER CENTER
PO BOX 7188   DEPT # ST
MADISON, WI 53707

Or visit them on the web: **www.kraftfoods.com/oscar-mayer**

Nuts About Nuts

If you're crazy about nuts, *All The Goodness of Hawaii* is the catalog for you. You can order anything from Macadamia Nuts to Kona Coffee. For your free copy, send a postcard to:

MAUNA LOA GIFT CENTER
1 MACADAMIA ROAD
H. C. 01, BOX 3
HILO, HI 96720
www.maunaloa.com

Staying Young At Heart

Are you one of the 60 million Americans with high blood pressure? If so you should learn how to eat right. Send for the free booklet, *So You Have High Blood Cholesterol* from:

INFORMATION CENTER
NATIONAL HEART, LUNG, & BLOOD INSTITUTE
7200 WISCONSIN AVE.
PO BOX 30105
BETHESDA, MD 20824
Also check out their web site: www.nhlbi.nih.gov

Creole Cooking

If you enjoy the unique taste and flavors of cajon and creole food, this one's for you. For a free copy of chef Paul Prudhomme's Magic Spice Book showing you how to use creole seasoning to create old-fashioned Louisiana taste delights. Call toll-free:
1-800-457-2857
www.chefpaul.com

Sizzling Lamb Recipes

The American Lamb Council has several recipe collections that will show you exciting ways to make your dinners more delightful. The collection includes *Make It Simple, Make It Sizzle,* and *Festive Lamb Recipes,* plus several others. You'll find wine-basted, marinated, grilled, roasted and broiled recipes using fresh American lamb. Send a long SASE to:

THE AMERICAN LAMB COUNCIL
6911 S. YOSEMITE ST. SUITE 200
ENGLEWOOD, CO 80112
Visit their web site at: www.lambchef.com

Bringing Home The Bacon

If you like bacon, be sure to get your copy of *Savor The Flavor, Round The Clock With Oscar Mayer Bacon.* In it you'll discover tasty recipes and cooking ideas featuring bacon. They will also include party & cookout recipes using Oscar Mayers Little Wieners & Little Smokies plus Nutrition Facts. Send a postcard to:

BACON BOOKLETS
OSCAR MAYER CONSUMER CENTER
PO BOX 7188
MADISON, WI 53707
www.oscarmayer.com

Delicious Skinny Beef

Looking for something easy but delicious for your family's meals? How about meals that are perfect for anyone watching their weight? Try something different… like 'beef, pasta & artichoke toss' or 'quick steak & vegetable soup'. For some great recipes visit the Meat Board Test Kitchens on the internet at:

www.beef.org (then click on 'kitchen')

How To Comfort

Now you can make some great desserts, drinks and even coffee using that versatile liquor from Kentucky — Southern Comfort. If you would like some delicious recipe ideas, write to:

SOUTHERN COMFORT COMPANY
DEPT. GT, BOX 1080
LOUISVILLE, KY 40201

Wine And Dine With Gallo

The Gallo recipe collection will show you dozens of palate pleasing ways of using Gallo to enhance your next meal. Included is a delightful recipe for a Goumet Pizza and lots more. These recipes will help you turn everyday cooking into an adventure. Write to:

E & J GALLO WINERY
MODESTO, CA 95353

New Recipes For Using White Wine

Wine lovers delight in trying new wines and new ways to enjoy familiar wines. With this compact collection of recipes called, *White Wine Recipes,* you'll create tasty new meals using the fine wines of Widmer. Free from:

WIDMER WINE CELLARS
116 BUFFALO ST.
CANANDAIGUA, NY 14424
1-800-836-5253
www.widmerwine.com

Free Wine Tasting Tour

Beaulieu Vineyards describes and pictures the Beaulieu line of fine wines. Also includes a card for a free wine tasting tour of their vineyard. Write to:

BEAULIEU VINEYARDS
PO Box 329
RUTHERFORD, CA 94573

Virgin Island Rum

Cruzan Rum is an exceptionally clean tasting rum that works well with mixers or on its own. For your copy of the free *Imported Rum Recipes* and get great rum cake recipes too...write:

CRUZAN RUM DISTILLERY
PO Box 218, FREDERIKSTED
ST. CROIS, VL 00840
www.cruzanrums.com

The Finest Cordial Recipes

Hiram Walker has put together a selection of over 30 famous food and drink recipes from around the world. These recipes all feature their fine line of cordials. Just ask for their free, *The Best Of Kahlua*. Pink Chinchilla Pie anyone? Visit this web site:

www.kahlua.com

The Marvelous Liqueur

Chambord is a liqueur made with small black raspberries plus other fruits & herbs combined with honey. For new ways to enjoy this magnificent liqueur, send for the free *Chambord Recipe Book* from:

CHAMBORD RECIPES
2633 TRENTON AVE
PHILADELPHIA, PA 19125
1-800-523-3811

For Home & Garden

"Trash The Germs"

The makers of Bounty paper towels want to send you their informative booklet *Trash the Germs*, to help reduce the spread of household germs. Most of us are not aware of how we can prevent the spread of household germs before they cause serious problems. Using paper towels to dry your hands and discarding it after handling meat or poultry products reduces the risk of leaving any bacteria to linger and multiply on a cloth dish towel. Learn to have good home hygiene ask for *Trash the Germs*. Call toll-free:
1-800-9-BOUNTY
www.quickerpickerupper.com

Dirty Secrets

Wisk will be happy to send you their free *Dirty Secrets* brochure with tips on how to handle all those dirty laundry problems. To get your copy, just call them toll-free at:
1-800-ASK-WISK
Or visit their web site at: **www.wisk.com**

Powerful Hand Cleaner

Ink Solv is great hand cleaner that will remove those ugly hard to clean ink and paint stains from your hands. If you are tired of scrubbing ink and paint stains, give them a call. They're offering a free sample if you need a heavy duty soap in your work. Call them toll-free:
1-800-383-0251

Free Potpourri Bonnets

These delightful miniature straw hat bonnet magnets are

filled with potpourri and ready for your refrigerator door or bathroom. They are yours for six first class loose stamps. Send to:

VALERIE'S HATTERY
13435 S. CEDAR RD
CEDAR, MI 49621

Putting Solar Energy To Work

The day will come when your home will be heated and powered with free energy from the sun. Here are the answers to many of the most frequently asked questions about putting solar and other kinds of renewable energy to work for you. Write to:

EREC
EE90
1000 INDEPENDENCE AVE. SW
WASHINGTON, DC 20585

There is also a toll-free phone number you can call to get in touch directly with an expert who can answer specific questions you may have about renewable energy. There are also a large number of free booklets dealing with every aspect of renewable energy. They are all available by calling the same toll-free number.
CALL: **800-363-3732.**

Finally, if you have a computer and modem you can access the Department of Energy and Renewable Resources, on the Worldwide Web. They even have free software you can download. Their web site is located at:
www.eren.doe.gov

Important Tips To Save Energy

Saving energy not only makes America less energy dependent on other nations - it will save you a tidy sum of money too. The Department of Energy has put together a package chuck full of useful energy-saving information they would

like you to have. Ask for the *Energy Saver booklets*. They're
yours free from:
D.O.E. TECHNICAL INFORMATION CENTER
BOX 62
OAK RIDGE, TN 37830
www.osti.gov

How Does Fiberglas Work?

All About Insulation and *Owens-Corning Fiberglas* are two
of the useful guides found in the *Fiberglas information series*. You'll find out how Fiberglas is made and how it's used
for insulation, dust-stops and air filters. It's yours free from:
OWENS CORNING
ONE OWENS CORNING PKWY
TOLEDO, OH 43659
1-800-438-7465
www.owenscorning.com

Let The Sun Shine In

If you're planning on building or remodeling a house, have
you thought about which new windows and doors are right
for you? *Window Scaping* pictures and describes all of the
various types of windows and doors available to help you
decide for yourself. It's free from:
PELLA CO.
102 MAIN STREET
PELLA, IA 50219
1-888-84-PELLA
www.pella.com

Home Remodeling Ideas

Are you getting ready to build or remodel a home? If so the
Insider's Look At Building Your Home and *Insider's Look At
Remodeling Your Home* are an absolute must. Your creative
juices will begin to flow as you thumb through these beautifully illustrated idea books. The answer books will provide

help in solving your remodeling problems whether you're adding a room or simply changing a window. Write to:
ANDERSEN CORP.
BAYPORT, MN 55003
1-800-426-4261 EXT 2837
Or visit them on the web at: www.andersenwindow.com

Emergency Stain Removal

This helpful *Emergency Spot Removal Guide* will help you get rid of some of the trickiest stains you may get on your carpets or draperies. It is free for the asking and will come with discount coupons. Drop a postcard to:
COIT DRAPERY & CARPET CLEANERS
DEPT. ABJ, 897 HINKLEY RD.
BURLINGAME, CA 94010
1-800-367-2648
Find out how to remove any stain, go to: **www.coit.com**

Beautify & Protect Your Home

Red Devil would like to show you the right way to beautify your home with wall coverings and protect it from cracks and drafts with caulk. Ask them for the *free wallcovering and caulk booklets.* Write to:
RED DEVIL INC.
CONSUMER RELATIONS
PO BOX 3133, UNION, NJ 07083

"The Story Of Hardwood Plywood"

If you are a handyman, you'll enjoy this informative booklet which tells the whole story of plywood. Best of all you'll receive a set of 4 different plans showing you how to build a bookcase, room divider, saddle seat desk and TV trays (planter/desk/stereo, etc.) All free from:
HARDWOOD PLYWOOD MANUFACTURERS
PO BOX 2789
RESTON, VA 22090

Building A House You Can Afford

You may still be able to afford the home you've always wanted. For the past quarter century DeGeorge Homes has helped over 15,000 people enjoy home ownership with their step-by-step instructions and pre-cut material. For a free copy of their 80 page *color catalog* with 50 exciting models to choose from, contact:

DeGeorge Homes
55 Realty Drive
Cheshire, CT 06410
1-800-342-7576

"Save Water"

Wasting water even from a slow leak over time can cost you a bundle. To help you prevent this, here's a fully illustrated guide on how to pinpoint water waste in your toilet and what to do about it. You'll also receive a packet of dye you can use to detect leaks. Send a postcard to:

Fluidmaster
30800 Rancho Viejo Road
San Juan Capistrano, CA 92675
1-800-631-2011
www.fluidmaster.com

The Right Way To Clean A Carpet

Hoover will send you a free guide to carpet care. *The Consumer Guide to Carpet Cleaning* is loaded with carpet care tips and facts, cleaning alternatives, a stain removal chart and more. This 16 page booklet provides important information you should know. Ask for *Consumer Guide to Carpet Cleaning.* Send a long SASE to:

THE HOOVER COMPANY
CONSUMER EDUCATION, DEPT. FC
101 E. MAPLE ST.
NORTH CANTON, OH 44720

Do-It-Yourself

If you love to fix up your home yourself, you're going to love this web site. On it you will find highly informative handyman articles on fixing your basement, attics, plumbing, painting and lots more. Check it out at on the internet at:
www.handyman.com

Save On Wallpaper By Mail

This great *catalog* offers you an excellent selection of high quality wall covering products at guaranteed lowest prices. To get a copy of their catalog with over 375 of the most popular patterns with free shipping and a 100% satisfaction guarantee plus a coupon for 10% off your first catalog order call:
American Blinds, Wallpaper & More
TOLL-FREE AT **1-800-575-8016**
Or visit them at their web site:
www.DecorateToday.com

"Guide To Paint & Varnish Removal"

In this handy guide you will learn some great and easy ways to improve the appearance of your house. There are quick and easy methods for removing both mildew stains and paint or varnish from all interior and exterior surfaces. These helpful hints are a must for any tough cleaning or renovating job. Send for your free guide to:
SAVOGRAN COMPANY
P.O. BOX 130
NORWOOD, MA 02062
1-800-225-9872
www.savogran.com

Alarm Your Home For Security

To protect your family and home, a home security alarm system is essential. To help you decide on what type of protection is best for you and your family, ask for the free *Amgard Security Planning Guide.* Write to:

AMGARD SECURITY OFFER
AMWAY CORPORATION-33A-2J
ADA, MI 49355

The All-Purpose Wonder

Want to save money and look good too? Send for *This Little Box With A House Full of Uses.* In it you will learn how to use baking soda in ways you never thought of...in the kitchen, bathroom, basement, even on your pet. Write to:

ARM & HAMMER
CONSUMER RELATIONS
CHURCH & DWIGHT CO.
PRINCETON, NJ 08543
1-800-524-1328
www.armhammer.com

Stain Removal Guide

Most stains can be removed if you know how. The people at Maytag have an excellent stain removal guide they will send you just for the asking. Remember, once you master the steps it's easy to remove just about any stain by referring to this handy guide. You'll also receive *Facts of Laundry.- Choosing The Right Laundry Additives.* Send a postcard to:

MAYTAG COMPANY
CUSTOMER SERVICE
240 EDWARDS STREET
CLEVELAND, TN 37311
1-800-688-9900
www.maytag.com

Carpet Care

If you are thinking of adding or changing carpets in your home but are confused by the many choices you have to make, call The Carpet and Rug Institute's information line for answers to your questions related to carpeting your home
1-800-882-8846
www.carpet-rug.com

How To Stay Warm This Winter

Stay warm this winter with insulated clothing, outdoor equipment and toasty down comforters that you make yourself — with the help of a Frostline kit. For a copy of their free catalog, send a postcard to:
FROSTLINE KITS
PO BOX 3419
GRAND JUNCTION, CO 81502
1-800-548-7872

Keeping Your Silver Glistening

If you would like to keep your silverware shining like new, try storing it in Hagerty's Tarnish Intercept Bags. Once the silverware is placed inside and the bag zipper is closed, it locks out tarnish. The inside of the bag will blacken when it has absorbed all the corrosion-causing gases. You then remove the silver and place it in a new bag. For information on their line of precious metal care products, call:
1-800-348-5162 x103
W. J. HAGERTY SONS, LTD.
P.O. BOX 1496
SOUTH BEND, IN 46624.
OR VISIT THEIR WEB SITE AT:
www.hagerty-polish.com

Shingle Your Home Inside & Out

Lots of remodeling ideas are contained in this great *Red Shingle & Shake package*. It shows how to use shingles and

shakes outside and inside your house. These guides also show how to do-it-yourself and save. Drop a card to:
Cedar Shake & Shingle Bureau
PO Box 1178
Sumas, WA 98295
www.cedarbureau.org

Stain Out Hotline

Do you have questions about problem stains on your favorite garments? What do you do if it's an unknown mystery stain and you don't know where to begin? The Dow Stain Experts, the makers of Spray 'N Wash, have the answers for you. Give them a call at on their toll-free hotline:
1-800 260-1066
www.reckitt.com

Free Spot Removal Guide

Here are lots of helpful tips from the clean clothes professionals at Clorox on keeping your clothes clean, bright and stain free. Ask for *Emergency Spot Removal Guide*. Drop a postcard to:
The Clorox Co.
1221 Broadway
Oakland, CA 94612
1-800-292-2200
www.clorox.com

How To Choose The Right Carpet

If you are thinking of buying new carpets, Dupont Company would like you to have this free booklet *Consumer's Guide To Choosing Carpets* to help answer all your questions about carpet selection and care. Send a postcard to:
Dupont Co.
Room G 40284
Wilmington, DE 19898
1-800-4-DUPONT
www.dupont.com

Brighten Up Your Garden

Would you like to add a colorful look to your garden next spring? Consider planting Holland or domestic tulip bulbs. For a full color catalog, write to:

VAN BOURGONDIEN
PO 1000
BABYLON, NY 11702
1-800-622-9997
www.dutchbulbs.com

Start An Herb Garden On Your Window Sill

This catalog is packed with everything you can imagine to start your vegetable, flower or fruit garden. They have seed starter kits and plants. You'll even find garden helpers, bird houses and fun seed kits for kids. Grow your own herb garden right on your kitchen window sill. When you call or write mention OFFER *#82* and in addition to their new *Flowering Bulb and Perennial Catalog*, you'll also receive a special $5.00-off coupon. Free from:

BURPEE & CO.
300 PARK AVE
WARMINSTER, PA 18974
OR CALL 1-800-888-1447
www.burpee.com

Start A Community Garden

In the last few years backyard community gardens have been popping up all over the nation. Bring your community together add beauty to your community and save money too - start a community garden. You'll also

receive teaching tools to help young minds grow. Ask for
Growing Ideas. It's yours free from:
NATIONAL GARDEN ASSOCIATION
1100 DORSET ST.
SOUTH BURLINGTON, VT 05403
WWW.NATIONALGARDENING.COM

Why Plants Fail

The question of why some plants fail to grow even when they
are carefully tended to, has always been somewhat of a mystery. Now Gurney Seed and Nursery would like to throw
some light on the subject so you can have a more beautiful
garden. They will also send you the new *Gurney Catalog*. It
features over 4000 items—many shown in full color. You'll
find how-to-grow-it tips plus planting charts and moisture
guides along with many special offers. If you'd like a packet
of giant sunflower seeds, include a quarter. Write:
GURNEY'S SEED & NURSERY CO.
PO BOX 4178
GREENDALE, IN 47025
www.gurneys.com

Growing An Organic Garden

How To Grow An Organic Garden will get you started raising your own delicious and naturally pure vegetables. It even
includes a plan for a sample garden. Get your free copy and
let Mother Nature do her thing. Visit their web site at:
www.harmonyfarm.com

1,300 Exotic Imported Plants

Do you enjoy unusual and out-of-the ordinary type plants?
If so, this one's for you. The new *Stokes seed catalog* features
1300 varieties including many imported from England, Europe, and Canada. Get your free catalog from:

STOKES SEEDS INC.
BOX 548
BUFFALO, NY 14240
1-800-396-9238
www.stokeseeds.com

Terrific Nursery Guide

In this nursery catalog and planting guide, you'll find a new seedless grape, virus-free berries and several pages of tested recipes and a whole lot more. Miller Nurseries has put together a broad selection of their most popular nursery items. Ask for their new *Catalog & Planting Guide*:

J. E. MILLER NURSERIES
5060 WEST LAKE ROAD
CANANDAIGUA, NY 14424
1-800-836-9630
www.millernurseries.com

To Grow The Perfect Lawn

Here's a super 5-star special for anyone with a lawn or garden. To help improve lawn, flowers, vegetable garden, trees and shrubs - call the experts at Scott Lawn Products on their toll-free phone. They have the answers to any and all questions about lawn growing, diseases, fertilizing, problem areas and more. They'll also give you a free subscription to *Lawn Care* with loads of useful information (plus money saving coupons). They're happy to send you any of the dozens of booklets, magazines and brochures that will help you grow the perfect lawn or garden. Excellent. Call toll free:

1-800-543-TURF OR WRITE:
SCOTT LAWN PRODUCTS
14111 SCOTTS LAWN RD.
MARYVILLE, OH 43041
Or visit their web site: www.scottscompany.com

Would You Like A Great Lawn?

To create a great lawn, check out this terrific web site. It has everything you ever wanted to know about how to plant, grow and maintain the perfect lawn. Visit them at:
www.doityourself.com/lawn

Imagine – Full-Sized Fruit From Dwarf-Size Trees!

If your yard is too small to grow as many fruit trees as you'd like, take a look at this free catalog. These dwarf trees grow only 8 to 10 feet tall but grow full size apples, peaches, pears, cherries, and nectarines. This catalog features almost 400 varieties of fruit, shade and nut trees plus shrubs, vines, ornamentals, and award-winning roses. Send a postcard for the catalog and special offers to:

STARK BROTHER NURSERIES
BOX 1800, HIGHWAY 54W
LOUISIANA, MO 63353

1-800-775-6415
www.starkbrothers.com

Free Fertilizer

Free manure is available to gardeners through Extension Services located throughout the country. To find the one nearest you, call your local U.S. Department of Agriculture Extension Service. You'll find their phone number in the blue pages of your local phone book.

Great Gardens

The Burreil Seed Growers have a nice seed catalog every home gardener will want to have. It features all kinds of wonderful ideas on creating a beautiful garden. Before you get ready to plant your next garden, be sure to get a copy of this catalog. Send a postcard to:
D.V. BURREIL SEED GROWERS
PO BOX 150
ROCKY FORD, CO 81067

Gardener's Handbook

If you want to learn how to have a beautiful fruitful garden, be sure to get a free copy of *The Park Gardener's Handbook.* In it you will find all kinds of useful information that will help you to get more productive results from your gardening efforts. You can also choose from over 3000 new and rare varieties of flowers and vegetables as well as the more familiar types—all available in the full color Park catalog you'll receive. Send a postcard to:
GEORGE W. PARK SEED CO. INC.
ONE PARKTON AVE
GREENWOOD, SC 29649
1-800-213-0076
www.parkseed.com

For Pet Lovers

Being Kind To Animals

If you care deeply for animals, The American Society For The Prevention of Cruelty to Animals...the ASPCA has an information packet including booklets about caring for or traveling with your pets. To get a full list of their helpful information, write to:

AMERICAN SOCIETY OF PREVENTION OF CRUELTY TO ANIMALS
PUBLIC INFORMATION DEPT.
424 E. 92ND ST.
NEW YORK, NY 10128

Or visit them on the Internet at:
www.aspca.org

How About A Free Pet?

If you have ever stopped by a pet shop in the mall to play with the delightful puppy they had sitting in the window, you learned that to take that puppy home would make a deep dent in your wallet. There's no reason to spend hundreds of dollars when your local newspaper and supermarket bulletin boards may have ads giving away free kittens and pups when their pets have litters. Also, don't forget that animal shelters also have delightful free pets dying for a home. Usually they'll only ask you to pay for the shots. Call your local animal shelter for more information.

Free Animal Calendar And Datebook

For pet lovers everywhere, The Animal Protection Institute has a handy informative *Animals Calendar and Datebook*. In addition to being a datebook and calendar it is full of hundreds of fascinating facts about animals plus a listing of important animal events. If you love animals, this is definitely for you. Write to:

ANIMAL PROTECTION INSTITUTE
1122 S STREET
SACRAMENTO, CA 95814
1-800-348-PETS
www.api4animals.org

Caring For A Dog With Arthritis

Does your dog have difficulty getting up after a nap or a hard time climbing? Most people just assume that it's old age and that nothing can be done about it. The problem may very well be osteoarthritis which afflicts 1 dog in 5. Pfizer Dog Care has a toll-free number you can call for information on what you can do for your dog if it suffers from this problem. Call:

1-800-720-DOGS
www.rimadyl.com

Taking Special Care Of Your Cat

Special Care for Special Cats is a cat chow that helps maintain the urinary tract health for your cat. It's made with real chicken for a great taste. For information call:

1-800-7-PURINA   or visit their web site: **WWW.PURINA.COM**

Your Dog Will Love You More

Purina One Reduced Calorie Dog Formula is made with real turkey, that makes it nutritious and tasty. Your dog will love

it! For your free sample plus useful information, call:
1-800-787-0078 Ext. 43

If You're Allergic To Pets

If you would love to have a pet but are allergic to animal hair and dander, there may be a new way to help eliminate those allergies around the house with a new vacuum by Nilfisk, Inc. of America. Call:
1-800-645-3475
www.pa.nilfisk-advance.com/index.html

Free Vet Care For Your Pet

Remember if you live near a university that has a Veterinary school, you may be able to get free vet care for your pet especially if you are a senior citizen. Call them and ask about the services they offer.

Also, if you need assistance with an ailing pet, contact:
CENTER FOR VETERINARY MEDICINE
U.S. FOOD AND DRUG ADMINISTRATION
7500 STANDISH PLACE
ROCKVILLE, MD 20855
301-827-3800
www.fda.gov/cvm

You And Your New Puppy or New Kitten

Are you thinking of getting a new puppy or kitten? If so, this freebie from Iams Company is for you. *You & Your New Puppy* and *You & Your New Kitten* will give you useful advice on feeding, house-training, health care, grooming, training of a new pet and lots more. Write to:
THE IAMS COMPANY
PUPPY/KITTEN INFORMATION CENTER
BOX 1475
DAYTON, OHIO 45401
WWW.IAMS.COM

Caring For Your Pet

If you have a dog or are planning to get one, make sure you write for *free pet information* from the folks at Ralston Purina dog food products. They have an excellent freebie that will not only give you a brief history of dogs, but also give you tips on feeding your dog, grooming, obedience training, keeping your dog healthy and traveling with your dog. They may also include discount coupons and a Purina dog food guide to balancing nutrients to meet your dog's needs. Also ask for *Guide To Caring For Your Dog* and *Help...My Pet Refuses To Eat.* These freebies are a must if you've ever thought of getting a dog for a pet. Write to:

NESTLE PURINA PET CARE COMPANY
DOG FOOD DIVISION
CHECKERBOARD SQUARE
ST. LOUIS, MO 63164.
1-800-778-7462
www.purina.com

This Cake Is For The Birds

Lafeber's Avi-Cakes Gourmet Bird Food will provide a perfectly nutritious snack to satisfy bird munchies. Avi-Cakes is a nutritionally complete bird treat with proper vitamins and delicious flavors. Get your free trial size sample now. Ask for the *Avi-Cakes Sample* Write to:

LAFEBER COMPANY
24981 N. 1400 EAST RD
CORNELL, IL 61319

Fish Are Fun

Fish are educational, fun and something the whole family can enjoy. Now you can learn step-by-step how to set up a year round backyard pond and stock it with hardy fish. Send for your free *We Are The Water Garden Experts*. Drop a postcard to:

TETRA POND
3001 COMMERCE ST.
BLACKSBURG, **VA 24060-6671**
1-800-526-0650
www.tetra-fish.com

Raising A Healthy Pet

If you have a dog, cat, bird or virtually any other pet for that matter, PetsMart, one of America's largest pet care retailers has a host of specific information you will find useful. Just go to their web site and you will find great guides, tips and hints that will show you how to care for and raise a healthy pet. To explore this great web site go on the internet to:

WWW.PETSMART.COM

More Than A Friend

To millions of people their pet is a real member of the family. And love of animals has inspired many to follow a career path to becoming a veterinarian. For these people, the American Veterinary Association has an interesting booklet called *Today's Veterinarian* about the opportunities available today in this interesting field. For your free copy, send a postcard to:

AMERICAN VETERINARY ASSOCIATION
1931 NORTH MEECHAM RD. SUITE 100
SCHAUMBURG, **IL 60173**
www.avma.org

Caring For Your Pets

The American Humane Association has a whole series of informative booklets available for pet owners. These booklets tell how to care for dogs, cats, horses, birds and fish. For a complete listing, write for their free *catalog of publications.* From:

AMERICAN HUMANE ASSOCIATION
63 INVERNESS DRIVE E.
ENGLEWOOD, CO 80112
1-800-227-4645
www.americanhumane.org

Better Pet Care And Nutrition

If you'd like any information about proper pet care and pet nutrition, the makers of Kal Kan pet food would like to help you. They will send you *Understanding Your Dog* and *Understanding Your Cat.* Write to:

KAL KAN CONSUMER ADVISORY SERVICE
3386 EAST 44TH ST.
P.O. BOX 58853
VERNON, CA 90058
WWW.KALKAN.COM

Craft & Hobbies

Free Bead Supply Catalog

Are you looking for an interesting and challenging hobby? The Frantz Bead Company has put together an informative newsletter and supply catalog to help teach you the art of bead making. You'll get the free newsletter plus a catalog with a full assortment of terrific bead supplies. Simply send a postcard to:

FRANTZ BEAD COMPANY
1222 SUNSET HILL ROAD
SHELTON, WA 98584
www.frantzartglass.com

Beautiful Christmas Craft Ideas

If you love to make truly unique Christmas ornaments, you will definitely want to visit this web site. You'll learn how to make beautiful hand-made stocking stuffers that will quickly become the centerpiece of your holiday decorations. Many of these crafts are also great for holiday sales. When you visit their web site be sure to sign up for their free crafts newsletter. Visit them at:
http://mycraftbook.com/

Fun With Ribbons

Learn to create colorful and fun projects with ribbons. You'll be amazed at what you can create using ribbons of all sizes, colors and textures. This is a great rainy day project

and you can even use the finished projects to raise money
for a special cause. Write to:
C M Offray & Son
857 Willow Circle
Haggerstown, MD 21740
1-800-344-5533
www.offray.com

If You Like Duplicate Bridge

Do you enjoy playing duplicate bridge? If so you'll want this
catalog and product source guide with just about anything
you might want or need for this game. Write to:
American Contract Bridge League
2990 Airways Blvd.
Memphis, TN 38116
1-800-467-2623
www.acbl.org

Playing Better Chess

Learn the official rules of this challenging game of chess and
also receive another publication to join the U.S. Chess Federation. Chess helps you develop your ability to think
analytically. Ask for *Ten Tips To Winning Chess.* Send
a long SASE to:
U.S. Chess Federation
3054 US Route 9W
New Windsor, NY 12553
Or call: 1-800-388-5464
www.shopuschess.org

Crocheting A Doll

If you love to crochet you'll want this free pattern for a pair
of Raggedy Ann and Andy dolls. Crocheting these dolls are
just half the fun ...giving them as a gift and seeing the joy
they bring is the rest. Send a long SASE and $1.00 postage
and handling to:

NP PATTERNS
341 4TH TERRACE
EGG HARBOR, NJ 08215
WWW.CRAFTOWN.COM/FREE.HTM

For Collectors of Mechanical Toys

If you are a collector of fine mechanical toys, this beautifully illustrated catalog is for you. In the 32 pages of this catalog you will find a unique collection of classic cars. Ask for Lilliput Catalog from:

LILLIPUT
PO BOX 447
YERINGTON, NV 89447
OR CALL: **1-800-TIN-TOYS**
WWW.LILLIPUTMOTORCOMPANY.COM

Free Numismatic News

Here's a newspaper every coin collectors will want to have. Simply write and request a free copy of *'Numismatic Weekly.'* You'll enjoy its many interesting articles on all aspects of this fascinating hobby. Send a card to:

NUMISMATIC NEWS WEEKLY
KRAUSE PUBLICATIONS
700 EAST STATE STREET
IOLA, WI 54990
www.amnumsoc.org

Star Search

Do you have a favorite recording artist or special movie star? Well here's your chance to get an autograph of that famous star. You'll receive a listing of over 100 superstar names and addresses along with a brief bio as well as helpful hints on making your star search productive. Send a long SASE to:

JIM WEAVER'S AUTOGRAPHS IN THE MAIL
322 MALL BLVD., #345
MONROEVILLE, PA 15146-2229

Free Celebrity Autograph

Have you always wanted to collect a celebrity's autograph but didn't know how to get it? Now there's someone who will teach you how. When you write, you'll receive a free address of a celebrity and instructions on how to request an 8x10 autographed celebrity photo. The first time you write, the celebrity's address you receive will be Mr. Greenhill's choice. He's been doing this for 10 years so he knows what he's doing. To get on the celeb bandwagon, send a long SASE to:

DAVID GREENHILL
2306 CEDAR WAY
DALLAS TX 75241

Help From Kodak on How To Take Great Photos

This 48 page guide in full color shows you how to take the best snapshots under any circumstances. It's easy to understand and deals with topics such as lighting, flash photography, action and more. So start taking better pictures now. Ask for *Hot Shots With Any Camera*. Call:

1-800-242-2424
www.kodak.com

Crochet Time

These free crochet instructions will show you how to make some beautiful hand made ornaments, that you could sell, give as gifts or enjoy yourself. You can make seven simple thread snowflakes and 10 easy yarn ornaments. So get started now and send for your free instructions. Ask for: Crochet Tree-Trim Pattern, SASE to:

LORRAINE VETTER-SR
7924 SOPER HILL ROAD
EVERETT, WA 98205

Home Sewing Basics

If you're thinking of decorating anything from a single room to an entire house, be sure to get, *Sewing - It's Sew Soothing*. Discover how much fun it is to make your own curtains, slip covers and pillow shams. To get your copy, send a long SASE to:

HOME SEWING ASSOCIATION
PO BOX 1312
MONROEVILLE, PA 15146
www.sewing.org

Win At Blackjack

If you enjoy playing blackjack, two free Blackjack Strategy Cards are yours for the asking. These pocket-sized cards give you invaluable strategies, based on what you are dealt and and lists all the correct...hit, stand, split, and double down decisions. Various combinations of hands and dealer show cards are printed right on an easy to read chart. Gambling, blackjack in particular, can be fun if you're able to combine luck with a little strategy. Ask for the *Blackjack Strategy Cards*. Send $1.00 for postage & handling to:

THOMAS CASINO SERVICES
5380 OVERPASS ROAD SUITE E DEPT BF
SANTA BARBARA, CA 93111

Beat The Odds In BlackJack

Thousands of people love the challenge and excitement of blackjack. If this describes you, you may have wondered if there was any way you could improve your chances of winning. To help you better your odds, send for a wallet-size free mini-magnetic strategy card. Send a SASE and ask for *Winning Blackjack Strategies* to:

S. J. LEE ENTERPRISES
PO BOX 333-H, DEPT. BSR
SCARSDALE, NY 10583

Having Problems With Your Polaroid?

Have your Polaroid photos been coming out the way you'd like? If not there's a toll-free hotline to call where an expert will answer any questions you may have. Call toll free 8AM -8PM Monday through Saturday at: **800-343-5000.** Polaroid has a wonderful policy of complete customer satisfaction. Your problem may lie with defective film which they'll replace at no charge. Send defective film or photos to:

POLAROID CUSTOMER CARE SERVICE
1265 MAIN STREET W-7
WALTHAM, MA 02451
www.polaroid.com

Just For Knife Collectors

This catalog is packed with hundreds of knives, swords, specialty and novelty knives, sharpening systems, accessories and more. Now you can find that special carving knife for meat, cheese or fruitcake. If you are a collector of swords and sheaths there are several to choose from. Write:

SMOKY MOUNTAIN KNIFE WORKS
2320 WINFIELD DUNN PARKWAY
SEVIERVILLE, TN 37876
WWW.OHWY.COM/TN/S/SMMTKNWK.HTM

Taking Better Photos

Kodak has a terrific freebie for anyone who wants to take perfect (or at least better) photographs. Call their toll-free phone number and ask for the beautifully illustrated book, *365 Days to Better Pictures.* Call:

1-800-599-5929
www.kodak.com

Can You Picture This?

Kodak has a great web site that will help you take better photos. You will find... Top 10 techniques for good photos;

Problem-pictures remedies; Picture taking tips for any situation plus a host of other topics and chat rooms relating to digital, general and professional photography.
Also be sure to visit their web site at:
WWW.KODAK.COM

Enjoying Play Clay

Did you know you can create your own unique gifts, decorations and jewelry with 'play clay'? You'll learn how to make play clay from Arm & Hammer Baking Soda. To get this freebie. Send a postcard and ask for *Play Clay to*:
ARM & HAMMER CONSUMER RELATIONS
PLAY CLAY BROCHURES
PO BOX 1625
HORSHAM, PA 19044-6625
1-800-524-1328
WWW.ARMHAMMER.COM

Creating Beautiful Letters

If you are interested in learning how to create handcrafted lettering, this is for you. With the *Hunt Lettering Charts* you will receive a super collection of Roman Gothic, Old English and Manuscript lettering charts plus helpful hints. Send a card to:
SPEEDBALL ART PRODUCTS
PO BOX 5157
2226 SPEEDBALL ROAD
STATESVILLE, NC 28677
WWW.SPEEDBALLART.COM

The Art of Ventriloquism

Do you remember Howdy Doody, and Edgar and Jerry Mahoney? Well now you can learn all the same techniques they used. Here is your chance to learn about what a ventriloquist is and how to become one. You will also learn how to build a puppet and even put together and market a show. You will learn how to start the show, the direction to go in and lots more. To receive this 32 page booklet on *How To Become A Ventriloquist,* write to :

THE NORTH AMERICAN ASSOCIATION OF VENTRILOQUISTS
BOX 420
LITTLETON CO 80160
Or visit their web site at: www.maherstudios.com/naav.htm

If You Collect Zippo Lighters

Somewhere in your attic or basement you may stumble across an old Zippo lighter known for their reliability and quality for over 50 years. Instead of throwing it out as junk, find out whether that old Zippo has any real value. Send for a *Collectors Guide To Zippo Lighters*:

ZIPPO MANUFACTURING CO.
33 BARBOUN ST.
BRADFORD, PA 16701
www.zippo.com

Just For Comic Book Collectors

While rumaging through the attic many people have stumbled across comic books they've had since they were kids bringing back wonderful memories of their childhood. For some that is the beginning of an enjoyable hobby of collecting old comic books. If that describes you, you'll want to send for a *giant list of back issues of Marvel comics.* Send 50¢ postage to:

R. CRESTOHL
4732 CIRCLE RD.
MONTREAL, CANADA

Old-Time Stamp Collection

There's an old-time collection of 26 different stamps waiting for you. Each stamp is 50 to 100 years old. The stamps are worth $4.00 at catalog prices but are yours for only $1.00 postage. You'll also receive other stamps on approval but there's no obligation to buy anything. Write to:

JAMESTOWN STAMP CO,
341 EAST 3RD STREET
JAMESTOWN, NY 14701
1-888-782-6776
www.stamp-company.com

Start A Stamp Club

If you're interested in collecting stamps, you will probably enjoy the hobby more in the company of other stamp collectors. If this sounds like something you might be interested in, ask for your free copy of *You Can Start A Stamp Club*. Write to:

AMERICAN PHILATELIC SOCIETY
P.O. BOX 8000
STATE COLLEGE, PA 16803
WWW.STAMPS.ORG

Learn A New Craft

If you are interested in learning a new hobby, why not consider needlecraft? To help you get started with this fun hobby, here are a few kits you will want to get. While the kits are free, include a $2.00 shipping and handling charge for each one you want. Be sure to specify the kits you want.

Needlepoint Kit: Includes a full colored canvas, yarn, needle and instructions.

Quilting Squares: A set of 26 pieces of fabric and complete instructions for three 12" X 12" projects.

Counted Cross Stitch Kit: This kit includes fabric, yarn, needle and full instructions.

Send your request along with postage & handling to:

SUPRISE GIFT OF THE MONTH CLUB
PO BOX 11
GARNERSVILLE, NY 10923

NOTES:

Computers & The Best Internet Sites

They'll be a time in the not too distant future that having a computer will be as common as having a telephone...and just as essential. One of the main reasons for having a computer is to gain access to the Internet (sometimes called the World Wide Web or just the 'Web'). What this means is that just by typing in an address of a web site, your computer is instantly transported to a place that could very well be on the other side of the world...all for the price of a local phone call!

If you don't have a computer yet but would like to see just what the Internet is all about, here are a number of ways of getting started.

First, virtually all libraries across the nation have computers you can use free of charge with access to the Internet. It's very easy to use and the librarian will be happy to show you how to get started.

Next, if your budget will allow it, you might want to get your own computer and 'modem' (a little box that hooks you up via your phone line to the Internet.) The most affordable way to get started is with a used computer which you can buy for as little as $100-$200 at stores like Computer Renaissance which sells only used computers. (Incidentally, to use the Internet it isn't necessary to have the newest or fastest computer. However it is good idea to get a fast modem (cost: $50-$120) which will speed your access to the Internet.

Finally, if your budget will allow, there is now a computer called the Apple iMac (under $1,000) which is already set up as it comes out of the box with everything including a built-in modem to get you online in a matter of ten minutes.

Free Computer Services

One of the big advantages of owning a computer is that it puts the world right at your finger tips. At a touch of a key you have instant access to people and sources of information that may be on the other side of the globe. In an instant you can surf the Internet with thousands of fascinating web sites. To get started with free software and in many cases with free online trials, call these toll-free numbers:

AMERICA ONLINE (AOL) GENERAL INFO: **1-800-827-6364**

   TO GET UP TO **1025** FREE HOURS TO GET STARTED
   ON AMERICA ONLINE, CALL: **1-888-265-8002**

COMPUSERVE: **1-800-848-8199**

MICROSOFT NETWORK: **1-800-386-5550**

SBC YAHOO / PRODIGY: **1-800-776-3449**

EARTHLINK: **1-800-876-3151**

Free Computer Supplies

Right now there's intense competition going on between several nationwide computer retailers. Just to get you into their store, each of them offers free computer supplies with a full rebate. For example, in the last several weeks the authors have received several hundred computer diskettes, surge protectors, laser paper, a keyboard, a computer mouse, and other computer related items all of which came with a 100% rebate. Hundreds of dollars in supplies absolutely free! Check your local newspapers for full page ads and inserts for CompUSA, Circuit City and other chain stores.

Free Screen Savers

Screen savers can turn a dull gray computer screen into a beautiful work of art. For hundreds of free screen savers, visit the following web sites:

www.freesaver.com
www.cinemadesktopthemes.com
www.topdesktop.com

Best Deals on PC's & Macs

If you are looking for the best deals around in computers, software and accessories, some of the best prices you will find are from mail order companies. Even if you decide to buy from a local store, calling mail order companies will allow you to comparison shop to get the lowest price. Each of the companies listed here have been in business for a number of years and have an excellent reputation for customer satisfaction. When you call, ask for their latest catalog which will be full of important information to help you make an intelligent buying decision. Most companies have a 24-hour customer service line and your orders arrive promptly, often the very next day

PC CONNECTION: 1-800-800-1111
MAC CONNECTION: 1-800-800-0002
PC WAREHOUSE & MACWAREHOUSE:
1-800 255-6227
DATACOM: 1-800-328-2261
MACZONE: 1-800-248-0800
PC ZONE: 1-800-258-2088
TIGER: 1-800-888-4437
MACMALL: 1-800-222-2808
MEI: 1-800-634-3478

Free Apple Assistance

If you own a Macintosh or are thinking of buying one and have questions you need answered, there's a toll-free number you can call for help.
APPLE HELP LINE: 1-800-SOS-APPL (THAT'S 1-800-767-2775)
Or visit their web site: www.apple.com

Free Computer Business Information

Computer Business Services will send you free cassettes and color literature on one of today's quickest growing industries. We all know the computer industry has taken off like a rocket, and now it's possible for you to be a part of it. To receive free cassettes and color literature on their business opportunities, call **1-800-343-8014**, or write to:
COMPUTER BUSINESS SERVICES
CBSI PLAYA, STE. 1180
SHERIDAN, IN 46069

Free Computer Supply Catalog

If you or your company owns a computer, you will want to get a copy of the *Global Computer Supplies Catalog*. This full color catalog lists thousands of computer-related products of all types. Drop a postcard to:

GLOBAL COMPUTER SUPPLIES
11 HARBOR PARK DRIVE
PORT WASHINGTON, NY 11050
OR CALL: 1-800-8-GLOBAL (THAT'S 1-800-845-6225)

Free On The Internet

Thousands of pieces of software are available absolutely free on the Internet. If you have a computer and a modem, accessing the Internet is a simple and easy way to open up a whole new world. Among other things, you will find 'freeware', 'shareware' and free computer application upgrades waiting for you to download into your computer. You will also find full text of hundreds of useful government booklets and reports on a host of fascinating subjects all of which you can download free.

Exploring the Internet...
Web Sites Just For Seniors

Here are the Internet addresses of sites on the World Wide Web that are of special interest to mid-life and older Web users. Be sure that when you type in the address that you are careful to type it in perfectly. Even a small change like the addition or deletion of a space or period will mean you will not be able to access the site

AMERICAN ASSOCIATION OF RETIRED PERSONS:
www.aarp.org

A.A.R.P. GUIDE TO INTERNET RESOURCES RELATED TO AGING:
www.aarp.org/cyber/guide1.htm

ACHOO:
www.achoo.com

AGE OF REASON:
www.nih.gov/nia/health/pubpub/pubpub.htm

ANDRUS FOUNDATION:

www.andrus.org

BRINGING THE FUTURE TO SENIOR CITIZENS: CAREGIVER ALLIANCE:
www.caregiver.org

CHRONICNET:
www.chronicnet.org

ELDERHOSTEL:
www.elderhostel.org

ELDERPAGE: INFORMATION FOR OLDER PERSONS AND FAMILIES:
www.aoa.dhhs.gov/elderpage.html#wal

FAMILYPC'S GUIDE TO SENIOR CITIZEN COMPUTING:
www.zdnet.com/familypc/content/970411/cover/cover.html

FOCUS ON THE INTERNET:
www.aarp.org/cyber

THE GEEZER BRIGADE:
www.thegeezerbrigade.com

GENERATIONS UNITED:
www.gu.org

DEALING WITH DEATH AND GRIEVING: GRIEFNET:
rivendell.org

HEALTH A TO Z:
www.healthatoz.com

INTERNET DEVELOPMENT FOR THE AGING NETWORK: ONLINE
RESOURCES:
www.aoa.dhhs.gov/aoa/pages/guidrev.html

MAPQUEST:
www.mapquest.com

NATIONAL AGING INFORMATION CENTER:
www.aoa.dhhs.gov/naic

NATIONAL COUNCIL ON THE AGING:
www.ncoa.org

NEW LIFESTYLES:
www.newlifestyles.com

OLD-TIME RADIO WEB PAGE:
www.old-time.com

TOO OLD FOR COMPUTERS? VISIT:
WWW.SENIORSINCYBERSPACE.ORG/OLD.HTM

OLDER JOKES FOR OLDER FOLKS:
seniors-site.com/funstuff/jokes97.html

ONLINE RESOURCES FOR FINANCIAL AND RETIREMENT PLANNING:
www.aoa.dhhs.gov/aoa/pages/finplan.html

PLAY BRIDGE HAND GENERATOR:
www.playbridge.com

SSA DIRECT: PERSONAL EARNINGS AND BENEFIT ESTIMATE STATEMENT BY MAIL:
www.ssa.gov/pebes

THE SENIOR CENTER
www.senior-center.com
This is a web site especially for seniors. The Senior Center has all kinds information for senior citizens. You can send a personal e-mail message to the President, Majority Leader of the House of Representatives, the Majority Leader of the U.S. Senate or your own Congressman or Senator.
The Senior Center will also tell you about free and low cost travel bargains at:

SENIOR CONNECTION
www.senior.com

SENIORLAW HOME PAGE:
www.seniorlaw.com:80

SENIORNET:
www.seniornet.org

SENIOR STAFF JOB INFORMATION DATABANK:
www.srstaff.com

SILVER THREADS:
www.winnipeg.freenet.mb.ca/sthreads

SPRY FOUNDATION:
www.spry.org

THIRDAGE:
www.thirdage.com

www.dreamscape.com/frankvad/Internet.html

WEATHER CHANNEL:
www.weather.com

TO HELP YOU USE THE NET - FOLKS ONLINE:
www.folksonline.com

SENIORS SITE FOR FOLKS OVER 50
www.seniors-site.com

Use These Web Sites For Online Tips For Navigating The Web

BEGINNERS CENTRAL:
www.northernwebs.com/bc

THE HELPWEB:
www.imagescape.com/helpweb

INTERNET STARTER KIT:
ss2.mcp.com/resources/genInternet/frame_iskm.html

INTERNET WEB TEXT INDEX:
www.december.com/web/text

Bigtime Savings With Online Auctions

If you love shopping for bargains, you're in for the time of your life with these Internet auction sites. You can bid on everything from cameras to computers and golf clubs… anytime day or night, 24 hours a day, all without ever leaving the comfort of your home. But just remember that as with a traditional auction you must be careful not to get caught in a bidding frenzy and bid too much just to get something you could have bought for less in a store.

A couple of tips: Find out whether the item is new, used or refurbished. New products should come with a manufacturer's warranty. Check the warranty and return policies.

When buying from someone online, be wary of sellers with e-mail accounts which could be used to mask the seller's identity. Wherever possible, pay for your purchase with your credit card since that will offer you the best protection in case there's a problem. In some instances you are buying from a private individual but in others (like egghead.com) you are buying directly from a large company which adds an additional layer of protection.

Here are several of the most popular Internet auction sites:
www.ebay.com

This is the largest Internet auction site with everything imaginable from antiques to Beanie Babies. To find the items you are interested in you can enter key words and they will do the work of finding a match for the item you are interested in.

This site is operated by egghead.com. You'll find all kind of computer equipment and other electronics. Also at **www.egghead.com** you'll find a continuous auction on every kind of item imagineable such as Yamaha keyboards and cordless phones. In addition, at egghead.com you'll find an online liquidation center called surplus direct which is a great place to shop for super bargains of all kinds.

www.auctionwarehouse.com
This site focuses strictly on computer-related equipment.

www.onsale.com
Here you'll find an ongoing auction featuring a wide range of items from tech stuff to vacuum cleaners.

www.ubid.com
At this auction site you'll find not only computer products but all kinds of consumer electronics as well.

www.webauction.com
This auction site is operated by one of the largest computer mail order companies, MacWarehouse.

Free Internet Access

If you are paying too much for your internet access, maybe you should check out Juno.com and NetZero.com. These two web 'portals' will give you an entry point to surf the web. They both feature a totally free option for those who only use the internet infrequently. They also offer a low priced option that will give you unlimited access 24 hours a day, 7 days a week. Check out each at:
www.juno.com
www.netzero.com

Learning Something New

One of life's true joys is exploring the world and discovering something we never knew before. We enter life with an enormous inborn curiosity about the world around us. Unfortunately once we enter school for many of us learning becomes a chore, a job, something we are forced to do to get good grades or a good job. But once we reach a certain age and the pace of life becomes less frantic, we can once again recapture that excitement of learning something new and feeling like a kid again.

Senior Summer School

That's right Summer School for seniors- two to ten weeks of learning and fun centered around 7 college campuses in the U.S. and Canada. Here's your chance to meet new friends and see the world. The sessions last from 2-10 weeks with no marks, no grades and no mandatory attendance. WOW – school was never like this.

The only requirement is a desire to learn something new. All the programs offer social events too. Write to:

SENIOR SUMMER SCHOOL
PO BOX 4424
DEERFIELD BEACH, FL 33442-4424
YOU CAN ALSO CALL: 1-800-847-2466
OR VISIT THEIR WEBSITE:
www/seniorsummerschool.com

Back To School With Elderhostel

Elderhostel offers senior study programs around the world all year long. You'll live in conference centers on college university campuses and enjoy the cultural and recreational resources that go with them. So if you have an adventuresome spirit and are looking to be challenged by new ideas and experiences, this is for you. You must be 55 years or older to be eligible. Here's your chance to go back to college and experience dorm life as a more seasoned veteran. For information, be sure to get the free catalog of senior study programs from:

ELDERHOSTEL
11 AVENUE OF de LAFAYETTE
BOSTON, MA 02111
CALL THEM AT: **1-877-426-8056**
OR VISIT THEIR INTERNET SITE AT:
www.elderhostel.org

Free College Extension Courses

If you've always wanted to return to college, there's no time like the present. First, check the *Directory of Colleges With Special Programs For Seniors* in the back of this book. They all offer free or very low cost tuition for seniors.

CONGRATULATIONS

Also, don't forget you can check your local telephone directory for state and community college extension courses. These courses are not given for credit but they are a lot of fun.

Next, contact your local senior centers to see what they have. Museums, nature centers, libraries and church groups also offer courses and seminars that are educational and fun and many instances free or almost free.

Finally, check your local newspaper for seminars and other educational activities in your area.

Are You A Sky Gazer?

If you enjoy studying the heavens, you will want to get a copy of *Essential Magazines of Astronomy* with a catalog of some of the finest astronomy books that will delight all star gazers. Write to:

SKY PUBLISHING CORP.
49 BAY STREET RD.
CAMBRIDGE, MA 02138
1-800-253-0245
www.skyandtelescope.com

A Share Of America

Getting Help When You Invest and *Understanding Stocks and Bonds* and two fascinating guides that tells all about how the stock market works and the important role it plays in our nation's economy. The New York Stock Exchange also has an excellent series of educational aids, huge wall posters, ticker tape, teacher guides and more. Write to:

N.Y. STOCK EXCHANGE
EDUCATIONAL SERVICES
11 WALL ST.
NEW YORK, NY 10005
www.nyse.com

What Are Quarter Horses?

Whether you are presently an owner of horses or perhaps thinking of buying one - check out American Quarter Horses, the world's most popular breed of horse. Here's an interesting booklet you will want to have, *For An American Quarter Horse*. For a copy of this fascinating booklet (and a colorful bumper sticker too), drop a postcard to:

AMERICAN QUARTER HORSE ASSN.
PO BOX 200
AMARILLO, TX 79168
WWW.AQHA.COM

Tennessee Walking Horse

Here's one every equestrian will want to have. Send a postcard and ask for the booklet, *Tennessee Walking Horse* plus a colorful postcard showing the three horses chosen by the breeder's association as the world's greatest pleasure and show horses. Write to:

TENNESSEE WALKING HORSE
BOX 286
LEWISBURG, TN 37091-0286
1-800-359-1574
www.twhbea.com

KEEP IN MIND: If you don't have a computer or Internet access at home, most libraries have computers you can use and librarians who are happy to show you how to use them.

Protecting Your Home From Fire

Don't take any chances when it comes to protecting your home from fires. Learn what you can do to protect your family and your house with smoke detectors—a must for all homes. Send a card to:

"HOME FIRE DETECTION,"
NATIONAL FIRE PROTECTION ASSOCIATION
BATTERYMARCH PARK
QUINCY, MA 02269

Look To The Heavens

Man has always been fascinated by the sky at night. With the recent discovery of planets circling around distant stars, one can't help but wonder whether life exists elsewhere in the universe. To find out more about our distant neighbors, send for the *skywatching series of booklets* dealing with our solar system and beyond. Send to:

PUBLIC AFFAIRS OFFICE
HARVARD SMITHSONIAN CENTER FOR ASTROPHYSICS
60 GARDEN ST.
CAMBRIDGE, MA 02138
http://cfa-www.harvard.edu

The Wright Brothers

With men on the moon and rockets to Jupiter it's hard to believe that manned flight began less than a 100 years ago with an historic 120 foot journey that lasted all of 12 seconds. All the fascinating details are found in this historical recap, *The Wright Brothers.* Send a card to:

WRIGHT BROTHERS NATIONAL MEMORIAL
ROUTE 1, BOX 676
MANTEO, NC 27954

The Truth About Nuclear Energy

Is nuclear energy the answer to our energy needs or are the risks of nuclear disaster just too great? To help you answer this question, here is an excellent package of books that is free for the asking. Topics covered include nuclear power plants, the structure of the atom, magnetic fusion, the story of nuclear energy and a whole lot more. They will also include information about wind energy and conservation. Ask for the *Nuclear Energy information package.* Very informative. All free from:

U.S. DEPARTMENT OF ENERGY
PO BOX 62
OAK RIDGE, TN 37830

What Is Australia Like Today?

What is life like 'down-under'? *Australia Now* will give you a look—in full color-at what's happening in Australia today. You'll also receive vacation planning, travel tips and information on locations, tours and accommodations. Drop a postcard to:

AUSTRALIAN CONSULATE GENERAL
630 FIFTH AVE. SUITE 420
NEW YORK NY 10111

The Facts About Oil

This nicely illustrated guide to petroleum tells all about the history of oil exploration and shows how the search for oil is conducted. Ask for the *energy information series* and you'll receive a great package of excellent booklets dealing with many forms of energy including wind, nuclear, geothermal, coal, oil and more. Send a postcard to:

AMERICAN PETROLEUM INSTITUTE
PUBLICATIONS SECTION
1220 L ST. N.W.
WASHINGTON, DC 20005
www.api.org

How To Shop Smart

Everyone spends money, but not everyone knows how to do it right. Spending money wisely takes skill, time and experience. To help you learn how to shop smart, the FTC and the National Association of Attorneys General have put together a fun activity booklet called *The Real Deal*. To get your free copy, write to:

YOUR STATE ATTORNEY GENERAL
OFFICE OF CONSUMER PROTECTION
YOUR STATE CAPITAL
OR TO: THE FEDERAL TRADE COMMISSION
600 PENNSYLVANIA AVE., NW, ROOM 130
WASHINGTON, DC 20580
1-877-FTC-HELP
www.ftc.gov

Would You Drive An Aluminum Car?

Today, through greater use of aluminum parts, our cars are getting far better miles per gallon. This is just one of the many uses of aluminum. If you would like a better understanding of the history of aluminum, the ways it is made and how it's used, ask for the free *Story of Aluminum* and *Alcoa* from:

ALCOA
150 ALCOA BUILDING.
PITTSBURGH, PA 15219
www.alcoa.com

Cleaning Up The Environment

Bethlehem Steel would like you to know what they are doing to clean up the air and water. For example, at one plant they have spent over 100 million dollars for air and water quality controls. For a free copy of *Steelmaking & The Environment,* send a postcard to:

BETHLEHEM STEEL CORP.
PUBLIC AFFAIRS DEPT., ROOM 476MT
BETHLEHEM, PA 18016

Learn About Coal

If you're curious about coal and how it is found, extracted, transported and used, be sure to get the informative booklets and poster available free from the American Coal Foundation. When you write, be sure to indicate exactly what your interests are so they can provide appropriate materials for you. A few of the items available include:

Coal Poster - A large colorful poster with important coal information

Coal: Ancient Gift Serving Modern Man

Let's Learn About Coal - includes puzzles and word games explaining how coal is formed.

What Everyone Should Know About Coal Describes the different types of coal, how it is used and how it effects the envirnment.

Coal Science Fair Ideas - to help spark interest in coal plus tips to help you get started with a learning project.

Write to:

AMERICAN COAL FOUNDATION
1130 17TH ST NW, SUITE 220
WASHINGTON, DC 20036-4604
WWW.ACF-COAL.ORG

Pitch This One!

Did you know that former President George Bush used to pitch horseshoes? If you think you might find this sport interesting, and would like to find out more about it, now's the time. To discover more about this fun sport and to learn all the rules and tips for throwing the perfect horseshoe pitch, send for your free copy of the *Official Rules For Horseshoe Pitching,* visit their web site at:

www.horsepitching.com

Learning To Be More Romantic

Since the beginning of time, women have accused men of not being romantic enough. Finally there's help and it's called *The RoMANtic.* Each newsletter gives dozens of practical, creative and inspiring ideas and stories on dating, gift-giving, anniversary celebrating and more. To learn how to rekindle the romantic spark and have more fun in your relationships, check out their web newsletter

To HECK OUT SAMPLE ISSUES GO TO THEIR INTERNET site at:
www.TheRomantic.com

Invite A Bird Over For Lunch

This large colorful poster-like guide will show you how to *Invite Birds To Your Home.* It tells how to attract birds with proper tree plantings that specific species prefer. You also might want to ask for *Your Hometown, Clean Water Town.* For your free copy write:

SOIL CONSERVATION SERVICE
U.S.D.A.
Box 2890
WASHINGTON, DC 20013

Preserving Our Forests

The book you're reading right now and the lumber in the house in which you live are just two of the many products we take for granted that come from our nation's forests. It is essential that we take care to preserve and renew our forests. The U.S. Forest Service has a booklet you will want to have: *Making Paper From Trees* shows how a tree goes from the forest and ends up as paper. Send a postcard to:

FOREST SERVICE

U.S. DEPT. OF AGRICULTURE

BOX 2417

WASHINGTON, DC 20013

Money For College

If you're a parent with children in college or about to go off to college, you have discovered just how expensive it is. The good news is that there are all kinds of financial assistance programs available for virtually everyone. All that is necessary is to go through a series of steps in your search for the money you will need.

Here we've listed a number of important and easy to use resources to help you effectively direct your search for college money. One of the most efficient ways of locating financial assistance that applies to you is to use the Internet. Naturally this means having access to a computer. If you do not yet own a computer, you can check with your local library or ask a friend who has a computer to allow you to use theirs. Also most schools today have computers your child can use.

Free College Aid

It's a little known fact but there are literally billions of dollars in financial aid available to help students pay for their college education. This money is available from thousands of public and private sources. Much of this money is available as outright grants that never has to be repaid. Still more money for college is available through low-cost loans and work-study programs. The first place to check is with the financial aid office of the college of your choice. Counselors will help you locate all the sources of money including scholarships, grant-in-aid, work study programs and low interest government-backed student loans. Next, you will definitely want to use the Internet as a tool to search for financial assistance. In the listings that follow, you'll find the most important sources.

Free Computer Search To Locate College Scholarships And Grants

Are you looking for money for college? The Internet is the very best way to search for the financial aid that is waiting for you. Start your search with this computerized web site which was developed by the nation's financial aid administrators. At this web site you will find a number of great scholarship searches that are entirely free.

What you will do is fill out a detailed questionnaire on your computer screen while you are online. The information you list about yourself and your background on this questionnaire will be compared to the information in huge databases and you will be notified of the grants, scholarships and loans you qualify for. To begin your search go to the web site:

www.finaid.org/finaid

Once you are at the finaid.org web site you will find several other sites (listed below) where you will find the questionnaires that will begin your search. They will ask you to answer several pages of specific questions about your background and financial situation. Based on the answers to your these questions it will set up a personalized profile that will match your specific skills, needs and interests. It will begin the search through its massive database for all of the money that is available for you. Once the search is completed, it will report to you exactly what assistance you qualify for and exactly how to get it.

And despite the enormous value of this search and the fact that other organizations have charged up to $300 for this service, there is no charge to you for these extensive searches!

• **FastWEB:** A database of more than 300,000 private-sector scholarships, grants, fellowships and loans is the Internet's largest free scholarship search site. Also, FastWEB Classifieds offers a tailored search of employment opportunities across the U.S. that is available to students absolutely free.

www.fastweb.com

• **SRN Express:** A version of the Scholarship Resource Network (SRN) database with information from several hundred thousand financial aid sources with a special focus on scholarship information. They also have information on student loan forgiveness programs for college graduates who need alternatives for loan repayment.
www.srnexpress.com

Low Cost Loans To Pay for College

Sallie Mae is the leading source of money for college loans. They will be delighted to help you find the money you will need to pay for college.

The College Answer Service. First, they have a toll free hotline where you can speak to a financial aid expert who will answer your questions dealing with paying for college, loans, aid packages, advice on financial aid applications, deadlines, and lots more. You will also learn how to save hundreds of dollars with the lowest cost student loans available. Due to the low interest rates they offer, loans with Sallie Mae can cost a lot less to pay back. Call them Monday through Friday between the hours of 9am to 9pm EST at: **1-888-2-SALLIE**
Sallie Mae also has a number of helpful booklets including *Paying For College* and *Borrowing For College.*

Paying For College is a comprehensive guidebook which provides thorough advice on planning for a college education. The book addresses key financial aid terms, formulas for calculating the 'Expected Family Contribution', an overview of the federal student loan program and a summary of loan repayment programs ...many of which reward students for on-time payment.

Borrowing For College helps students and their parents choose low-cost student loan lenders in their area. To get free copies call: **1-800-806-3681**

www.sallie.mae.com One visit to their web site and you will see just how valuable it is. You will be able to do a free online search for scholarship money available from over

300,000 sources. Plus you can e-mail your financial aid questions and get quick advice from experts.

Student Loans & Grants

If you're a college student or plan to be one and are short of money to continue your education, be sure to get a free copy of *Funding Your Education* and *The Student Guide.* They are the most comprehensive resources of student financial aid from the U.S. Department of Education. It covers major aid programs including Pell Grants, Stafford Loans and PLUS loans. Contact:

THE **U.S.** DEPARTMENT OF EDUCATION,
400 MARYLAND AVE. **S.W.** ROOM **2097**
WASHINGTON. **D.C. 20202**
OR CALL THEIR INFORMATION HOTLINE:
1-800-4-FED-AID

Also, for information on Federal student aid backed by the U.S. Government, be sure to visit the Department of Education's web site at:
www.ed.gov

Paying For College

With the costs of going to college spiraling out of sight many students are not able to attend college without financial assistance. This guide will help you with all the many questions you have about paying for your college education. Ask for *Meeting College Costs,* free from:

THE COLLEGE BOARD
45 COLUMBUS AVE.
NEW YORK, NY **10023-6992**

Comparing College Costs

Computer users can quickly compare the cost of more than 1500 public and private colleges and get an estimate of what

it will cost to attend. When you call, ask for *College Savings Plus,* a free computer disk available from John Hancock Mutual Life Insurance Company. After you ask for the free computer disk, a John Hancock agent will likely call to ask if you want help devising a savings plan. Call:
1-800-633-1809

College Planning

T. Rowe Price's College Planning Guide helps parents project what a college education may cost for their young children so you can plan ahead and start saving now. It's free. Call:
1-800-225-5132
Also visit them on the web: **WWW.TROWEPRICE.COM**

$1,500 To Pay For College

Paying for college can be a huge burden, but now there's hope. In fact it's called the 'Hope Scholarship' and actually it's even better than a scholarship because it's an income-tax credit aimed at middle income people. There are no applications to fill out. All you do is when you file your tax return, you subtract the amount of the credit right from the amount you owe. In effect, the government gives you up to $1,500 back per student. Here's how it works:

• The income tax credit equals 100% of the first $1,000 paid in college tuition and fees plus 50% of the next $1,000, for a total of $1,500.

• The credit is for you, your spouse or your dependent children in their first and second academic year as long as they're enrolled at least half time in a 2 year or 4 year college or in a trade school.

• You can claim as many credits as you have qualified students. So for example, if you have two children in their first or second year of college, you get $3,000.

• To qualify for the full credit your adjusted gross income

must be under $40,000 if you are single (between $40,000 and $50,000 you still get a partial credit) or $80,000 if you are married (between $80,000 and $100,000 you still get a partial credit.)

- Tuition must be paid in the same year you claim the credit. For example, you must have paid the tuition in 2003 to claim a credit on your 2003 tax return.

- In addition to the Hope Scholarship, there is also the Lifetime Learning credit of $1,000 which can be taken for any student of any age, for any number of years and even for a single adult education course, for example. Right now this credit is worth up to $1,000 (20% of the first $5,000 paid in tuition and fees) and you can take just one credit per tax return no matter how many students you may have in school. While you can't take both credits at once for the same student, you can take the Hope credit for one and the Lifetime Learning credit for another.

If you qualify, these tax credits can be an important source of additional money for college. For more information, ask the IRS or your accountant.

Religion

Free Devotional Reading For Each Day

Our Daily Bread provides inspirational readings from the scriptures for each day of the month. You'll get a new book each month. Ask them to add your name to their mailing list for this devotional guide plus discovery series booklets as well as a campus journal for young people. All free from:

RADIO BIBLE CLASS
P.O. BOX 2222
GRAND RAPIDS, MI 49555

Free Catholic Information

The Knights of Columbus has dozens of booklets available on all aspects of the Catholic religion. The only cost is a nominal postage charge (generally 25¢ per booklet). They also have a 10 part home-study Catholic correspondence course that is free for the asking. The course is for both Catholics and non-Catholics who would like to learn more about Catholicism. It is sent in an unmarked envelope. For a complete listing of publications or to get your free correspondence course write to:

CATHOLIC INFORMATION SERVICE
KNIGHTS OF COLUMBUS
BOX 1971
NEW HAVEN, CT 06521

You Can Make A Difference In This World

News Notes are inspirational brochures published by the Christophers 10 times a year and are free for the asking. The Christophers exist for one purpose: to spread the message that one person can make a difference in this world. Write and ask for information on titles available in any of these categories, *News Notes*, books, videocassettes, they even have Spanish language material. Drop a postcard to :

THE CHRISTOPHERS
12 EAST 48TH ST.
NEW YORK, NY 10017

Inspiration And Prayer

The Lutheran Laymen's League has several religious publications you might like to have. A few of the titles currently available are: *'Escape From Loneliness'*, *'I Am An Alcoholic,'* *'Stress - Problem or Opportunity?'* and *'The Truth About Angels.'* All of them are free from:

INTERNATIONAL LUTHERAN LAYMEN'S LEAGUE
660 MASON RIDGE CENTER
ST. LOUIS, MO 63141

Free From The Worldwide Church Of God

The Worldwide Church of God has an excellent series of booklets available without charge (nor will they make any solicitations of any kind). Titles change frequently so drop a card for a current list of books available. Write to:

WORLDWIDE CHURCH OF GOD
PASADENA, CA 91123
OR CALL TOLL-FREE: **1-800-423-4444**

Beautiful Inspiration

Often in our daily lives events become too much to handle. The Salesian Missions have a beautiful series of booklets that are a pleasure to read and provide inspiration to help make our lives more fulfilling. Excellent! Send a postcard and ask for the *free inspirational booklets* from:

SALESIAN MISSIONS
2 LEFEVRES LANE
NEW ROCHELLE, NY 10801

Free Gospel Of
Saint John Course

If you would like to learn more about the life of Christ, you can receive a free Gospel of John in English or Spanish (please specify) and a Gospel of John Correspondence Course. Drop a postcard to:

THE POCKET TESTAMENT LEAGUE
PO BOX 800
LITITZ, PA 17543

Free King James Bible

If you would like a 764 page copy of the King James version of the Bible, it's yours free from The Church of Jesus Christ of Latter Day Saints...The Mormons. They may ask if you would like to speak with a church member but that is your option and is not required to receive the free bible. They also have a beautifully produced video called *Lamb of God* that is yours for asking. For a free copy of the *King James Bible* or the *Lamb of God* video (both of which will be sent by mail), call:

1-800-535-1118

Free Bible Reading Guides

For a new understanding of the Bible, you may want to receive the simplified Bible Reading Guides that are yours free from the Real Truth Ministries. To enroll in this bible course, call toll free:
1-800-863-5789

Cars & Drivers

Does Your Car Really Need That Tune-up?

Whether you have a new car or an older one, you want to be prepared for any trouble you may encounter. Most of us are very trusting souls when it comes to a car repair. We rely on the mechanic as the expert. When he tells us the car needs a tune-up or has any other problem, we have him check it out immediately. The Car Council wants us to be aware of *"Tune-ups For Changing Seasons."* It's full of easy to understand advice on what to look for before it's too late. To get your free copy simply write to:

THE CAR COUNCIL DEPT T
4600 EAST WEST HWY. STE 300
BETHESDA, MD 20814
WWW.CARCARECOUNCIL.ORG

Call This Toll-Free Number First If You Bought A Lemon

If you're having problems with your car and can't seem to get satisfaction from the dealer or manufacturer don't despair - help is on the way. The Auto Safety Hotline is anxious to hear about your complaint so they can get to work on it. They've even set up a toll-free hotline and an Internet site for you to contact them to report your problem. To report

your problem, call toll-free:
1-800-424-9393. OR WRITE TO:
NATIONAL HIGHWAY AND TRAFFIC SAFETY ADMINISTRATION
400 7TH ST., S.W.
WASHINGTON, DC 20590
OR VISIT THEIR INTERNET SITE AT:
www.nhtsa.dot.gov

If at this point you would just like to gather more information about recalls and auto defect reports, call this toll-free number operated by the Technical Information Services division of NHTSA:
1-877-382-4357

NHTSA does not get involved in individual cases of complaints between the consumer and the dealer or manufacturer. If you have such a complaint, visit the Federal Trade Commission's web site at:
WWW.FTC.GOV

Car Shopping On The Internet

Thinking of buying a car? Want to negotiate the best deal and save thousands of dollars? The Internet has scores of Web sites with auto information. The most useful ones reveal invoice cost, road-test performance and rebates and incentives. Try these:

For up-to-date information, analyses and columns from auto industry experts, check out the **Car Connection**'s web site at:
www.thecarconnection.com

Use this Web site to go to the **Auto Channel**, which has links to every automaker's Web site for lease help, chat rooms and more.
www.excite.com/autos

Edmund's Vehicle Price Guide. Find out how much the car dealer pays for the car you are thinking of buying. You will also discover how much the "holdback" allowance is. The holdback allowance is an additional profit that the manufacturer later gives back to the dealer after the car is sold. It usually runs about 3 percent of the suggested retail price. The site also has information on rebates and incentive plans. **www.edmunds.com.**

The Kelly Blue Book web site can give you a good idea what your trade in is worth, or the real value of a used car you want to buy. **www.kbb.com**

Consumer Product Ratings site offers ratings of cars, hotels, restaurants volunteered by online users. (They are not affiliated with Consumer Reports magazine.) You can reach them on the Internet at: **www.consumeratings.com**

What Does Consumer Reports Think?

If you would like to see just what Consumer Reports thinks of the car you are thinking of buying, visit their Internet site. You will find evaluations of over 120 makes of new cars. Access to their site costs $4.95 a month but you can visit their *Best of the Best* page for free. **www.consumerreports.org**

Save Thousands On Your Next Car Purchase Or Lease

One of the very best ways of saving a lot of money on the purchase or lease of a vehicle is to use the online vehicle brokers. They have nationwide networks of thousands of dealers of every make of auto or truck.

CONSUMER CAR CLUB

In addition to offering you online auto insurance quotes, an auto comparison guide and a loan-versus-lease cost comparison, they also offer three ways to buy a car or truck. First, they will refer you to a dealer at no charge. They also offer a factory direct ordering service for $179 and a Personal Shopper service for $179. Visit their site at:
www.carclub.com

NATIONWIDE AUTO BROKERS

They will sell you a car and even bring it right to your front door. How's that for convenience! Their advertised prices range from $50 to $125 over dealer invoice. They charge $11.95 for the first price quote on the car of your choice and $9.95 for each additional quote. Check out their Web site at:
www.car-connect.com

CARS@COST

They offer many models of new cars at dealer invoice plus their fee. Their fees range from $249 to $499 depending upon the car you are buying.
www.carscost.com

Dealer Referral Services

As a smart shopper it's essential to inform yourself fully before you go out to buy your next car. One of the best ways to gather the information you'll need to make an intelligent choice and get the very lowest price is by visiting these online Internet sites where you will not only learn lots of valuable information about cars, but also get referrals to auto dealers in your local area.

AUTO-BY-TEL

With several million customers, this is one of the largest and most useful web sites around. They have links to six car pricing sites, over 2,700 dealers in their referral network and a great reputation to boot. You'll find a lease-buy comparision calculator and even an online finance application. Visit their web site at:
www.autobuytel.com

AUTOWEB.COM

At this site you'll find well organized information that will help you buy a new car, buy or sell a used car, check out insurance rates from State Farm on the car you are thinking of buying, check financing from Nations Bank and find a list of dealers in your area. Visit them on the Internet at:
www.autoweb.com

AUTOBUYER

There's not too much detailed information but this is a great place to visit to get a dealer quote on the car of your choice without the pressure of a car salesman in the showroom. Their web address is:
www.autobuyer.com

CARSMART

A great consumer buying guide with loads of very useful information on topics like financing, best time to buy a new car, air bags, anti-lock brakes and much more. You can even

get insurance and financing quotes, links to dealer and manu-facturers' sites and vehicle pricing reports ($4.90 each report).
www.carsmart.com

Microsoft CarPoint

This Online Car Buying web site previews various car models and offers "test drives" of selected cars. You'll find lots of reviews, photos and reports on safety, road tests, and more. You'll also find very useful features like side-by-side comparisons and even an affordability calculator. Check it out before you buy your next car. Their web address is:
www.carpoint.msn.com

For AAA Members

If you're a member of AAA, you should know that they offer an excellent tour service. Contact your local AAA office and tell them the destination you would like to drive to and they'll give you detailed road maps with your route outlined in pencil. Many local offices also offer members a car buying service that can save you thousands of dollars on your next auto purchase or lease. Contact AAA at:
1-888-859-5161
www.AAAmidatlantic.com

10 Ways To Slash Auto Insurance Costs

1. MAINTAIN A GOOD DRIVING RECORD. Accidents and speeding tickets are a fast way to drive up your premiums. Drive carefully and defensively. Consider walking or taking other means of transportation or car pooling to reduce your risk of accidents.

2. RAISE YOUR DEDUCTIBLES. This is the amount you must pay for any loss before your insurance kicks in. If your current deductible is $250 or less, raising it to $500 can save you 15%-30%.

3. PROTECT AGAINST THEFT. Security devices like care alarms and even having your serial number etched on the window saves you 15% on your comprehensive auto insurance.

4. ASK ABOUT DISCOUNTS. Insurance companies offer special deals and discounts if you are retired, belong to a business association, have been insured with a company for a number of years, insure all your cars or have your home and car with the same firm.

5. TAKE A DRIVER IMPROVEMENT COURSES to get a discount. For example, AAA has a Driver Improvement Program for people 55 and older that leads to car insurance discounts.

6. REDUCE YOUR COVERAGE OR ELIMINATE COVERAGE YOU DON'T NEED. For example, many new cars now come with towing or road service included. If that's the case you can eliminate that coverage from your auto insurance.

7. MANY INSURERS GIVE DISCOUNTS TO DRIVERS OVER 50 OR THOSE WITH LOW ANNUAL MILEAGE. Others give students with good grades a 5% discount. If your child maintains a B average or better in school or has taken driver's education you may be eligible for discounts. If you child is away at college as long as the car stays home and college is 100 miles or more away depending on the insurance

company, you may also be eligible for discounts.

Rates are also much lower when the teenage driver is considered only an occasional driver of the parent's cars.

8. CHECK INSURANCE RATES *BEFORE* YOU BUY A CAR. The cost of insuring a Porsche is much higher than the cost of insuring an inexpensive family car.

9. SHOP AROUND. Talk to friends and neighbors about their insurance coverage and rates. Get quotes from several companies, compare rates and coverage.

10. GET A CAR WITH ANTI-LOCK BRAKES AND AIR BAGS AND SAVE AN ADDITIONAL 5%.

Should You Buy That Car Or Lease It?

If you can't decide whether to buy or lease a vehicle you need to have this guide...*A Consumer Guide to Vehicle Leasing.* It's your free from the Federal Reserve Board.
CALL 202-452-3244
Or check it out on the internet at www.federalreserve.gov

What To Do If You Have A Car Accident

- Write down names and addresses of all persons and all witnesses involved.
- Notify the police immediately
- Get medical attention if needed
- Contact your insurance agent and do not admit liability or discuss your accident with anyone except your insurance representative or the police.

Be A Good Neighbor...
Be A Good Friend

State Farm wants to help give you, your college, civic group or professional organization free *designated driver presentation items*. They're a colorful way to remind your friends and associates of the importance of safe driving. They will send your group a free designated driver kit. It has a presentation guide, video and sample speeches. Write to:

STATE FARM INSURANCE COMPANIES
ACTION NETWORK-PUBLIC AFFAIRS
DESIGNATED DRIVER PROGRAM
ONE STATE FARM PLAZA
BLOOMINGTON, IL 61710
www.statefarm.com

How Safe Are Your Tires?

Did you know that when you keep your tires properly inflated that the air provides a cushion of protection when you hit a pothole? If the tire is under inflated you could damage the wheel. If it is over inlated the tire will be damaged. For the best information around for caring and protecting your tires, send for a free copy of *The Motorist Tire Care and Safety Guide*. Send a long SASE to:

RUBBER MANUFACTURERS ASSN.
1400 K ST NW SUITE 900
WASHINGTON, DC 20005
202-682-4800
www.rma.org

A Safer Car

Before you go shopping for your next car, be sure to get a copy of *Injury, Collision and Theft Losses - Shopping For A Safer Car*. This informative booklet will help you make an intelligent choice about which is the safest vehicle for you. It provides you with an excellent safety and loss comparisons for hundreds of passenger cars, vans, pick ups and utility vehicle models. Write to:

INSURANCE INSTITUTE FOR HIGHWAY SAFETY
HIGHWAY LOSS DATA INSTITUTE
COMMUNICATIONS DEPARTMENT
1005 NORTH GLEBE RD. SUITE 800
ARLINGTON, VA 22201
www.hwysafety.org/pubs.htm

Automobile Hotline Numbers

If you thinking of buying or leasing a car in the near future, be sure you get all the information you need to make an intelligent decision before you go to the dealer showroom. Your first step should be to call the toll-free hotline phone number for the cars you are interested in. The manufacturers will send you beautiful color product information booklets and even video tapes featuring their cars.

ACURA	1-800-TO-ACURA
BMW	1-800-334-4BMW
BUICK	1-800-4-RIVIERA
CADILLAC	1-800-333-4CAD
CHEVROLET	1-800-950-2438
CHRYSLER	1-800-4-A-CHRYSLER
DODGE	1-800-4-A-DODGE
FORD	1-800-392-3673
GMC SIERRA	1-800-GMC-TRUCK
HONDA	1-800-33-HONDA EXT 435
HYUNDAI	1-800-826-CARS
INFINITI	1-800-826-6500
ISUZU	1-800-726-2700
JAGUAR	1-800-4-JAGUAR

NOTES:

Free For Sports Fans

Senior Sports

Healthy eating and exercise are the keys to keeping fit, feeling great and living longer. Keeping active physically also keeps us alert mentally. Whatever your favorite sport Go out and *DO IT!* If you are unable to participate in a fitness program, WALK.

Did you know that there is a Seniors Softball World Championship and a Seniors Softball World Series each year?

Believe it or not Senior Softball was started in 1930 by a hotel owner in Florida who was looking for something for her elderly guests to do. She organized the *'Three-Quarter Century Club.'* Members had to be at least 75 years old. Think about that the next time you're too tired and feel you can't exercise.

For more information on Senior Athletic Competition like Senior Softball, write to:

NATIONAL SENIOR GAMES ASSOCIATION
PO Box 82059
BATON ROUGE, LA 70884
225-766-6800
WWW.NSGA.COM

Also contact your local senior center, city recreation dept, library or YMCA.

Women: Get Involved With Sports

This organization encourages women

to get involved in sports. They will offer your group or school free films of women in sports to help encourage other women to be active and stay active. They also publish a guide listing scholarships to American colleges and universities for women who are into sports. It's a myth that only men get sports scholarships to college. Call them toll-free:
1-800-227-3988
or visit them at their web site:
www.womenssportsfoundation.org

Outdoor Sports

L. L. Bean, the outdoor sporting specialists for 67 years, would like to send you a copy of their *catalog*. It features fine quality apparel and footwear for the outdoorsman or woman as well as equipment for camping, fishing, hiking and canoeing. Call toll-free:
1-800-441-5713
www.llbean.com

The Story Of The Olympic Games

The History of The Olympics gives you the complete story of the Olympics starting with the earliest recorded game in 776 B.C. and traces the game's history right up to through the present. You'll find a ton of addtional information when you visit them on the internet at:
www.olympic-usa.org

99 Tips For Family Fitness

One of the best ways to stay in shape is by involving the whole family in a fitness progam. In *99 Tips* you'll find a slew of fun fitness activities for kids and parents alike. You'll also find advice from notable athletes like Troy Aikman. Just send a postcard to:
99 TIPS FOR FAMILY FITNESS

MET-Rx Foundation For Health Enhancement
2112 Business Center Drive
Irvine, CA 92715

Free Hockey Cards

If you are a hockey fan, you'll definitely want to send for this freebie. When you request it you will receive 10 free hockey cards. To get your cards, just send a long SASE and 50¢ to:
DANORS, Department **H**
5721 Funston Street Bay 14
Hollywood, FL 33023

Free From Your Favorite Team

Do you love sports? How would you like to receive photos of your favorite teams? Most sports clubs have all kinds of freebies for their loyal fans. These neat freebies often include team photos, souvenir brochures, stickers, fan club information, playing schedules, catalogs and lots more. All you have to do is write to your favorite sports teams at the addresses in this book. Tell them you're a loyal fan and ask them for a "fan package."

Even though it's not always necessary, it's always nice idea to send a long self-addressed-stamped envelope with your name and address written in so they can return your freebie right in your own envelope.

Also, if you have a favorite player on the team, write his name on the envelope.

Sometimes it takes a while to get an answer since most teams are flooded with mail. Just be patient and you'll hear from them.

Hockey

National Hockey League
1251 Avenue of the Americas
New York, NY 10020
www.nhl.com

EASTERN CONFERENCE

Atlanta Thrashers Hockey Club
Atlanta, GA 30348-5366
www.atlantathrashers.com

Boston Bruins
One FleetCenter Ste. 250
Boston, MA 02fi4-1303
www.bostonbruins.com

Buffalo Sabres
Marine Midland Arena
One Seymore H. Knox III Plaza
Buffalo, NY 14203
www.sabres.com

Carolina Hurricanes Hockey Club
Entertainment & Sports Arena
1400 Edwards Mill Rd.
Raleigh, NC 27607
www.caneshockey.com

Florida Panthers Hockey Club
One Panthers Pkwy.
Sunrise, FL 33323
www.floridapanthers.com

Montreal Canadiens
1275 St. Antoine St West
Montreal, Quebec Canada H3C 5L2
www.canadiens.com

New Jersey Devils
Continental Airlines Arena
50 Route 120 North
E. Rutherford, NJ 07073
www.newjerseydevils.com

New York Islanders
Nassau Veterans Memorial Coliseum
1535 Old Country Rd.
Plainview, NY 11553
www.newyorkislanders.com

New York Rangers
Madison Square Garden
Two Pennsylvania Plaza, 14th flr.
New York, NY 10121
www.newyorkrangers.com

Ottawa Senators Hockey Club
Corel Centre
1000 Palladium Dr.
Kanata, Ontario
Canada K2V 1A5
www.ottawasenators.com

Philadelphia Flyers
Wachovia Center Complex
3601 S. Broad St.
Philadelphia, PA 19148
www.philadelphiaflyers.com

Pittsburgh Penguins
Mellon Arena
66 Mario Lemieux Pl.
Pittsburgh, PA 15219
www.pittsburghpenguins.com

Tampa Bay Lightning
Ice Palace Arena
401 Channelside Dr.
Tampa, FL 33602
www.tampabaylightning.com

Toronto Maple Leafs
Air Canada Centre
40 Bay St.
Toronto, Ontario
Canada M5J 2X2
www.mapleleafs.com

Washington Capitals
Market Square North
401 Nitnth St. NW, Suite 750
Washington, DC 20004
www.washingtoncaps.com

WESTERN CONFERENCE

Anaheim Mighty Ducks
Arrowhead Pond of Anaheim
2695 Katella Ave.
Anaheim, CA 92806
www.mightyducks.com

Calgary Flames
Pengrowth Saddledome
PO Box 1540, Station M
Calgary, Alberta
Canada T2P 3B9
www.calgaryflames.com

Chicago Blackhawks
United Center
1901 W. Madison St.
Chicago, IL 60612
www.chicagoblackhawks.com

Colorado Avalanche
Pepsi Center
1000 Chopper Cir.
Denver, CO 80204
www.coloradoavalanche.com

Columbus Blue Jackets
Nationwide Arena
200 W. Nationwide Blvd.
Suite Level
Columbus, OH 43125
www.bluejackets.com

Dallas Stars
Dr. Pepper StarCenter-Valley
Ranch
211 Cowboys Pkwy.
Irving, TX 75063
www.dallasstars.com

Detroit Red Wings
Joe Louis Arena
600 Civic Center Dr.
Detroit, MI 48226
www.detroitredwings.com

Edmonton Oilers
Skyreach Centre
11230 110 St.
Edmonton, Alberta
Canada T5G H7
www.edmontonoilers.com

Los Angeles Kings
Staples Center
1111 S. Figueroa St.
Los Angeles, CA 90015
www.lakings.com

Minnesota Wild
317 Washington St.
St. Paul, MN 55102
www.wild.com

Nashville Predators
501 Broadway
Nashville, TN 37203
www.nashvillepredators.com

Phoenix Coyotes
Alltel Ice Den
9375 E. Bell Rd.
Scottsdale, AZ 85260
www.phoenixcoyotes.com

San Jose Sharks
525 W. Santa Clara St.
San Jose, CA 95113
www.sjsharks.com

St. Louis Blues
Savvis Center
1401 Clark Ave.
St. Louis, MO 03103-2709
www.stlouisblues.com

Vancouver Canucks
General Motors Place
800 Griffiths Way
Vancouver, BC
Canada V6B 6G1
www.canucks.com

BASKETBALL

Atlanta Hawks
Centennial Tower
101 Marietta St NW
Atlanta, GA 30303
www.nba.com/hawks

Boston Celtics
FleetCenter
151 Merrimac St., 5th f1r.
Boston, MA 02114
www.nba.com/celtics

Charlotte Hornets
100 Hive Dr.
Charlotte, NC 28217
www.nba.com/hornets

Chicago Bulls
United Center
1901 W. Madison St.
Chicago, IL 60612-2459
www.nba.com/bulls

Cleveland Cavaliers
One Center Court
Cleveland, OH 44115
www.nba.com/cavs

Dallas Mavericks
The Pavilion
2909 Taylor St
Dallas, TX 75226
www.nba.com/mavericks

Denver Nuggets
1000 Chopper Circle
Denver, CO 80204
www.nba.com/nuggets

Detroit Pistons
Palace of Auburn Hills
Two Championship Dr.
Auburn Hills, MI 48326
www.nba.com/pistons

Golden State Warriors
1011 Broadway, 20th flr.
Oakland, CA 94607
www.nba.com/warriors

Houston Rockets
Toyota Center
1510 Polk St
Houston, TX 77002
www.nba.com/rackets

Indiana Pacers
125 S. Pennsylvania St.
Indianapolis, IN 46204
www.nba.com/pacers

Los Angeles Clippers
Staples Center
1111 S. Figueroa St.
Los Angeles, CA 90015
www.nba.com/clippers

Los Angeles Lakers
Staples Center
I1111 S. Figueroa St.
Los Angeles, CA 90015
www.nba.com/lakers

Memphis Grizzlies
175 Toyota Pl., Ste. 150
Memphis, TN 38103
www.Grizzlies.com

Miami Heat
American Airlines Arena
601 Biscayne Blvd.
Miami, FL 33132
www.nba.com/heat

Milwaukee Bucks
Bradley Center
1001 N. Fourth St.
Milwaukee, WI 53203
www.nba.com/bucks

Minnesota Timberwolves
600 First Ave. N
Minneapolis, MN 55403
www.nba.com/timberwolves

New Jersey Nets
390 Murray Hill Pkwy.
E. Rutherford, NJ 07073
www.nba.com/nets

New York Knicks
Madison Square Garden
Two Pennsylvania Plaza
New York, NY 10121
www. nba.com/knicks

Orlando Magic
8701 Maitland Summit Blvd.
Orlando, FL 32810
www.nba.com/magic

Philadelphia '76ers
First Union Center
3601 S. Broad St.
Philadelphia, PA 19148
www.nba.com/sixers

Phoenix Suns
America West Arena
201 E. Jefferson St.
Phoenix, AZ 85004
www.nba.com/suns

Portland Trail Blazers
One Center Court, Ste. 200
Portland, OR 97201
www.nba.com/blazers

Sacramento Kings
Arco Arena
One Sports Pkwy.
Sacramento, CA 95834
www.nba.com/kings

San Antonio Spurs
SBC Center
1 SBC Center
San Antonio, TX 78219
www.nba.com/spurs

Seattle Sonics & Storm
351 Elliott Ave. W., Ste. 500
Seattle, WA 98119
www.nba.com/sonics

Toronto Raptors
Air Canada Centre
40 Bay St.
Toronto, Ontario
Canada M5J 2X2
www.nba.com/raptors

Utah Jazz
Delta Center
301 W. South Temple
Salt Lake City, UT 84101
www.nba.com/jazz

Washington Wizards
MCI Center
601 F Street NW
Washington, DC 20004
www.nba.com/wizards

FOOTBALL

National Football League
280 Park Ave.
New York, NY 10017
www.nfl.com

AMERICAN CONFERENCE

Baltimore Ravens
M & T Bank Stadium
1101 Russell St.
Baltimore, MD 21230
www.BaltimorRavens.com

Buffalo Bills
One Bills Dr.
Orchard Park, NY 14127
www.buffalobills.com

Cincinnati Bengals
One Paul Brown Stadium
Cincinnati, OH 45202
www.bengals.com

Cleveland Browns
1085 West 3rd St.
Cleveland, OH 44114
www.clevelandbrowns.com

Denver Broncos
13655 Broncos Parkway
Englewood, CO 80112
www.denverbroncos.com

Houston Texans
711 Louisiana, 33rd flr.
Houston, TX 77002-2716
www.houstontexans.com

Indianapolis Colts
7001 W. 56 St.
Indianapolis, IN 46254
www.colts.com

Jacksonville Jaguars
One ALLTEL Stadium Pl.
Jacksonville, FL 32202
www.jaguars.corn

Kansas City Chiefs
One Arrowhead Dr.
Kansas City, MO 64129
www.kcchiefs.com

Miami Dolphins
Pro Player Stadium
7500 SW 30th St.
Davie, FL 33314
www.miamidolphins.com

New England Patriots
One Patriot Place
Foxboro, MA 02035
www.patriots.com

New York Jets
Giants Stadium
East Rutherford, NJ 07073
or
1000 Fulton Ave.
Hempstead, NY 11550
www.newyorkjets.com/
index2new.php

Oakland Raiders
7000 Coliseum Way
Oakland, CA 94621
www.raiders.com

Pittsburgh Steelers
3400 S. Water St.
Pittsburg, PA 15203
www.steelers.com

San Diego Chargers
4020 Murphy Canyon Rd
San Diego, CA 92123
www.chargers.com

Tennessee Titans
One Titans Way
Nashville, TN 37273
www.titansonline.com

NATIONAL CONFERENCE

Arizona Cardinals
8701 S. Hardy Dr.
Phoenix, AZ 85284
www.AZcardinals.com

Atlanta Falcons
4400 Falcon Pkwy.
Flowery Branch, GA 30542
www.AtlantaFalcons.com

Carolina Panthers
Ericsson Stadium
800 S. Mint St.
Charlotte, NC 28202
www.panthers.com

Chicago Bears
Halas Hall
1000 Football Dr.
Lake Forest, IL 60045
ww.chicagobears.com

Dallas Cowboys
Texas Stadium
2401 East Airport Freeway
Irving, TX 75063
www.dallascowboys.com

Detroit Lions
222 Republic Dr.
Allen Park, MI 48101
www.detroitlions.com

Green Bay Packers
1265 Lombardi Ave.
Green Bay, WI 54304
www.packers.com

Minnesota Vikings
Hubert H. Humphrey Metrodome
9520 Viking Dr.
Eden Prairie, MN 55344
www.vikings.com

The New Orleans Saints
5800 Airline Dr.
Metairie, LA 70003
www.neworleanssaints.com

New York Football Giants
Giants Stadium
East Rutherford, NJ 07073
www.Giants.com

Philadelphia Eagles
Nova Care Complex
One Nova Care Way
Philadelphia, PA 19145
www.PhiladelphiaEagles.com

San Francisco 49ers
4949 Centennial Blvd.
Santa Clara, CA 95054
www.sf49ers.com

Seattle Seahawks
11220 N.E. 53 St.
Kirkland, WA 98033
www.seahawks.com

St. Louis Rams
901 North Broadway
St. Louis, MO 63101
www.stlouisrams.com

Tampa Bay Buccaneers
One Buccaneer Pl.
Tampa, FL 33607
www. buccaneers. com

Washington Redskins
21300 Redskin Park Dr.
Ashburn, VA 20147
www.redskins.com

Baseball

Major League Baseball
MLB Advanced Media
New York, NY 10011
http://mlb.com

AMERICAN LEAGUE

Anaheim Angels
Angel Stadium
200 Gene Autry Way
Anaheim, CA 92806
http://anaheim.angels.mlb.com

Baltimore Orioles
Oriole Park at Camden Yards
333 W. Camden St.
Baltimore, MD 21201
http://
baltimore.orioles.mlb.com

Boston Red Sox
Four Yawkey Way
Boston, MA 02215-3496
http://bostonredsock.mlb.com

Chicago White Sox
333 W. 35 St.
Chicago, IL 60616
www.whitesox.mlb.com

Cleveland Indians
Jacobs Field
2401 Ontario St.
Cleveland, OH 44115-4003
http://clevelandindians.mlb.com

Detroit Tigers
Commerce Park
2100 Woodward Ave.
Detroit, MI 48201

http://detroittigers.mlb.com

Kansas City Royals
One Royal Way
Kansas City, MO 64129
http://kansascity.royals.mlb.com

Minnesota Twins
Metrodome
34 Kirby Puckett Pl.
Minneapolis, MN 55415
http://minnesota.twins.mlb.com

New York Yankees
Yankee Stadium
161st St. and River Ave.
Bronx, NY 10451
http://newyork.yankees.mlb.com

Oakland Athletics
7677 Oakport St., Ste. 200
Oakland, CA 94621
http://oakland.athletics.mlb.com

Seattle Mariners
SAFECO Field
1250 First Ave. S.
Seattle, WA 98134
http://seattle.mariners.mlb.com

Tampa Bay Devil Rays
Tropicana Field
One Tropicana Dr.
St. Petersburg, FL 33705
www.devilrays.mlb.com

Texas Rangers
1000 Ballpark Way, #4oo
Arlington, TX 76011
www.rangers.mlb.com

Toronto Blue Jays
One Blue Jays Way, Ste. 3200
SkyDome
Toronto, Ontario
Canada M5V 1J1
www.bluejoys.mlb.com

NATIONAL LEAGUE

Arizona Diamondbacks
Bank One Ballpark
401 East Jefferson St.
Phoenix, AZ 85001
http://
arizona.diamondbacks.mlb.com

Atlanta Braves
755 Hank Aaron Dr.
Atlanta, GA 30315
http://atlanta.braves.mlb.com

Chicago Cubs
Wrigley Field
1060 W. Addison
Chicago, IL 60613
http://chicagocubs.mlb.com

Cincinnati Reds
100 Cinergy Field
Cincinnati, OH 45202
http://cincinnati.reds.mlb.com

Colorado Rockies
Coors Field
2001 Blake St.
Denver, C0 80205-2000
http://colorado.rockies.mlb.com

Florida Marlins
Pro Player Stadium
2269 Dan Marino Blvd.
Miami, FL 33056
http://florida.marlins.mlb.com

Houston Astros
501 Crawford St.

Houston, TX 77002
http://houston.astros.mlb.com
Los Angeles Dodgers
Dodger Stadium
1000 Elysian Park Ave.
Los Angeles, CA 90012-1199
http://losangeles.dodgers.mlb.com

Milwaukee Brewers
One Brewers Way
Milwaukee, WI 53214-3652
http://milwaukee.brewers.mlb.com

Montreal Expos
4549 Avenue Pierrede Coubertin
Montreal, Quebec
Canada HIV3N7
http://montreal.expos.mlb.com

New York Mets
Shea Stadium
123-01 Roosevelt Ave.
Flushing, NY 11368-1699
http://newyork.mets.mlb.com

Philadelphia Phillies
Veterans Stadium
3501 S. Broad St.
Philadelphia, PA 19148
http://philadelphia.phillies.mlb.com

Pittsburgh Pirates
PNC Park at North Shore
115 Federal St.
Pittsburgh, PA 15212
http://pittsburg.pirates.mlb.com

St. Louis Cardinals
250 Stadium Plaza
St. Louis, MO 63102
http://stlouis.cardinals.mlb.com

San Diego Padres
8880 Rio San Diego Dr. Suite 400
San Diego, CA 92112
http://sandiego.padres.mlb.com

San Francisco Giants
Pacific Bell Park
24 Willie Mays Plaza
San Francisco, CA 94107
http://sanfrancisco.giants.mlb.com

Money Matters

Do You Need A Financial Planner?

Are you are always having difficulty making ends meet? Maybe you would like to have more money to enjoy your retirement. You might need the help of a financial planner. *When and How to Choose a Financial Planner* is a free booklet available from the National Endowment for Financial Education, that will help you choose a planner. This 12 page guide gives basic information on when you should seek advice, as well as how to go about choosing a financial planner. To get your free copy, write to:

NATIONAL ENDOWMENT FOR FINANCIAL EDUCATION
5299 DTC BLVD. SUITE 1300
GREENWOOD VILLAGE, CO 80111
www.nefe.org

Finding The Right Financial Adviser

Everybody with assets to protect, regardless of their age, should have a financial advisor. Just remember, you worked hard for your money and now it's time to make your money work harder for you. Oppenheimer Funds has published a guide, *Finding A Financial Adviser Who's Right For You.* It will take you through the process step-by-step of selecting names, conducting interviews, making the final decision, and maintaining a relationship that will be profitable. This is a must for anyone looking for help in making intelligent financial planning decisions. To order your free copy call:

1-888-470-0862
www.oppenheimerfunds.com

How To Make Educated Investments

American Century Investments is offering free investor education materials you might find useful. Here are some of the more popular ones:

IRA CHOICES AND CHALLENGES, a 16 page booklet that compares the different types of IRAs created by the 1997 Tax Relief Act

INVESTING WITH A PURPOSE, a 26 page booklet that explains the concepts of diversification and asset allocation, offers four sample portfolios based on your stage in life, and includes a do-it-yourself investor profile questionnaire

COLLEGE PLANNER, a slide-rule calculator for determining college costs

POST-RETIREMENT CALCULATOR, a slide-rule calculator for determining how long your savings will last, depending on how much you spend

FAST TAXFACTS, a laminated card with tax rates and general information on IRA rules and IRA Rollovers and much more. For your free copy of any or all of these booklets or calculators, call American Century Investments toll-free at:

1-800-345-2021
www.americancentury.com

Tax Saving Investments

If would like to lower your income taxes maybe you should be looking at investments that are completely or partially free of federal, state or local income tax. Lebenthal, one of the nation's leading municipal bond dealers has the *Lebenthal Municipal Bond Information Kit* that will show you the advantages of investing in tax-exempt bonds. For your kit, call them toll-free at:

1-888-425-6116
www.lebenthal.com

Before You Buy A Franchise

Did you ever think of starting your own business maybe by buying one of the thousands of franchises that are available? Before you decide to make your mark as an franchise entrepreneur, you owe it to yourself to learn more about franchising. Some valuable sources to contact are:

The *ACCESS Franchise Directory*, the most comprehensive database of franchise information on the Internet. This site lists more than 2500 franchises at their web address: **www.entremkt.com.**

The Federal Trade Commission, which has an excellent 12 page pamphlet called *A Consumer Guide to Buying a Franchise*. You can download it from the FTC's Web site: **www.ftc.gov.**

Free Help Starting A Business

Service Corps of Retired Executives (SCORE) can give you free advice on starting a small business. This is a group of working and retired executives and business owners who donate their time and expertise to provide individual confidential business counseling and business workshops for aspiring entrepreneurs and small business owners. To find the SCORE office nearest you, call them at: **1-800-634-0245** **www.score.org**

Money To Start A Business

For some seniors the definition of retiring is to stop doing your usual job and starting up something new. If you've always wanted to start a business, now's your chance. The U.S. Small Business Administration (SBA) is a great resource you can use for starting that business. They have a variety of programs including a loan guarantee program you might want to use. The SBA has offices throughout the U.S. But to find out more, first call the SBA Answer Desk at: **1-800-827-5722**

Or visit the U.S. Small Business Administration web site: **www.SBAonline.SBA.Gov**

Searching the Web for the Best Mortgage Loans

Before you shop for a new mortgage, be sure to find out what rates are being charged in your area, find out mortgage trends and use repayment calculators. Even a slightly lower interest rate can often save you thousands of dollars over the repayment period of your loan. Once you've become an informed consumer you can then shop intelligently for a mortgage loan either on the Internet or at your local financial institution. Here are three online sites where you can find up-to-date rate information and lots more. They do not offer mortgages directly but will provide you with all kinds of highly useful information you can use:

FANNIE MAE
www.fanniemae.com
Provides all kinds of mortgage and home refinancing information. They also list the co-op, condos and houses that they own due to foreclosures throughout the nation. A great place to shop for a terrifc buy on your next home.

MORTGAGE MARKET INFORMATION SERVICE, INC.
www.interest.com
Employs an easy-to-use click-on map to find up-to-date information about mortgage rates and lenders in specific areas around the country.

MICRO SURF
www.microsurf.com
This site is the largest independent source of mortgage information on the Internet. While they are not lenders or brokers, they do allow you to compare the rates offered by 1,300 lenders nationwide who update their rates daily.

Save Thousands By Shopping For Your Mortgage Online

Your home mortgage is the most important financial transaction your family is likely to ever make. But if you have ever shopped for a mortgage you know how long, tedious... and expensive the process can be. Now there may be a better way...online mortgages.

With the application filed out on your home computer and sent electronically, online mortgage applications offers you a combination of speed, convenience and cost savings. Financial experts agree that getting your mortgage online will almost definitely save you money. In fact, sometimes the savings can total tens of thousands of dollars over the term of the mortgage! The reason is that the online mortgage companies deal with lenders throughout the country and they are constantly searching for the very best rates to offer you. Mortgage approval can often be a matter of minutes instead of weeks or even months that it takes the traditional way.

In addition, several of the online mortgage companies offer you a variety of additional services that include help in finding a home, tips on negotiating and inspecting the home you plan to buy and lots more. Here are three of the leading online mortgage companies you can contact directly through their Internet sites:

Intuit Inc.: www.quickenmortgage.com

E-Loan: www.eloan.com

I Own: www.iown.com

Do You Have Unclaimed Money Waiting For You?

Did you know that there are actually $300 billion dollars in unclaimed funds waiting for their rightful owner to come along? What often happens is that people move and forget to notify everyone of their new address. You may have a bank account from years ago with money that was never withdrawn. Also, there are 3 million stock brokerage accounts with securities that belong to shareholders who are currently lost. If you think there's even a remote possibility that you have funds or securities you have forgotten about, be sure to check at these web sites and see what you have and how you can claim your funds. It's like winning the lottery!

The first Internet website is for a lost funds search company called The CapitaLink. Their web address is: **www.ifast.com**

And, 25 states with web sites have a combined site where you can search by name for unclaimed property they hold. Check out this web site at: **www.unclaimed.org**

Download Coupon Savings

One of the traditional ways of saving money is to clip coupons and use them in your shopping. The trouble is that it takes a lot of time to scour the newspapers to find the coupons you will use. Now there's an easier way of getting those same savings without the hassle...dowloading them from the Internet.

One of the leading companies helping you get these coupons online is called *CoolSavings*. Their electronic method of couponing has met with great success and their web site has quickly become one of the most visited Internet sites. The way it works is that you go to their web site and fill out a brief online questionnaire, select the coupons you want, download them into your computer and print them out. You'll find a vast array of companies at their web site including everything from local pizza delivery stores to national chains like J.C. Penney, Toys 'R Us and

McDonalds. To check out their free web site go to:
www.coolsavings.com

IRA - Roth IRA – What's The Difference?

You probably know that Individual Retirement Accounts commonly known at 'IRA's' are allowed to help you save tax sheltered money for retirement. But do you know what the difference is between an IRA and a ROTH IRA? To help taxpayers learn more about all kinds of IRA's and so you can determine which is right for you, the IRS has updated its 'Publication 590' that focuses on these types of accounts. Call them at:
1-800-829-1040
Or visit their website at: www.irs.gov

How To Avoid Phone Scams

Be careful…unscrupulous individuals and companies have a phone scheme that preys on consumers and especially on seniors. Without your knowledge they 'slam' or 'cram' your phone.

'Slamming' means switching your phone service to their company without your permission.

'Cramming' is the practice of charging you for services you never ordered.

Here are tips from the National Fraud Information Center, on how to avoid slamming and cramming, and what to do if you think you've been defrauded.

Check every page of your phone bill as soon as you get it for unauthorized charges. If you find something that is unclear call your local phone company.

Read the fine print before filling out any contest form or coupon offer.

Take care when calling 800 or 900 numbers. Be especially wary of following instructions that say, "enter activation code numbers or of answering 'yes' to questions that may result in your authorizing unwanted telephone services.

Here's what to do once you feel you have been defrauded:

• Call the National Fraud Information Center at:

1-800-876-7060

• Send a letter describing what happened and enclose a copy of your bill to the

FEDERAL COMMUNICATIONS COMMISSION
CONSUMER PROTECTION BRANCH
445 12TH STREET SW
WASHINGTON, **DC 20554**
1-888-225-5322
www.fcc.gov

• File a complaint with your local attorney general and telephone regulators.

Planning For Retirement

Whether you are just starting to invest or already have a plan, Charles Schwab has a free source book that will help you with those important financial decisions. *The Essential Investor* will help you plan for a more secure financial future. It includes a checklist of investing essentials to get you started as well as sample portfolios and even a quick retirement planner. Ask for *Smart Answers For Today's Market* when you call:

877-488-6762
www.schwab.com

Women and Money

The *Money Minded* web site is designed specifically for women. It addresses questions about saving, family goals, and investing mostly from a woman's perspective. On the site you'll find featured entrepreneurs and financial risk-

takers who offer their great advice and important information for women and their money. Their web address is:
www.moneyminded.com/index.htm

The Best Online Broker

Gomez.com ranks Charles Schwab as the #1 overall online broker. If you buy or sell securities on the Internet and would like to get important financial information about Schwab's brokerage services, check them out on their web site:
www.schwab.com

Understanding Mutual Funds

A Guide to Understanding Mutual Funds is available free from the Investment Company Institute, the mutual fund industry's principal trade group. This guide describes the various types of funds and explains the risks involved, discusses how funds are structured, and how to set up an investment plan. They also discuss important tax considerations and give you a guide to finding and analyzing information on funds yourself. To get your free copy, call:
202-326-5800
www.ici.org

Mutual Fund Report Card

Are you holding the right mutual funds? Charles Schwab has a series of report cards for different mutual funds that give you their ratings, performance and growth records. You can request up to three reports for any mutual funds even if they're not available through Schwab. There's no cost or obligation. Call them toll-free at:
1-877-476-2370
Or visit their web site at www.schwab.com

Mutual Fund Info

Waterhouse Securities, Inc. will send you the *Top Performing Mutual Funds Guide* and the *Mutual Funds Information and Comparison Guide*. If you invest in mutual funds or are thinking of investing, you'll definitely want these free guides. Call toll-free:
1-800-934-4448
Or visit them at their web site: www.tdwaterhouse.com

Getting Your Budget In Shape

To help you keep your budget in shape, the Internet has a number of helpful sites that will help you:

SMART CALC:
You'll find a number of very useful calculators at this web site that will help you budget your spending, determine how much your mortgage payments will be... and lots more.
www.smartcalc.com

HEALTHY CASH
Are you an overspender? Are there things you can do to avoid the devastating effects of this habit? To discover your 'Spending Personality,' take a self-test online at *Healthy Cash* which is at the Health World Online Web site at:
www.healthy.net/library/articles/cash

THE MONEY WISE HOME GUIDE:
www.mpicture.com/homeguide/financial/debt.htm

Tips To Get Financially Fit

- Pay off your credit card debt to reduce interest expenses. Start with the credit cards that have the highest finance charge. If possible pay off your balance every month.
- Switch to using credit cards with no annual fees.
- Be a smart shopper and always shop around before you buy something especially big ticket items.

- If you do find it necessary to carry balances on your credit card, be certain you are not using a card that charges a high percentage rate on unpaid balances. Remember, you can get the interest rate lowered with most credit cards just by asking for a lower rate. Tell them you are thinking of dropping their card and using another one that charges a lower interest rate. You'll be amazed at how often they will offer you a substantially lower rate rather than lose you as a customer.
- Join a credit union if you're eligible. Credit unions generally charge lower fees than banks especially if you maintain only small balances in your checking and savings accounts.

Money Facts

The Federal Reserve Bank of Atlanta has a free fascinating booklet that describes how currency is designed, printed, circulated and eventually destroyed. There's even a section on how to redeem bills that might have been damaged in a fire or chewed up by the family dog. Ask for *Fundamental Facts About U.S. Money*. Write to:

FEDERAL RESERVE BANK OF ATLANTA
PUBLICATIONS DEPARTMENT
1000 PEACH TREE STREET NE
ATLANTA, GA. 30309
www.frbatlanta.org

Fast Banking

The American Bankers Association's free brochure on *A Dozen Ways to Save Time and Money at the Bank* offers a variety of tips on money management. It will help you take charge of your finances. For a free copy, write to:

ATTENTION: *'A DOZEN TIPS.'*
THE AMERICAN BANKERS ASSOCIATION
1120 CONNECTICUT AVE. N.W.
WASHINGTON, D.C. 20036

Choosing The Mortgage That's Right For You

Are you ready to shop for a mortgage? This easy to read 40 page guide can help. It walks you through the mortgage shopping process in three easy steps. Discover how big a mortgage loan you can afford, how to choose the mortgage that's right for you, and how to compare terms commonly used among lenders. This guide is free from:

FANNIE MAE FOUNDATION
4000 WISCONSIN AVE. NW
NORTH TOWER SUITE **1**
WASHINGTON, DC 20016
OR CALL 1-202-274-8000
www.fanniemaefoundation.org

Tax Do's & Don'ts For Mutual Fund Investors

This helpful 20 page booklet, *Tax Do's & Don'ts For Mutual Fund Investors*, lists 13 points to consider about the tax aspects of mutual fund investing. For example , it warns you *not* to assume that all fund distributions are the same, that you owe no taxes on reinvested dividends or that you owe no tax if you exchange shares from one fund for shares of another in mutual fund 'families.' For a copy of the free booklet, write to:

ICI
1401 H ST. N.W., SUITE **1200**
WASHINGTON, D.C. **2005**

Investing For Retirement

IRA Transfers is a free brochure that explains tax-sheltered retirement investing. It can help you get the most from your investments. It is published by the AARP Investment Program from Scudder, Stevens & Clark - a group of no-load mutual funds designed for members of the AARP, but open to investors of any age. (No-load means there is no sales

commission.) For free a copy, call:
1-800-322 2282

The State Tax Laws: A Guide for Investors Aged 50 and Over is another free publication from AARP. Scudder prepared this 112 page guide in conjunction with the National Conference of State Legislatures. For a copy call:
1-800-322-2282
www.aarp.scudder.com

Finding The Right Tax Professional

When tax time comes around it's always an excellent idea to have a tax pro help you. To help you through the difficult process of choosing the right tax pro, you might want to start by getting the names of professionals in your area and interviewing a number of them. For the names of tax experts in your area, call the National Association of Enrolled Agents at: **1-303-212-9608**
Or visit their web site: www.naea.org

Before You Go Into Business

If you've ever thought of going into business and starting a new corporation, here's a booklet you will definitely want to get. *Starting Your Own Corporation* will answer many of the questions you may have regarding setting up the right kind of corporation. For your free copy, call the 'Corporation Company' at:
1-800-818-0204
www.corporate.com

Personal Finance Helplines

If you are not sure where to turn for good advice regarding your personal finances, here are several toll-free hotlines you can turn to for help. They will either provide you with the information you need or they will tell you where you can go for further assistance.

Financial Planning

THE INSTITUTE OF CERTIFIED FINANCIAL PLANNERS - FOR BROCHURES & REFERRALS, CALL: 1-800-282-7526

THE AMERICAN INSTITUTE OF CERTIFIED PUBLIC ACCOUNTANTS' PERSONAL FINANCIAL PLANNING DIVISION CALL: 1-888-777-7077

THE FINANCIAL PLANNING ASSOCIATON
CALL: 1-800-647-6340

THE NATIONAL ASSOCIATION OF PERSONAL FINANCIAL ADVISERS. CALL:
1-800 366-2732

THE AMERICAN SOCIETY OF CLU AND ChFC.
CALL: 1-800-392-6900

Choosing The Right Stock Broker

The best way to find a good stockbroker is to ask for referrals from friends, professional acquaintances or from your family. If you have any questions and would like to check on a particular broker's background, call:
THE NATIONAL ASSOCIATION OF SECURITIES DEALERS:
1-800-289-9999
www.nasd.com

Savings Bond Redemption

Did you know that all Series E Savings Bond issued since 1941 are still earning interest? If you own any bonds tucked away in a safety deposit box and would like to know exactly how much they're worth today, write for *Tables of Redemption Values For Savings Bonds* from:
BUREAU OF PUBLIC DEBT
SAVING BOND OPERATIONS
PARKERSBURG, WV 26101-1328
OR VISIT THEIR WEB SITE: www.savingbonds.gov

Buying U.S. Government Securities

Americans have been buying Series E Savings bonds for many years. But few people know they can also buy Treasury Bonds and Bills that pay even higher interest. For more information on how you can get in on this no-risk, high-yield investment, write for *U.S. Securities Available to Investors.* From:

TREASURY DIRECT
PO Box 9150
MINNEAPOLIS, MN 55480
1-800-722-2678
www.publicdebt.treas.gov

Recovering Lost Money

Did your dog chew up some money you left on the table? Did it get partially destroyed in a fire? Well the U.S. Department of Treasury can help get that money back for you. Drop them a line with a plausible detailed explanation. Once the claim is processsed and verified, the actual payment is made by federal check. For more information write:

U.S. DEPARTMENT OF THE TREASURY
BUREAU OF ENGRAVING & PRINTING
14TH AND C STREETS SW
WASHINGTON, D.C. 20228
OR CALL: 1-202-874-3019
www.moneyfactory.com

Getting A New Mortgage

If you are looking for a new mortgage either to buy a new house or to take advantage of lower mortagage rates, it is important that you learn how to evaluate the type of mortgage that is best for you. As a first step you might call First Financial Equity on their toll-free number for more information and for answers to your mortgage questions. Call:

1-888-951-1010
www.ffec.com

Evaluating Your Investments

Before you make any significant investment, learn what to look for to find the one that's best for you. Also discover how to evaluate your investment and determine how well it meets your objectives. The first step is to ask for *Evaluating Investment Performance,* when you contact:
NEUBERGER & BERMAN
INDIVIDUAL ASSET MANAGEMENT GROUP
605 THIRD AVE.
NEW YORK, NY 10158
OR CALL 877-672-7329
www.nb.com

Savings Just Because You're Over 50

Now that an ever growing part of the population is over 50 years old, there are lots of bargains and discounts available just for the asking. Remember if you don't ask you'll never know. In any store you shop in always check to see if there are certain days or certain times when seniors are offered discounts or specials. Many hotels offer discounts on their rooms as well as discounts if you eat in their restaurants. You can also apply for a travel club card if you are a member of AARP...The American Association of Retired Persons. Their toll-free phone number is:
888-687-2277
www.aarp.scudder.org

Learning About Mutual Funds

If you would like to learn all about mutual funds and find out which are the best ones for you, check out the Strong Equity Performers from Dreyfus. Call them toll-free at:
1-800-782-6620
Or visit a Dreyfus Financial Center via the Internet at:
www.dreyfus.com

Global Utilities Fund

Basic utilities such as water and electricity are always in demand and telecommunications is growing in all countries. That's why the Franklin Global Utilities Fund might be a growth fund for you. They will manage a portfolio especially designed for you. If this sounds like something you would consider, call today for a free brochure and prospectus:
1-800-632-2301
www.franklintempleton.com

The Lowest Cost Life Insurance - Guaranteed!

If you are looking for the maximum life insurance coverage at the lowest cost...this one's for you. A company called Quotesmith actually guarantees they will find the lowest term life rates in America or they'll send you $500.00! That's quite a claim but it's worth checking them out.

What they do when you request a quote by calling their toll-free number is scan the 350 insurance companies in their database and give you the lowest price quotes that that search comes up with. There is no charge for their service so you may want to give them a try. It could save you a bundle. You can call them at:
1-800-556-9393
www.quotesmith.com

Fund Raising Kit

If your school or organization needs money, this *free fund-raising kit* will teach you how. This kit will help show your group how to collect member's recipes and publish them into a great cookbook. Write for your free kit to:
FUNDCRAFT
410 HIGHWAY 72 WEST
BOX 340
COLLIERVILLE, TN 38017
1-800-853-1363
www.fundcraft.com

Lower Your Insurance Premiums

Did you know that if you're in the market for Medicare and Medigap policies for health insurance for yourself or a parent, your premiums will be lowest if you enroll between three months before, to four months after your 65th birthday? After that the premiums may grow by 10 percent each year you wait. For more information, ask for The Social Security Administration's free *Guide to Health Insurance for People with Medicare.* Contact:

THE HEALTH INSURANCE ASSOCIATION OF AMERICA
PUBLICATION OFFICE
555 13TH ST. NW SUITE 600-E
WASHINGTON, D.C. 20004
OR CALL TOLL-FREE: 1-800-772-1213

Mutual Funds For Investors Over 50

You've worked hard to save money for your retirement and to help it grow, now you must be sure you do everything you can to preserve and protect that important investment. *Understanding Mutual Funds: A Guide for Investors Aged 50 and Over*, defines the basics to help older individuals choose funds appropriate for their needs. It's your free! Contact:

AARP INVESTMENT PROGRAM
SCUDDER PROCESSING CENTER
BOX 5014
JANESVILLE, WI 53547.
OR CALL: 800-322-2282, EXT 4884

Check Out Money Market Funds

If you want higher interest than you will get in a bank but still want instant access to your money, be sure to check out the money market funds. To find out more about money market funds, contact one or more of these large funds and ask for their *prospectus and information package:*

DREYFUS SERVICE CORP.
200 PARK AVENUE
NEW YORK, NY 10166
1-800-645-6561
WWW.DREYFUS.COM

FIDELITY INVESTMENTS
P.O. BOX 77001
CINCINNATI, OH 45277
CALL: 1-800-544-3902
www.fidelity.com

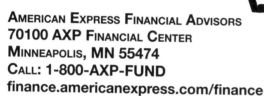

AMERICAN EXPRESS FINANCIAL ADVISORS
70100 AXP FINANCIAL CENTER
MINNEAPOLIS, MN 55474
CALL: 1-800-AXP-FUND
finance.americanexpress.com/finance

Tax-Free Income Fund

If you are in a high tax bracket and would like to lower your tax bite, did you know you can start earning tax-free income with as little as $1,000 with instant liquidity and no sales or redemption fee? For more information on tax-free investing, call:
1-800-638-5660
www.trprice.com

IRS Or H&R Block?

Few people realize that the IRS is committed to giving tax-payers every legitimate deduction they're entitled to. The IRS has toll-free numbers throughout the country you can call for assistance and/or forms. As a start, for answers to your income tax questions, call The Internal Revenue Service's tax hotline toll-free:
1-800-829-1040

The IRS also has a series of helpful publications such as *Federal Income Tax* available free of charge. Call the toll-free number for this publication or a list of the others available. In the internet go to: **www.irs.gov**

The IRS also has a toll-free number to assist deaf/hearing-impaired taxpayers who have access to TV-Phone/Teletype-writer equipment (800-829-4059).

"Congratulations! You've Just Won...."

Even though the world is full of people who would never think of doing anything dishonest, there are still plenty of people out there who wouldn't give a second thought to conning you out of your life savings. One of the most common scams is calling elderly people with an exciting announcement such as... *"Congratulations, Mr. Jones, you're name has been selected as the winner of an exciting cruise. Isn't that great? All you need to do to claim your prize is to put up a good faith deposit by sending us a check for $$$$$$."*

Hang up the phone right there. One rule you must always follow is:

Never...EVER buy anything or pay money to claim your *'free prize.'* No reputable company will ever ask you to send them money to get a 'free' prize.

For more information on these scams and what you can do to keep from falling prey to one, get your free copy of *Telemarketing Travel Fraud.* It's your free from:

PUBLIC REFERENCE
FEDERAL TRADE COMMISSION
CRC 240
WASHINGTON, DC 20580
1-877-382-4357
www.ftc.gov

Be Your Own Broker

If you have a computer and like to make your own investment decisions without the help of a stockbroker, this one may be for you. Charles Schwab has free computer software you can use to buy and sell securities over the Internet for just $29.95 for up to 1,000 shares. The software also allows you to do your own research using various Internet databases, track the stocks you are interested in and lots more. For more information call: **1-800-E-SCHWAB.**

For a listing of online brokers that allow you to trade

for a small fraction of what it would cost you from a full service broker, see the listings at the end of this section.

Six Ways To Protect Your Family With Estate Planning

1. CREATE A WILL

   The will is an essential part of your estate plan. It should detail how and when to distribute your assets and who will manage your estate upon your death. If your kids are minors, under age 18, you also should appoint legal guardians in case both you and your spouse die. In the event that you don't name a guardian, the court will select one for your kids. In addition, if family members fight over custody, your estate pays the legal fees. Also, if you die without a will the court chooses an executor to distribute your assets. In many cases, a court administrator is chosen and he or she gets paid from your estate.

The court, regardless of your intentions, may divide your assets between your surviving spouse and children, even if your spouse needs the children's share to meet day-to-day expenses.

2. **TAKE ADVANTAGE OF TAX EXEMPTIONS**

    With the proper planning, you can structure your estate plan to take advantage of valuable tax exemptions. There has recently been a change in the tax laws that will allow an increasing amount of your estate to pass tax exempt to your heirs. The exempt amounts will change but in 2005 the first $1,500,000 of your assets is exempt from federal estate and gift tax. After that, a marital deduction will allow you to transfer an unlimited amount of property tax-free to your spouse. When your spouse dies, $1,500,000 of assets in the estate is shielded from estate taxes. Couples with modest estates can plan ahead and minimize their taxes by dividing their assets. This way, each spouse owns no more than $1,500,000 in assets.

3. **USE TRUSTS TO REDUCE YOUR TAXABLE ESTATE.**

    If you have more than $1,500,000 in assets, a By-Pass Trust allows you to pass more assets directly to your heirs. A typical Bypass Trust enables the surviving spouse to receive income from the trust. At his or her death, the principal would then pass to the heirs. Since the assets are in a trust, they are not included in the taxable estate of your spouse.

4. **CONSIDER GIFTING.**

    If your assets far exceed any possible use you may have for them in your lifetime, you might consider giving portions of your assets to those you would want to have them.

5. **UNDERSTAND THE VALUE OF YOUR ESTATE.**

    Simply put, your estate includes everything you own. Most of us don't realize how quickly your assets add up.

Make a personal financial statement that totals up the value of your home, any other real estate, stocks, bonds and investment interests, even the value of your life insurance policies, as well as any valuables you may own.

6. SPEAK TO A PROFESSINAL

Tax laws are confusing and change periodically. Before you decide on any estate plan you may be considering, be sure to consult with an accountant or attorney who specializes in tax law.

Save Hundreds of Dollars On Every Stock Trade By Trading Online

14 ONLINE BROKERS CHARGING $20 PER TRADE OR LESS

If you are an active trader or investor in stocks and make all of your own buying and selling decisions without the advice of a broker, you can save a lot of money on your trades by using an online broker.

Here are stock brokerage firms that charge $20.00 per transaction or less for online trades. Some, like Ameritrade and Datek, even charge less than $12 for trades that would cost several hundred dollars at a full-service firm! The services they offer, speed of execution and investor financial requirements vary from one firm to the next. Most firms also let you trade using their toll-free phone number but they generally charge somewhat more for these trades than those you make online. To find out more, check out their Internet sites at the web addresses listed here or call their toll-free phone numbers.

BROKER	INTERNET ADDRESS	TOLL-FREE
Ameritrade	www.ameritrade.com	800-454-9272
Brown & Co.	www.brownco3.com	800-822-2021
Buy and Hold	www.buyandhold.com	800-646-8212
e-Trade	www.etrade.com	800-786-2575
Freedom Investments	www.freedominvestments.com	800-944-4033
Harris Investor Line	www.harrisdirect.com	800-825-5723
Investex Securities Group	www.investexpress.com	800-392-7192
JB Oxford & Co.	www.jboxford.com	800-649-1776
Preferred Trade	www.preferredtrade.com	888-889-9178
Quick & Reilly	www.quickandreilly.com	800-793-8050
Scottrade	www.scottrade.com	800-619-7283
Strong	www.estrong.com	800-359-3379
TD WaterhouseSecurities	www.tdwaterhouse.com	800-934-4445
Wall Street Electronica	www.wallstreete.com	888-925-5783

Traveling Free Or At Huge Savings

The Four Best Ways To Get Free Travel

Most people don't know it but there are lots of ways you can get free or almost free travel. Here are a few of the best...

If you have a unique skill or hobby, many cruise lines will give you a free trip in exchange for giving a lecture about your specialty on one of their cruises. They often have theme cruises you might fit in with. For example, if you are a fitness specialist, they often look for people to teach aerobics on board. So if you have a unique skill...let's say you're an amateur magician or perhaps a financial advisor, the cruise line will often give you a free trip just for spending an hour a day instructing others while on the cruise. Check the travel section of your local newspaper or check the toll-free directory for the phone numbers of the cruise lines. If you have a computer, you can also reach the cruise lines via the Internet. See the Internet listings at the end of this section.

There are some courier services that will ask you to carry a package anywhere in the world they travel to. With that you get a free trip for carrying the parcel. Sometimes you can get to stay a few extra days as long as you can catch their plane on the return flight. For more information, contact the International Association of Air Travel Couriers at: **308-632-3273** or on the Internet at: **www.courier.org**

A common practice of all airlines is to overbook

their flights since they know from experience that a certain percentage of people do not show up for their flight and the airline wants to leave with a full plane. When too many passengers show up the the airlines will offer free tickets to anywhere they fly just for changing your flight. One great method of getting free airline tickets is as soon as you get to the airport for your next trip, volunteer to take the next flight out if they are overbooked in exchange for a free ticket on a future flight. (See the following report: *10 Tips On Getting Free Travel When Your Plane Is Overbooked.*)

Frequent flyer programs are still a good deal that costs you nothing. Many charge cards will give you frequent flyer miles just for using their cards. Check with your charge card company. Also, make sure you are a member of the airline's frequent flyer club if you plan on doing any airline travel. They usually don't put a time restriction on them.

When they travel, some families look for housesitters. In return for watching their home, you get a free place to live. If you like to travel, you can even trade apartments and homes with people in other parts of the country (or the world) through different real estate exchanges. Check the classified section of your local newspaper.

Adventure Tours For Seniors

A great number of seniors who are in fairly good physical condition want trips that involve challenges and cultural learning experiences. These seniors are looking for new adventures and also want to learn about local culture and nature in such places as Africa and South Africa. Elder Treks specializes in senior adventure tours to 30 different countries including Africa and South Africa. If you are looking for that adventurous tour call Elder Treks at:

1-800-741-7956
Or visit their web site: www.eldertreks.com

10 Tips On Getting Free Travel When Your Plane Is Overbooked

A lot of plane flights are overbooked. That means that the airline has sold more tickets than there are seats on the plane. The reason they overbook is that often people do not show up for their flights and the airline wants to fly with as full a passenger load as possible. When a flight is overbooked, the airline must offer inducements to passengers to voluntarily take a later flight. The inducement generally will be a voucher for free plane tickets on their airline. If the flight is very overbooked, you might be able to get an even better deal that might include vouchers for more than one flight, upgrade to first-class on their next flight, overnight hotel stay if there are no more flights until the next day and even cash. Here are ten useful tips:

1. Volunteer *before* airline representatives offer vouchers, if you think your flight may be oversold.

2. Make an informed decision. Ask how long it will be until the next flight leaves for your destination.

3. If there are no takers after a voucher is announced for a low amount and it's a popular flight don't raise your hand. The voucher value is likely to increase.

4. Use the voucher immediately. Most expire within a year and are not replaceable if lost or stolen.

5. Ask for a meal voucher.

6. When using a travel voucher, plan in advance. In some cases, limited seating may make it more difficult to redeem your free or discounted travel exactly when you want to.

7. If you have a travel agent, show him or her the front and back of your voucher to determine whether it qualifies for a particular flight.

8. Read the fine print. Some vouchers may not be used on certain days and holidays.

9. Many vouchers themselves are not transferable. But the recipient generally can buy a ticket for someone else,.

10. Be polite but don't be afraid to ask for more...for example, in addition to travel vouchers you might ask for an upgrade to first class on the next fight out. Remember, they *must* get people off the overbooked flight and will offer whatever it takes.

Travel Bargains For Seniors

One of the great benefits of becoming a senior are those discounts on just about everything from 'senior day' at your local retail store to movies, theater, restaurants and best of all...travel.

Next time you plan to venture out on any trip, be absolutely sure to ask about senior discounts.

There are a number of ways for seniors to get discount travel. For example, the airlines offer discount booklets you can purchase for substantial savings on your air fare.

Next, don't forget to become a member of AARP... The American Association of Retired Persons. (No, you don't have to be retired but you or your spouse must be 50 years of age or older.) For a small membership fee of $12.50 per year, (including your spouse) you'll receive a ton of benefits including a magazine, *Modern Maturity*, newspaper updates and a membership card that gets you discounts on just about everything (hotels, insurance, drugs and more.) Once you're a member, to get your discounts you simply show your membership card or call their member services toll-free phone number: **888-687-2277**

Or visit them on the Internet at:
www.aarp.org

Most of the airlines offer special programs for seniors. Before you book your plane reservation, check with the airline you are planning to travel on to be sure they offer at least 10% discount for seniors 62 and older. They also have programs where you can purchase coupon booklets or passport programs that allow you to travel domestically and internationally at substantial discounts.

CONTINENTAL AIRLINES has a Freedom trip booklet and Senior passport program that allows you to enjoy discounted domestic and international travel.
Call them from 6:30 am to 10 pm Central time.at:
1-800 441-1135 or 1-800-248-8996
www.continental.com

DELTA AIRLINES has a discount program for domestic and international for seniors 62 and older. Call: **1-800-221-1212**
www.delta.com

For information on AMERICAN AIRLINES SENIOR DISCOUNT program, call them at: **1-800-237-7981**
www.aa.com

American Airlines has a senior coupon book you can purchase for domestic travel plus they will include a coupon for 20% off international travel. Anyone 62 or older can take advantage of these great money savings programs. Call them toll-free at: **1-800-433-7300**

Lowest Air Fares

While planning your next trip, be sure you are getting the best fares to and from the cities you will be visiting. There are a number of companies that specialize in getting you the lowest fares available. They check constantly with the various airlines and track their prices to insure that when you contact them you will get the best fare. For example, recently Global Discount Travel Services had fares from New York to San Francisco of just $111 one way. While fares change constantly, similar savings are available to and from many other major cities both within the U.S. and on international flights. To check their fares, call them at:

1-888-777-2222   OR VISIT THEIR WEB SITE AT:
www.lowestfare.com

Also check the following web site where you can actually 'name your own price' for hotels and airfare:
www.priceline.com
OR CALL THEM AT: **1-800-PRICELINE**

Airline Coupons For Seniors

As a senior citizen you're now eligible to purchase *Senior Citizen Airline Coupons*. With Senior Citizen coupons you can fly anywhere an airline flies within the 48 states for no more than $298 round trip currently or even less on some airlines. Airlines that go to the U.S. Virgin Islands, Puerto Rico and the Bahamas, and several that fly to Canada even throw in those destinations for the same low price.

The coupons are usually sold in a book of four one-way flights. Prices change frequently so check with each airline to get the current prices and programs for seniors.

Each coupon is good for a one-way fare, and while some airlines require a 14 day advance reservation, you can also use them to fly standby. You don't have to travel round trip, so there's no minimum stay. *Senior Coupon* travel also earns you frequent flier miles. With most airlines a couple cannot share a coupon book.

Also, don't forget to check with all the airlines for special seniors' clubs and senior discounts. For example, American, Delta and United run senior clubs that currently offer zoned fares ranging from $98-$298, round trip, for travel within the lower 48 states, depending on distance. In other words, you pay no more than the usual senior-coupon price for a long trip, and get an even better price on shorter trips. Those clubs also offer discounted international travel that isn't available with the regular coupons. Remember as a senior you get at least a 10% discount but check with the airline for an even bigger discount and the best travel deal.

50% Discount On Hotels

Want to save a lot of money the next time you book a hotel reservation in a large city? Try using a 'hotel broker'.

Just like airline-ticket consolidators, hotel brokers are outlets through which hotels rent some of their vacant rooms... *cheap*.

Hotel brokers are given blocks of discounted rooms by big city hotels. They in turn pass the bulk of the savings onto you. They concentrate mainly on big cities...Boston, Chicago, Los Angeles, New York, San Francisco, Washington, and more. A few even handle larger cities overseas, such as London, Sydney, Paris and Hong Kong. Where they operate, these consolidators can cut your hotel costs by as much as 50%. The brokers are classified into two groups.

BOOKING-AGENT BROKERS:

Some brokers make a reservation for you at the discounted rate. Once you have your confirmed discounted reservation you simply check in at the hotel as you ordinarily would and pay the discounted amount when you check out.

PREPAY BROKERS:

Other brokers are like tour operators. They sell hotel rooms at the same reduced rates they would in package tours. Here you must prepay for your entire stay in order to get the best rate, and the broker sends you a voucher, which you use to pay upon arriving at the hotel.

When comparing the two types of brokers just keep in mind that with the first method where you pay at the checkout, you don't have to worry if you are forced to cancel or reschedule your trip.

The largest PREPAY-VOUCHER BROKER is HotelDiscount.com.
800-715-9887
Or visit their web site at: **www.hoteldiscount.com**

The largest BOOKING-AGENT BROKER is:
QUICKBOOK
You can call them toll-free at: **800-789-9887**
Or visit their Web site at: www.quickbook.com

Another BOOKING-AGENT BROKER is Express Reservations which specializes only in New York and Los Angeles hotel bookings:
EXPRESS RESERVATION:
Call them toll-free at: **1-800-407-3351**
Or visit them on the Internet at: **www.express-res.com**

If you plan to travel to Florida and would like to save money on hotels, be sure to check with the Florida Tourist Bureau, Inc. Despite the official sounding name they are not a state agency but rather a private travel company that specializes in saving you up to 50% on your hotel accomodations throughout Florida. They work on the prepaid voucher system where you book your room and pay in advance in exchange for a very substantial discount at the best hotels and motels. Call them toll-free at:
1-888-246-8728
www.2000FloridaTravel.com

Half-Price Hotels

Many people have found that membership in a discount club is an excellent way to save money on their travel. If you spend more than a few nights a year in hotels, the annual price of membership in a good hotel discount club can be a good investment.

Most clubs promise 50% discounts off rack rate, subject

to availability and the occupancy level the hotel expects. Here are some of the largest discount programs:

GREAT AMERICAN TRAVELER: **1-800-548-2812**
www.accessvalues.com

ONLINE TRAVEL SERVICE: **1-877-259-2691**
www.TravelersAdvantage.com

15% Senior Savings On Amtrak

For seniors who prefer to travel by train, Amtrak offers year-round discounts for anyone 62 and older. These discounts include 15% off regular fares, special one way fares, Explore America Fares and special group fares. They also have beautiful brochures describing their fun vacation packages. Call Amtrak toll-free at:
1-800-USA-RAIL (THAT'S **1-800-872-7245**)
Or visit the web site: www.amtrak.com

Jet Vacations

If you plan to travel to France and want to save money on everything... quality air travel, hotels, car rental, ski packages, sightseeing, call Jet Vacations This company specializes in trips to Paris, France and to the Riviera. Plan your trip early and save. Call them toll-free and learn how you can enjoy France 3,435 different ways. Call *Jet Vacations* at:
1-877-7-TRAVEL

Before You Travel

Planning a trip? Before you go you'll want to get a copy of *Lightening The Travel Load Travel Tips*. This handy booklet is filled with "how-to" materials on selecting, packing, traveling and caring for luggage. Send a postcard to:

SAMSONITE TRAVELER CONSUMER RELATIONS
PO Box 90124
ALLENTOWN, PA 18109
OR CALL: 1-800-262-8282
www.samsonite.com

Importing A Car

Can you save money by buying a foreign car on your next trip abroad? What are the customs requirements? What should you know about emission standards on a car you import yourself? For answers, send a postcard asking for *Importing A Car* and also *U.S. Customs Pocket Hints*. It's yours free from:

U.S. CUSTOMS SERVICE
1300 PENNSYLVANIA AVE. NW ROOM 6.3D
WASHINGTON, DC 20229
www.customs.ustreas.gov

Travelodge Directory

There's a *free directory* of the more than 500 TraveLodge motels and motor hotels waiting for you. It lists location, room rates and a map for each TraveLodge. You'll also find information on their new group rates, family plan and bargain break weekends. Contact TraveLodge International at:
1-800-578-7878
www.travelodge.com

Days Inn Directory

Quality accommodations for the American traveler at economical rates has been the motto of Days Inn since its founding in 1970. For a *free directory* of the 301 Inns and 229 Tasty World Restaurants with their rates, maps, toll free numbers and more, call: **1-800-325-2525**
www.daysinn.com

Holiday Inn Directory

For a complete listing of all Holiday Inns both in the U.S. and worldwide, request a free copy of their huge directory. In seconds you can locate any of the thousands of Holiday Inns with room rates, list of recreation activities, even a map for each hotel. Call toll free:

1-800-HOLIDAY

Or visit their web site:

www.ichotelsgroup.com

Enjoy A Club Med Vacation

Club Med's unique vacation resorts have delighted thousands of people tired of 'the same old thing'. If you're interested in a fun vacation that really is something different, get the free color *travel booklet*. Club Med offers seniors 55 and older a discount on stays of 7 nights or more. To get your free booklet or for more information on their clubs, contact them at Club Med:

CALL: **1-800-CLUB-MED**
(THAT'S **1-800-258-2633**)
Or visit their web site at: **www.clubmed.com**

Barefoot Adventure Cruise

Are you ready for something different? For a vacation unlike any you've ever been on, consider sailing a tall ship to a small island in the Caribbean. The full color *Barefoot Adventure* will tell you all about 'Barefoot' shipboard adventures aboard schooners that once belonged to Onassis, Vanderbilt and the Duke of Westminster. Call Windjammer Barefoot Cruises toll free:

1-800-327-2600
www.windjammer.com

Safety Guide

Did you ever wonder if you should be concerned about your

health and safety when you travel to foreign destinations? Travel Medicine has a free *Travel Safety Guide* that offers practical quick tips on insect protection, medical kits, mosquito nets, protective clothing and water filters and more. Before you venture out on your next travel adventure, make sure you send for this free guide. Write to:

TRAVEL MEDICINE
369 PLEASANT ST.
NORTHAMPTON, MA 01060
1-800-872-8633
www.travmed.com

Foreign Exchange

If you plan to travel abroad, did you know that you can now buy francs, pounds or yen over the Internet? This service can be useful for travelers who want to have small amounts of currency upon arrival in a foreign country. At their web site, International Currency Exchange lists rates at which they sell foreign currency. If you decide to buy, you can pay by check or credit card and receive currency in 2-4 days via express mail. You can call them toll-free at:

1-888-278-6628

Or visit their web site:

www.foreignmoney.com

A Diet For Jet Lag?

Do you travel frequently and find that you suffer from jet lag? If so this free wallet size card should help. It summarizes the amounts and types of food you should eat and tells you the best times to eat to reduce the effects of jet lag. Ask for *The Anti-Jet Lag Diet*. To get a copy, send a long SASE to:

ARGONNE NATIONAL LABORATORY
JET LAG DIET
9700 S. CASS AVE.
ARGONNE, IL 60439
www.anl.gov

Volunteer For A Free Vacation

Regardless of how young or old you are, one of the most fascinating ways to enjoy a wilderness experience in a national park is by being a volunteer.

A variety of government agencies including the U.S. Forest Service, The National Park Service, U.S. Army Corps of Engineers, plus individual state park systems welcome volunteers to serve as campground hosts in exchange for a free stay. Every year hundreds of thousands of people who love the outdoors volunteer their services for anywhere from one day to a full year.

In addition to acting as hosts, volunteers also help as caretakers, researchers, ranger assistants, trail repair crews, plumbers and carpenters. This reflects the growing interest in 'doing vacations' or educational travel. In exchange for their services, volunteers may receive free camping and other recreational privileges that often include cabins, house trailers or bunkroom accommodations at no cost. While some volunteers are given an expense allowance, most should expect to pay for food and transportation costs.

If this sounds like a vacation you might be interested in, you can contact the park, forest, refuge, fish hatchery or other facility that you are interested in or check with the following:

NATIONAL PARK SERVICE,

They are looking for 95,000 volunteers a year who are interested in a stay of up to one or three months in one of the nation's 369 parklands to help with trail projects, species control and campground hosts. To get a brochure listing all of the parks in the U.S. along with an application, send a postcard to the address below.
NATIONAL PARK SERVICE,
VOLUNTEERS IN PARKS COORDINATOR
1849 C ST. N.W. SUITE 7312
WASHINGTON, DC 20240
or visit their web site at: www.nps.gov

U.S. FOREST SERVICE

Check in your local telephone operator or in the phone book blue pages for the phone number of the nearest U.S. Forest Service office. In their *Volunteers in the National Forests Program* they have up to 100,000 volunteers every year to serve in one of the nation's 155 national forests or 20 national grasslands.

The U.S. Forest Service also has a program called *Passports In Time*. This program welcomes families for one day to one week stays that focuses on archaeological digs and historical restorations. Call them toll-free at:

1-800-281-9176
Or visit their web site: **www.fs.fed.us**

BUREAU OF LAND MANAGEMENT
ENVIRONMENTAL EDUCATION AND VOLUNTEER PROGRAM
1849 C ST., N.W. LS-1275
WASHINGTON, DC 20240
1-202-452-5078
www.blm.gov/nhp

They need roughly 20,000 volunteers a year for their National Volunteer Program. Volunteers will be restoring watersheds, building trails, staffing visitor centers, patrolling cultural sites, writing brochures and conducting educational programs in federal lands, mostly in the West.

U.S. FISH AND WILDLIFE SERVICE
DIVISION OF REFUGES
NATIONAL VOLUNTEER COORDINATOR OFFICE
4401 NORTH FAIRFAX DR., ROOM 22203
ARLINGTON, VA 22203

This service oversees hundreds of wildlife refuges and fish hatcheries throughout the nation. Volunteers are needed to help with raising fish, banding birds, restoring fragile habitats, and conducting tours of the habitats and fisheries.

To get a visitors guide and map with all of the national wildlife refuges, call:

1-800-344-9453
Or visit them on the web: **http://pacific.fws.gov/planning**

U.S. ARMY CORPS OF ENGINEERS
1-800-865-8337
www.usace.army.mil
They manage 460 lakes throughout the country. Volunteers are needed to help with a variety of programs that include archaeological digs, pest control and campground hosts.

ALASKA DIVISION OF PARKS AND OUTDOOR RECREATION
ALASKA STATE PARKS VOLUNTEER COORDINATOR
550 WEST 7TH AVE. SUITE 1380
ANCHORAGE, AK 99501
1-907-269-8708
www.alaskastateparks.org
Alaska has one of the most extensive summer volunteer programs to help out as archaeological assistants, back-country ranger assistants, researchers and trail crew members. They will pay transportation expenses from Anchorage plus a small expense allowance for commitments of two weeks to three months.

To volunteer closer to home, try checking your local phone directory for your state's Department of Parks and Recreation and ask about their parks volunteer programs.

Healthy Travel To Foreign Lands

If you are on medication and plan to travel abroad be sure to get this free booklet. Put out by the International Society of Travel Medicine, it lists over 500 medicine clinics in 44 countries (including the U.S.). You'll also find answers to questions you may have about health risks in the countries you are visiting, what shots are needed, which medicines to pack and how to get medical assistance while you are there. Ask for the *Travel Medicine Clinics booklet*. Free from:
ISTM CLINIC DIRECTORY
c/o IMODIUM A-D DRAWER D
1675 BROADWAY, 33RD FLOOR
NEW YORK, NY 10019

Before you travel, you may also want to check with the following organizations for updates on illnesses in the countries you will be visiting:

THE WORLD HEALTH ORGANIZATION
1-202-974-3000
www.who.int

THE CENTERS FOR DISEASE CONTROL & PREVENTION
1-800-311-3435
www.cdc.gov

INTERNATIONAL ASSOCIATION FOR MEDICAL ASSISTANCE TO TRAVELERS
Links travelers to doctors in 130 countries
1-716-754-4883
www.iamat.org

Internet Sites For Travelers

Surfing the worldwide web is one of the easiest and most convenient ways to simplify your travel planning and to save money. If you are planning to travel and have access to the Internet either at home, at work or at your public library, here are a number of sites you will want to visit.

TRAVELOCITY
www.travelocity.com
If you would like to quickly check for the lowest plane fares from any major city to any other major city in the U.S., be sure to check out this site. Updated on a daily basis, you will find a listing of the lowest air fares at that time. You will also find several other features of interest including:

• PRICESHOPPER - great buys on vacation and cruise packages in the U.S. and abroad.

• HOT DEALS - for steals, deals and all round great travel bargains worldwide.

- **FLIGHT PAGING** - Keeps you informed of changes to your flight's departure or arrival times and gate assignments - all sent to your alphanumeric pager.
- **FARE WATCHER E-MAIL** - Sends low fare updates directly to your e-mail quickly and reliably.
- **SHOP SAFE GUARANTEE** - They protect every credit card transaction you make on Travelocity
- **REVIEWS** - for independent, non-biased reviews of vacation choices.
- **WEATHER FORECASTS** - Complete updated weather forecasts for cities around the world.

Looking for the best fares to the world's big cities? While at the TRAVELOCITY'S web site, if you enter a multiple airport city code, www.Travelocity.com will search for the lowest fare available at all metropolitan airports. Here are a few cities where this feature is valid:

New York City (NYC)

Washington, DC (WAS)

Chicago (CHI)

London (LON)

Paris (PAR)

Dallas (QDF)

Houston (QHO)

In addition, you may enjoy significant savings if you are willing to fly into nearby airports. For example, when traveling to Los Angeles (LAX), you may want to consider flying into the Burbank (BUR), Orange County (SNA) or Ontario (ONT) airports.

Similarly, the cost of a trip to San Francisco (SFO) might be reduced by flying into San Jose (SJC) or Oakland (OAK), while travel to Miami (MIA) may be less expensive if you fly into Ft. Lauderdale, FL.

■ ■

www.weather.com

What's the weather like in the city you are about to fly to?

Are there any flight delays due to bad weather? For answers, go to this web site, a service of the Weather Channel. Before your next trip check to see what weather's in store for you.

■ ■

www.biztravel.com
Internet's largest portal on specialty travel. Search over 11,000 guided or self-guided specialty vacations offered by over 1,300 travel suppliers. Get in touch with the travel suppliers to ask questions, order free travel brochures, and book a trip.

■ ■

www.frommers.com
Arthur Frommer's budget travel site has excellent advice and travel discounts. You'll find Arthur's tip-of-the-day, hot-spot-of-the-month, and a daily newsletter. The site also also features bargain air fares, cruises, car rentals and destination information.

■ ■

www.thetrip.com
This site is designed to save the money for small business travelers. You can book airline tickets, hotel rooms and car rentals at lower rates. To help you save money 'thetrip' will automatically search for flights from alternate airports and for connecting flights. You will also find Frommer City Guides with restaurant and hotel reviews plus maps with point-to-point directions from anywhere in the U.S. to anywhere else.

■ ■

www.reservation.com
This is the web site for Preview Travel. It allows you to make airline and rental car reservation online.

■ ■

www.expedia.com
This is Microsoft's travel web site. While it is primarily geared

toward leisure travelers, business travelers will find a number of useful features including city maps and restaurant listing. Another nice feature is expedia's low-fare tracker that will alert you to discount fares for cities you select.

■■■■■■■■■■■■■■■■■■■■■■

www.webflyer.com
The ultimate site for the frequent flyer. You will find all kinds of special bonus mileage offers and exclusive discount fares available only online. It's best feature is the fact that it tracks all airline, hotel and car rental discounts by city and saves you time by listing them all at one site.

■■■■■■■■■■■■■■■■■■■■■■

www.quikbook.com
This web site has been called one of the web's best sites for hotel discounts by *Consumer Reports Travel Letter.* At this site you will find out where you can get big hotel discounts of up to 60% in major cities like New York, Atlanta, Los Angeles, Boston to name a few.

■■■■■■■■■■■■■■■■■■■■■■

www.cheapticket.com
At this web site you'll find some of the very best prices not only for airline travel but for vacation packages and cruises as well

■■■■■■■■■■■■■■■■■■■■■■

City.Net: www.city.net
Epicurious: www.epicurious.com (Gourmet Magazine & Conde Nast Web site)

The Travel Channel: www.travelchannel.com
Yahoo: travel.yahoo.com

■■■■■■■■■■■■■■■■■■■■■■

Cruise Lines Web Sites

If you are thinking of taking a cruise and aren't sure which cruise is right for you, before you book, be sure to check out the web sites of the cruise lines you are considering. Here's a selection of web sites of cruise lines:

Carnival Cruise Lines: www.carnival.com

Celebrity Cruises: www.celebrity-cruises.com

Clipper Cruise Line: www.clippercruise.com

Cunard Lines: www.cunardline.com

The Delta Queen Steamboat Co.: www.deltaqueen.com

Holland America Line: www.hollandamerica.com/intro.html

KD River Cruises of Europe: www.rivercruises.com

Norwegian Cruise Lines: www.ncl.com/ncl

Radisson Seven Seas Cruises: www.regalcruises.com

Regal Cruises: www.regalcruises.com

Royal Caribbean International: www.royalcaribbean.com

Silversea Cruises: www.asource.com/silversea/

Windjammer Barefoot Cruises: www.windjammer.com

Windstar Cruises: www.windstarcruises.com

World Explorer Cruises: www.wecruise.com/

5 Tips To Save Money On Plane Travel

www.travelocity.com

Finding the lowest fare isn't always easy. Discount fares typically have restrictions that can be difficult, sometimes frustrating, to interpret. If you're looking for the cheapest price, here are a few suggestions that will help.

1. Make your reservation early. Many discount fares require that you make a reservation 7, 14 or 21 days before your trip depending on the fare. The best international fares often require a reservation 30 days in advance. Making a reservation as soon as you know your travel dates increases your chances of finding a fare you can live with.

2. Flying on a weekday usually costs less. Flights on Tuesday, Wednesday and Thursday usually offer the lowest fares. Fares are sometimes (but not always) higher on Monday and Friday than on other weekdays. Saturday flights occasionally have discount fares, but as a rule it's more expensive to fly on a weekend than a weekday.

3. Stay over a Saturday night. Most low fares require that you stay over at least one Saturday night before your return flight. However, some fares may only require you to stay a minimum of 3 or 4 days.

4. **One airline is better than two.** It's almost always less expensive to use only one airline for the entire trip instead of two. In fact booking two airlines can, in some cases, cost hundreds of dollars more. Airlines sell only a limited number of seats at the lowest fares. When those seats sell out, the price goes up. If you don't at first succeed, try an earlier or later flight. To get the lowest roundtrip fare, that fare must be available on both the departing and return flights you select. If the fare is sold out on either of these, the price you end up with will be much higher.

5. **Try an earlier or later flight** if you can't find the fare you want or if possible, consider flying on another day.

Traveling The USA

Planning ahead can make all the difference in the world between having great fun and having a run-of-the mill trip.

One of the very best sources of information are the tourist offices for the states you plan to visit. These offices are set up to provide maps, brochures and other information about the tourist attractions, climate, restaurants and hotels for their states.

If you plan to tour any part of the U.S.A., call the tourist offices of each of the 50 states you intend to visit. When you call them, tell them which areas of the state you plan to visit and indicate any special sight-seeing interests you may have. Often they can provide you with additional materials on the areas that interest you most.

The following is a list of state tourism offices. Where a toll-free number or web site is available, it is given.

ALABAMA
Bureau of Tourism & Travel
1-800-ALABAMA
www.800alabama.org

ALASKA
907-929-2200
www.travelalaska.com

ARIZONA
602-230-7733
www.arizonaguide.com

ARKANSAS
1-800-NATURAL
(that's 1-800-628-8725)
www.arkansas.com

CALIFORNIA
1-800-TO-CALIF
(that's 1-800-862-2543)
gocalif.ca.gov

COLORADO
1-800-433-2656
www.colorado.com

CONNECTICUT
1-800-CT-BOUND
(that's 1-800-282-6863)
www.ctbound.org

DELAWARE
1-800-441-8846
www.visitdelaware.gov

DISTRICT OF COLUMBIA
1-800-635-6338
www.washington.org

FLORIDA
1-888-735-2872
www.flausa.com

GEORGIA
1-800 VISIT-GA
(that's 1-800-847-4842)
www.GeorgiaOnMyMind.org

HAWAII
1-800-464-2924
www.gohawaii.com

IDAHO
1-800-635-7820
www.accessidaho.org

ILLINOIS
1-800-2-CONNECT
www.enjoyillinois.com

INDIANA
1-888-ENJOY-IN
www.ENJOYindiana.com

IOWA
1-888-472-6035
www.traveliowa.com

KANSAS
1-800-2-KANSAS
www.travelks.org

KENTUCKY
1-800-225-TRIP
www.kentuckytourism.com

LOUISIANA
1-800-964-7321
www.louisianatravel.com

MAINE
1-888-624-6345
www.visitmaine.com

MARYLAND
1-800-MD-IS-FUN
www.mdisfun.org

MASSACHUSETTS
1-800-447-MASS
www.mass-vacation.com

MICHIGAN
1-800-5432-YES
www.michigan.org

MINNESOTA
1-800-657-3700
www.visitmississippi.org

MISSISSIPPI
1-800-WARMEST
www.mississippi.org

MISSOURI
800-877-1234
www.visitmo.com

MONTANA
1-800-VISIT-MT
www.visitmt.com

NEBRASKA
1-800-228-4307
www.visitmebraska.org

NEVADA
1 800-NEVADA-8
(that's 1-800-638-2328)
www.travelnevada.com

NEW HAMPSHIRE
1-800-FUN-IN-NH
www.visitnh.gov

NEW JERSEY
1-800-JERSEY-7
www.state.nj.us/travel

NEW MEXICO
1-800 545-2040
www.newmexico.org

NEW YORK
1-800-CALL-NYS (that's 1-800-225-5697)
www.iloveny.state.ny.us

NORTH CAROLINA
1-800-VISIT-NC
www.visitnc.com

NORTH DAKOTA
1-800-HELLO-ND
www.ndtourism.com

OHIO
1-800-BUCKEYE
www.ohiotourism.com

OKLAHOMA
1-800-652-6552
www.travelok.com

OREGON
1-800-547-7842
www.traveloregon.com

PENNSYLVANIA
1-800-VISIT-PA
www.experiencePA.com

RHODE ISLAND
1-800-556-2484
www.visitrhodeisland.com

SOUTH CAROLINA
1-800-872-3505
www.travelSC.com

SOUTH DAKOTA
1-800-SDAKOTA
(1-800-732-5682)
www.travelSD.com

TENNESSEE
1-800-836-6200
www.state.tn.us/tourdev

TEXAS
1-800-8888-TEX
www.travelTex.com

UTAH
1-800-200-1160
www.utah.com

VERMONT
1-800-VERMONT
(that's 1-800-837-6668)
www.1-800-Vermont.com

VIRGINIA
1-800-VISIT-VA
www.virginia.org

WASHINGTON
1-800-544-1800
www.experiencewashington.com

WASHINGTON, D.C.
See District of Columbia

WEST VIRGINIA
1-800-CALL-WVA
(that's 1-800-225-5982
www.callWVA.com

WISCONSIN
1-800-432-TRIP
www.travelWisconsin.com

WYOMING
1-800-225-5996
www.WyomingTourism.com

U.S. TERRITORIES

AMERICAN SAMOA
1-684-633-1093
www.AmSamoa.com

GUAM
1-800-US-3-GUAM
www.visitGuam.org

PUERTO RICO

1-800-223-6530
www.PRtourism.com

U.S. VIRGIN ISLANDS
For great duty-free shopping consider the U.S. Virgin Islands for your next vacation. No passports are needed, their language is English and they use U.S. cur-

rency. For full travel information contact:
U.S. Virgin Islands Tourism
1270 Avenue of the Americas
New York, NY 10020
1-800-372-8784
www.usVI.net

NATIONAL PARKS
Enjoy the great outdoors. Get back to nature. Visit our beautiful national parks. There's a series of interesting guides to the 7 most popular national parks free for the asking. Send for any (or all) guides you'd like:
• Rocky Mountain National Park, Colorado
• Mt. McKinley National Park, Alaska
• Mesa Verde National Park Colorado
• Hot Springs National Park, Arkansas
• Hawaii National Park
• Yellowstone National Park
• Carlsbad Caverns, New Mexico
You might also want the free map of the National Park System. Request by name the guides you would like. Write to:
Dept. of the Interior
National Park Service
Washington, DC 20240

INTERNATIONAL VACATIONLAND— 1000 ISLANDS
The 1000 Islands region features the best of two countries — U.S.

and Canada. Some of the many attractions include fishing, golf, tennis, biking, hiking, houseboat rentals, shopping and recreational sports in all seasons. Three tour packages are available for the asking:

1. Write: **1000 Islands, 43373 Collins Landing, PO Box 400 Alexandria Bay, NY 13607.** (In Canada write: 1000 Islands, Box 69, Landsdoune, Ontario KOE ILO Or call: **1-800-8-IS-LAND**

2. Write: **Kingston Bureau of Tourism, Box 486, 209 Ontario St., Kingston, Ontario K7L 2ZI Or call: 1-888-855-4555**

3. Write: **Rideau Lakes Thousand Islands, P.O. Box 125 Perth, Ontario K7H 3E3**

CHOCOLATE TOWN USA
If you are looking for a really fun time, why not try a special theme weekend at the fun Hershey Park in Hershey, Pennsylvania. For more detailed information, call:
1-800-HERSHEY

foreign Travel

Before you travel abroad be sure to contact the tourist office for the countries you plan to visit. They are delighted to send you a beautiful package of travel brochures, places to visit and a whole lot more.

ANGUILLA
Anguilla Tourist Information
271 Main Street
Northport, NY 11768

ANTIGUA & BARBUDA
Antigua & Barbuda Dept of Tourism
610 Fifth Avenue, Suite 311
New York, NY 10020
1-888-268-4227
www.antigua-barbuda.org

ARGENTINA
For maps and color brochures describing Argentina drop a card to:
Argentina Embassy
1600 New Hampshire Ave.
Washington, DC 20009
1-202-238-6400
www.embajadaargentinaeeuu.org

ARUBA
Go sailing, scuba diving in the turquoise Caribbean, casinos, discos and lots more. Ask for "Sun Worshippers" with hotel rates and tourist information. Write:
Aruba Tourist Office
1000 Harbor Boulevard
Weehawken, NJ 07087
1-800-TO-ARUBA
www.aruba.com

AUSTRIA
Write for the "Austrian Information package" and you'll receive a beautiful assortment of travel guides and student education opportunities. Drop a card to: **Austrian National Tourist Office**
PO BOX 1142
New York, NY 10180-1142
1-212-6880, fax: 1-212-730-4568
www.austria-tourism.at

BAHAMAS
Bahamas Tourist Office
1-800-422-4262
www.bahamas.com

BARBADOS
Discover the many sides of Barbados that make it a luscious vacation spot. A nice tow package including several huge wall posters are yours for the asking. Write: **Barbados Board of Tourism**
800 Second Ave.
New York, NY 10017
1-800-221-9831
www.barbados.org

BELIZE
Belize Tourist Board
New Central Bank Bldg. Level 2
Gabourel Lane
PO Box 325
Belize City, Belize
Central America
1-800-624-0686
www.travelbelize.org

BRAZIL
Brazil Reservations
1050 Edison St., Ste. C
Santa Ynez, CA 93460
1-800-544-5503
www.brazilres.com

BRITISH VIRGIN ISLANDS
British Tourist Board
1270 Broadway Suite 705
New York, NY 10005
1-212-696-0400
www.bviwelcome.com

BRITAIN
There's always something new to discover in England, Wales, Scotland & Ireland. Drop a card requesting the Britain Information package and you'll receive a beautiful color magazine, photos, maps, tours, etc. Send to:
British Tourist Authority
551 Fifth Ave.
New York, NY. 10176
1-800-462-2748
www.visitbritain.com

BRITAIN BY RAIL
Tour scenic Britain by rail. BritRail offers unlimited travel on most rail, bus & ferry routes. For a free guide travel hints as well as bargain ticket rates write to:
Europerail International
691 Richmond St.
London, Ontario, Canada N6A 5M1
1-888-667-9734
www.britainontrack.com

BERMUDA
Thinking of traveling to Bermuda? Don't go without this information package. It includes travel tips, a map, hotel rates, and more. Write to:
Bermuda Dept. of Tourism.
675 Third Ave.
New York, NY 10017
1-212-818-9800 for brochures

1-800-223-6106 Dept. of Tourism
www.bermudatourism.org

CANADA
"Touring Canada" is a big guide to 54 exciting tours of Canada. You'll learn where to go, what to see, what clothes to bring and much more. You'll find there's more to do in 'our neighbor to the north' than you had ever imagined. Write to:
Canadian Tourism Commission
55 Metcalfe St Suite 600
Ottawa, Ontario
Canada K1P 6L5
1-613-1000
www.canadatourism.com

CANADA-NOVA SCOTIA
Nova Scotia Information
2695 Dutch Village Rd., Ste, 501
Halifax, Nova Scotia
Canada B3L 4V2
1-800-341-6096
www.checkinnovascotia.com

CANCUN & COZUMEL
Caribbean Tourism Organization
80 Broad St., 32nd flr.
New York, NY 10004
1-212-635-9530
www.doitcaribbean.com

CARIBBEAN SUN FUN
Discover the fun and excitement each of the Caribbean islands has to offer. Ask for the travel package free from:
Caribbean Tourism Organization
80 Broad St., 32nd flr.
New York, NY 10004
1-212-635-9530
www.doitcaribbean.com

CAYMAN ISLANDS
PO Box 67
Georgetown, Grand Cayman
Cayman Islands

345-949-0623
www.cayman.org/tourism

CHINA - TAIWAN
Taiwan Visitors Association
One World Trade Center
New York, NY

CURACAO
Curacao Tourist Board
7951 SW 6th St Suite 216
Plantation, FL 33324
1-800-328-7222
www.curacao-tourism.com

EGYPT
Travel back in time to the cradle of civilization. Explore the pyramids and discover the old and new wonders of Egypt. Ask for the 'Egypt Information package.' Write to: **Egyptian Tourist Authority**
630 Fifth Ave. Ste. 1706
New York, NY 10111
1-212-332-2570
www.egypttourism.org

FRANCE
The 'France Information package' is a mini-tour of France with a large full color tour book plus Paris on a budget, a tour of Paris, hotels and motels in France off-season packages, and more. Contact:
French Government Tourist Office
444 Madison Ave. 16th fl.
New York, NY 10022
1-212-838-7800
www.francetourism.com

GERMANY
"Welcome To Germany" is a beautiful guide full of color photos that are absolutely breathtaking. This is just part of the Germany Tour package free from:
German National Tourist Office
122 E. 42 St., 52nd flr.
New York, NY 10168-7200

1-212-661-7200
www.visit-to-germany.com

GERMANY TRAIN TRAVEL
If you're planning a trip to Germany one of the best ways to tour the country is by train. With German Rail you will have unlimited travel plus discounts on many bus and boat routes. For free information write:
DER Travel Services
9501 W. Devon Ave., Ste. 1E
Rosemont, IL 60018
1-888-337-7350
www.dertravel.com
1-800-660-5300
w w w . e u r o r a i l . c o m /
germrail.htm

GREECE
To help you make your trip to Greece more enjoyable, here's a large packet of brochures, maps and booklets on the beautiful Greek Islands. Request the 'Greece Tour package' from:
Greek National Tourist Organization
645 Fifth Ave., 9th flr.
Olympic Tower
New York, NY 10022
1-212-421-5777
www.gnto.gr

GRENADA
Grenada Board of Tourism
317 Madison Ave. Suite 1704

New York, NY 10017
1-800-927-9554
www.grenada.org

GUYANA
Guyana Tourism
c/o Caribbean Tourism Organization
80 Broad Street 32nd flr.
New York, NY 10004
1-212-635-9630
www.doitcaribbean.com

HONG KONG
Hong Kong Tourism Board
115 E. 54 St., 2nd flr.
New York, NY 10022
1-800-282-4582
www.discoverhongkong.com/usa

HUNGARY
Like beautiful picture post cards, the color illustrations in this package will take you for a tour of the sights and attractions of Hungary. Ask for the Hungary Travel package which includes a map of the country. Send a card to:
Hungary National Tourist Board
150 E. 58th St. 33rd flr.
New York, NY 10155
1-212-355-0240
www.gotohungary.com

INDIA
Dozens of scenic color photos of India are included in the India Tour Kit yours free from:
Embassy of India
2107 Massachusetts Ave. NW
Washington, DC 20008
1-202-939-7000
www.indiamart.com

INDONESIA
For facts on the Indonesia archipelago including their history, geography, culture, maps, and more drop a card requesting their information package. Write to: **Consulate General of Indonesia**

Information Section
Five E. 68th St.
New York, NY 10021
1-212-879-0600
www.indony.org

IRELAND
Irish Tourist Board
345 Park Ave., 17th flr.
New York, NY 10154
1-800-SHAMROCK
1-800-223-6470
www.ireland.travel.ie

ISRAEL
If you enjoyed the book you'll love the country. For a nice collection of guide books and maps of Israel and the Holy Land write to:
Israel Government Tourist Office
800 Second Ave., 16 flr.
New York, NY 10117
1-888-77ISRAEL
www.goisrael.com

ITALY
A beautiful arm chair tour of Italy is in store for you. Write for "A Trip To Italy tour package" with road maps and marvelous full color guide books. It's yours free from:
Italian Government Travel Office
630 Fifth Ave., Ste. 1565
New York, NY 10111
1-212-245-4822
www.italiantourism.com

IVORY COAST
Learn about the rites of Panther Men and the fascinating culture of the Agri Kingdom. All this and much more in the travel kit from:
Ivory Coast Embassy

2424 Massachusetts Ave NW
Washington, DC 20008
1-202-797-0337
www.embassy.org/embassies/ci.html

JAMAICA

Soft beaches, jungle waterfalls, hot discos and sailing in the sunshine— it's all in a beautiful full color book that features 56 great vacations. Ask for the free "Jamaica Vacation Book" from:
Jamaica Tourist Board
810 7th Ave. 34th Floor
New York, NY 10019
212-698-4900
www.visitjamaica.com

JAPAN

The 'Japan Tour package' is an impressive collection of travel booklets in full color with marvelous illustrations. You'll receive a mini tour of Japan chuck full of facts about Japan's history with travel tips and many fascinating tid bits. Write to:
Japan Travel Bureau
810 Seventh Ave., 34th flr.
New York NY 10019
1-212-698-4900
www.jtbusa.com

MARTINIQUE

Martinique Promotion Bureau
444 Madison Ave., 16th flr.
New York, NY 10022
1-800-391-4909
www.martinique.org

MEXICO

For a set of over a dozen color brochures showing the sights and tourist attractions of Mexico, drop a card to:
The Magic of Mexico
1-800-44-MEXICO
www.visitmexico.com

MONTSERRAT

Caribbean Tourism Organization
80 Broad St., 32nd flr.

New York, NY 10004
1-212-635-9530
www.doitcaribbean.com

MOROCCO

Exotic Morocco has some of the most magnificent scenery in the world. For a kit of travel information and tour packages to this ancient kingdom drop a card to:
Royal Air Maroc
666 Fifth Ave.
New York, NY 10103
800-344-6726
www.royalairmaroc.com

PERU

In this package are colorful maps, charts and pictures of native birds, flowers and animals. You'll also find a listing of national parks and reserves, as well as interesting archaeological and historical highlights.
Explorations, Inc.
27655 Kent Rd.
Bonita Springs, Fl 34135
1-941-992-9660
http://members.aol.com/
xplormaya

PORTUGAL

Discover all the beauty of Portugal— its beaches, entertainment and hotels — all in this package of full color brochures.
Portugese National Touris Office
590 Fifth Ave., 4th flr.
New York, NY 10036
1-212-220-5772
www.portugalinsite.pt

PUERTO RICO

Find out why Puerto rico is called "the complete island". There is something here for everyone —

sightseeing, sports, night life, casinos and lots more. Call: **1-212-599-6262**

RUSSIA
Embassy of the Russian Federation
2650 Wisconsin Ave. NW
Washington, DC 20007
1-202-298-5700
www.russiaembassy.org

ST. MAARTEN
For beautiful travel brochures of the island of St. Maarten call:
1-800-ST-MAARTEN
www.st-maarten.com

SCOTLAND
For colorful brochures on Scotland, call toll-free:
1-800-343-SCOT
www.visitscotland.com

SINGAPORE
Singapore's the place where all Asia comes together. Here's a beautiful color package of things to do and see plus a map and even a recipe booklet with delightful meals of Singapore. Write to:
Embassy of Republic of Singapore
3501 International Pl. NW
Washington, D.C. 20008
1-202-537-3100

SOUTH AFRICA
Embassy of South Africa
4301 Connecticut Ave.
Washington, DC 20008
www.SouthAfrica.net

SPAIN
Tourist Office of Spain

666 Fifth Ave., 35th flr.
New York, NY 10103
1-212-265-8822

SWITZERLAND
For a mini-tour of the Alps send a postcard for the 'Swiss Tour package'. You'll receive beautifully illustrated booklets, maps, travel tips, recipes and more. All of this comes to you free from:
Swiss National Tourist Office
608 Fifth Ave., Ste. 202
New York, NY 10020
1-212-757-5944
www.myswitzerland.com

TAIWAN
Taiwan Visitors Association
405 Lexington Ave., 37th flr.
New York, NY 10174
1-212-867-1632
www.tbroc.gov.tw

THAILAND
Come to Thailand and enjoy its dazzling scenery, incredible shopping bargains and the special joy of sharing all they have. Drop a card to:
Tourism Authority of Thailand
61 Broadway Suite 2810
New York, NY 10006
1-800-THAILAND
www.tourismthailand.org

ZAMBIAN SAFARI
Zambia has a big package of travel & tourist information waiting for you. The beautiful color brochures are a mini-safari through the African bush. Write to:
Zambia National Tourist Board
2419 Massachusetts Ave NW
Washington, DC 20008
www.ZambiaTourism.com

free from The Government

The U.S. Government Toll-Free Helpline

Have you ever tried to find an answer to a simple question about the Federal Government and ended up on a merry-go-round of referrals. Or you may have had a question about the Federal Government that was so difficult you had no idea where to begin. Well relax! Now there's one toll-free number you can call for assistance. It's called the *Federal Information Center* and it's a clearinghouse of all government agencies. It is designed to help the average person find the information they need quickly and effortlessly.

They will also refer you to the government agency that deals with the type of problem or question they may have. Their Information Specialists are extraordinary when it comes to finding the exact place you should contact for help. Some of the things they can help you with are... who you can contact for help with your social security benefits, sales & auctions of siezed properties, consumer complaints, veteran's benefits, offices of the aging and virtually all other branches of the government. Their hours of operation are 8 a.m. to 8 p.m EST Monday thru Friday.

Call them toll-free at:

1-800-688-9889

(Disabled individuals using text phones [TDD/TTY] may call toll-free anywhere in the U.S. by dialing 1-800-326-2996).

If you have access to the Internet you can also find help on all government related questions by going to:

www.info.gov

Exactly How Much Social Security Will You Get?

If you've ever wondered exactly how much money your Social Security benefits will be once you retire, there's an easy way to find out...get your Personal Earnings and Benefit Estimate Statement. For an estimate of what your retirement benefits might be call the toll-free phone number and ask for an *'earnings estimate request'* to fill out and return.

The Social Security Administration will then do a free search of their records and send you a detailed printout of how much has been contributed each year and how much your benefits will if you retire at different ages. Find out what disability benefits you qualify for... and how the value of your benefits compares with the amount of Social Security taxes you have paid over the years. This statement is yours free from the Social Security Administration.

At the same toll-free number they are also happy to answer any other questions you may have relating to your Social Security. Call:

1-800-772-1213

You can also access them on the Internet at: www.ssa.gov

Do You Need Extra Money From Social Security?

Many low income seniors never realize it but even if they don't qualify for regular Social Security benefits, they may still qualify for thousands of dollars in extra income.

If you are over 65 and find that you have difficulty meeting your normal living expenses, or if you are blind or disabled at any age, you may qualify for a program called Supplemental Security Income (SSI).

This program was established to help seniors over the age of 65 who have too little income to pay for their basic needs and to help those who are not able to work because they are disabled regardless of their age.

To qualify you must meet a maximum asset and monthly income qualification but studies have shown that as many as half of the seniors who do qualify never receive SSI benefits because they don't realize that they are eligible for this extra income. However, once you do qualify for SSI, you will also automatically qualify for both Medicaid and Food Stamps.

To find out if you qualify, either contact your local Social Security office or call their toll-free helpline:
1-800-772-1213

Free Food For Seniors

When you live on a limited budget you learn to cut corners wherever you can. But one of the areas you should never cut corners on is in eating properly. If you are living on a limited budget even if you are living with someone else, you may qualify for food stamps that will save you thousands of dollars. And as a senior, if you are not able to travel to the social services agency to apply for the food stamps, they may visit your home or take the application right over the phone. Check the blue pages of you local phone book for a social services agency in your area. You can also get the address and phone number by calling the OFFICE OF THE AGING in your area. (See listings at the back of this book).

Locating A Missing Person

If you have a problem of trying to locate a missing relative or friend, a letter to the Social Security Administration may help. When you write be sure to include as much information as you can about the missing person including their last address and date of birth. Write to:

PUBLIC INQUIRIES
SOCIAL SECURITY ADMINISTRATION
6401 SECURITY BLVD.
BALTIMORE, MD 21235
1-800-772-1213
www.ssa.gov

Free Books & Magazines

Did you know that the National Library Service has a large collection of books , magazines, journals, music materials in Braille, large type and recorded format for those who have temporary or permanent vision loss or physical limitations? Special playback equipment is available on a loan basis from the Library of Congress, and cassettes and CD's are available from over 155 participating libraries. And if you are unable to hold a book or have a serious visual handicap, you can borrow these materials postage-free. They will even pay the postage in sending the materials back to them. Contact them at the address and phone number below or ask your local library to find out what's available to you.

HANDICAPPED READERS REFERENCE SECTION
NATIONAL LIBRARY SERVICE FOR THE BLIND AND PHYSICALLY HANDICAPPED
LIBRARY OF CONGRESS
WASHINGTON, DC 20542
800-424-9100

Or access them on the web:
www.loc.gov/nls

A Boat For $100.00?

Yes you can really own a boat, luxury car, fancy gems even a house with all its treasures for just a tiny fraction of its true value. All these treasures are confiscated from drug raids or other illegal activities. The government has no use for these goods and can't store them all so they have contracted with private companies to auction off these goods.

At these auctions you have an excellent chance of getting goods for practically nothing. You can get a free copy of the *National Sellers List* which lists the local sellers of the Marshall Services goods. To get that list you must reach them either by fax or at their Internet site or from the Consumer Information Catalog:

THEIR FAX NUMBER IS: **202-307-9777**

Their Internet address is:

www.usdoj.gov/marshals/assets/assets.html

The IRS also has auctions throughout the country of property of every kind ...everything from houses to cars, jewelry and lots more...all seized for non-payment of taxes. For a list of sales and auctions for properties siezed by the IRS, request the list from:

TREASURY SALES & AUCTIONS
EG&G SERVICES, INC
3702 PENDER DRIVE SUITE 400
FAIRFAX, **VA 22030**
OR CALL THEM AT: **703-273-7373**
www.ustreas.gov/auctions

Striking It Rich

Did you know that the U.S. Government will let you prospect on public lands? If you would like to find out how to strike it rich on government lands, send a card to the Forest Service. Ask for *A Guide To Your National Forests*. Write to:

U.S.D.A. FOREST SERVICE
COMMUNICATIONS OFFICE - PUBLICATIONS
PO BOX **96090   201 - 14**TH STREET SW
WASHINGTON, DC **20090**
www.fs.fed.us

Free Firewood

Did you know that in most of the 154 National Forests, firewood for your own personal use is free. To find out how you

can get free firewood and also how to select, purchase and use firewood ask for the *Firewood Information package*. Free from:
FIREWOOD #559,
FOREST SERVICE COMMUNICATIONS OFFICE
PO BOX 96090
201 - 14TH STREET SW
WASHINGTON, DC 20090
www.fs.fed.us

Buying U.S. Government Surplus

Every year the federal government buys billions of dollars of every kind of merchandise imagineable. Much of this is never used and eventually the U.S. Government must sell all this surplus property on a regular basis. To find out how to buy everything from binoculars to cars at super low bargain prices, write to:
GOVERNMENT LIQUIDATION
6263 NORTH SCOTTSDALE ROAD SUITE 371
SCOTTSDALE, AZ 85250
OR CALL THEM AT: 1-888-352-9333
www.drms.com
www.liquidation.com/buyer

You're Paying Too Much Income Tax

Wouldn't that be a welcome notice to receive from the IRS? Believe it or not many seniors really *are* paying a lot more income tax than they should be. The reason is that they just aren't aware of all the deductions and exemptions they are entitled to. To be sure you're not paying more taxes than you should, ask for a free copy of *Protecting Older Americans Against Overpayment of Income Taxes.*. Contact:
SPECIAL COMMITTEE ON AGING
U.S. SENATE
G31 DIRKSEN BUILDING
SENATE OFFICE
WASHINGTON, D.C. 20510
202-224-5364
www.senate.gov/~aging

You're Also Paying Too Much Real Estate Tax

Throughout the nation, states and local governments are recognizing that seniors deserve a break when it comes to the real estate taxes they pay on their home. After all by the time they are 65 years old most seniors no longer have children in public school. And yet they're still paying school taxes on their real estate.

For example, New York State recently instituted what it calls the 'STAR' program. Under this program, while all homeowners qualify for a reduction in school taxes, seniors aged 65 or older who own a home are entitled to a whopping 40% reduction in the school taxes they pay as part of their real estate tax. This reduction is not based upon low income or financial need. It is available to *all* seniors in NYS who ask for it. But they will not get the reduction unless they ask. What that means is that you must check with your local town or county tax assessor's office to see if they offer a senior citizen tax reduction. Until you apply you could be paying thousands of dollars too much in real estate tax.

What Else Does The Secret Service Do?

Did you know that the Secret Service does more than protect the President? It was originally created to suppress counterfeiting - a job they still perform. To learn more, ask for *"Counterfeiting and Forgery"* which shows how to detect a counterfeit bill. Write to:

U.S. SECRET SERVICE
PROCUREMENT DIVISION
950 H STREET NW SUITE 730
WASHINGTON, DC 20223

Just How Secure Is Your Home?

The F.B.I. would like every family to feel more secure. Learn how to better protect your family against crime. *A Way to Protect Your Family Against Crime* offers tips you and your family can safely use to take a bite out of crime. Ask for the free *Crime Resistance booklet.* You might also want a copy of the *Abridged History of the F.B.I.* All free from:

F.B.I. PUBLIC AFFAIRS DEPT.
935 PENNSYLVANIA AVE. NW
WASHINGTON, DC 20535
www.fbi.gov

Pension & Retirement Hotline

If you have tax questions dealing with your pension or retirement plans, now you can ask the tax attorneys at the IRS for help. These attorneys specialize in tax law dealing specifically with pension and retirement plans. Now you can get expert tax advice right from the source...for free! Call them between 1:30 pm and 3:30 pm EST, Monday through Thursday. Call: **1-877-829-5500.**

You're Too Old...You're Fired!!"

No you aren't likely to hear these exact words but that doesn't mean you won't be discriminated against because of your age. Just remember that if you are over 40 years old, the law is clear. It is against the law to discriminate against anyone because of their age when it comes to hiring, firing, pay, promotions and other conditions of employment. And to insure that an employer will not discriminate against you on the basis of your age, sex, race, or disability and get away with it, the government has set up The Equal Employment Opportunity Commission. If you feel that you have been a victim of discrimination by an employer (or potential employer), be sure to contact:

THE EQUAL EMPLOYMENT OPPORTUNITY COMMISSION
1801 L STREET NW
WASHINGTON, DC 20507
AND TO BE CONNECTED TO THE EEOC OFFICE NEAREST YOU JUST DIAL:
1-800-669-4000
www.eeoc.gov

Free Help Getting A New Job

With all the downsizing and early retirements, many older American's find themselves in a situation where they can't afford to live on just their Social Security and yet unable to find a new job because of their age or because they need new skills. Well now thanks to government programs aimed specifically at seniors, there is help. This help comes in the form of free job training programs, counseling, as well as financial and tax incentives for companies to hire graduates of these training programs. For more information on programs available in your area, refer to the listing in the back of this book under *"Job Training Programs for Seniors.*

Golden Passport To Fun

Did you know that as a senior you can buy a lifetime entrance to national parks, monuments, historic sites, recreation areas and national refuges for a one time fee of just $10.00! This also entitles you to a whopping 50% discount on fees for things like camping, swimming, parking, boat launching and cave tours. It's called the Federal Golden Age Passport and it could be worth its weight in gold. And for the blind and disabled there's the Federal Golden Access Passport which is completely free. To get your passport, call the National Park Service at: **202-208-4747**

$10,000 To Fix Up Your Home

Is your home in bad need of repair but you just can't afford the money to fix it up? Well now there's help in the form of grants of anywhere from $1,000 to as much as $10,000 with money coming from the U.S.D.A. Rural Housing Service.

Right now there are more

than 2.5 million substandard homes across the nation. The federal government is helping remedy this situation by giving money to local non-profit groups who must use this money to make low-interest loans and outright grants that never have to be repaid. This money is for low-income homeowners aged 62 and older who otherwise would have to live in homes that are a safety or health risk.

To apply for a loan or grant, check the blue pages of your phone book under 'federal government' for your local *U.S. Department of Agriculture – Rural Development'* office. If you can't find it in your local phone book, you can contact:

RURAL HOUSING SERVICE NATIONAL OFFICE
U.S. DEPARTMENT OF AGRICULTURE
ROOM 5037
SOUTH BUILDING 14TH ST. & INDEPENDENCE AVE SW
WASHINGTON, DC 20250-0780
202-720-4323
You can also check on the Internet at: www.rurdev.usda.gov

Free Legal Services

If you've ever needed the services of an attorney you already know just how expensive legal help can be. But did you know that you can get legal help worth thousands of dollars - all paid for with money from the federal government or from legal services donated by attorneys who volunteer for "pro bono" (free) service to help those who can not afford legal representation.

See the back of this book for the *Free Legal Services Directory* which lists hundreds of legal service and pro bono attorney offices across the country. Find the office nearest you and call them the next time you need the services of an attorney.

Valuable Information From The U.S. Government

The U.S. Government offers thousands of special programs and services that your tax dollars have already paid for. But to benefit from them you must know they are there.

To keep you informed about these programs and to help you with a wide range of problems you may have, the government has hundreds of highly informative booklets that are yours free or practically free. These booklets are distributed through an agency called...

Consumer Information in Pueblo CO 81002

All of the publications listed here are either free or are available for a very nominal handling charge. You can order up to 25 free publications by enclosing $2.00 as a processing fee.

CARS

BUYING A NEW CAR
Here's a step-by-step guide that is a helpful tool for bargaining with dealers. 2 pp. **301M. $1.00.**

BUYING A USED CAR
Discusses your limited rights when buying from a dealer or private owner 16 pp. **302M. $1.00.**

FINDING THE BEST USED CAR
Covers what to look for on the test drive, warning signs of hidden damage, and how to verify the car's history. 10 pp. **590M. Free.**

GLOVE BOX TIPS
Six booklets to help you get your car ready for summer and winter driving, choose the right repair shop, and get the best work from your mechanic. 19 pp. **303M.** $1.00.

HOW TO FIND YOUR WAY UNDER THE HOOD & AROUND THE CAR
Instructions for 14 preventive maintenance services you can
perform on your car. 2 pp. **308M.** $1.00.

HOW TO GET A GREAT DEAL ON A NEW CAR
Step-by-step details for a proven negotiation technique to save
money on your next car. 4 pp. **305M.** $1.00.

NINE WAYS TO LOWER YOUR AUTO INSURANCE COSTS
Helpful tips on reducing your expenses. Includes a chart to
compare discounts. 2 pp. **307M.** $1.00.

TAKING THE SCARE OUT OF AUTO REPAIR.
Keep your car running smoothly with these practical tips on
spotting trouble, choosing a repair shop, and working with your
mechanic. 15 pp. **306M.** $1.00.

U.S. GOVERNMENT AUTO AUCTIONS
Explains the General Services Administration (GSA) Auto Auctions program and includes a handy checklist on how to buy a
quality car at a great price. 5 pp. **591M. Free.**

UNDERSTANDING VEHICLE FINANCING
Get the facts on dealership financing-what it is, how you apply,
special financing offers, cash back and rebates you may be eligible for, and more. 10 pp. **309M.** $1.00.

COMPUTERS

INTERNET AUCTIONS: A GUIDE FOR BUYERS AND SELLERS
Find out how Internet auctions work, payment options, and how
to protect yourself. 18 pp. **347M.** $1.00.

ONLINE SECURITY & SAFETY TIPS
Outlines three important steps you can take to protect your
computer and your personal information, with additional tips and
resources to consult for more information. 5 pp. **642M. Free.**

SHOP SAFELY ONLINE
Is it really safe? Here are the facts about buying over the Internet and how to protect yourself. 2 pp. **348M.** $1.00.

SITE-SEEING ON THE INTERNET
Learn how to navigate the Internet, learn the local customs and
lingo, and know what to avoid during your travels. 11 pp. **346M.**
$1.00.

EDUCATION

CHOOSING A SCHOOL FOR YOUR CHILD
Explains public and private school options available 'in many communities. Outlines steps to follow and provides questions to ask if you are not satisfied with your child's education. 39 pp. **352M.** $1.00.

FINANCIAL PLANNING FOR COLLEGE
Strategies to help you plan for tuition and fees, along with helpful charts for estimating future costs. 10 pp. 510M. **Free.**

GED INFORMATION BULLETIN
Explains the content of the GED Tests, how to prepare for them, and how to get more information. 16 pp. **512M. Free.**

AN INTERACTIVE GUIDE TO PROTECTING AMERICA'S DRINKING WATER
This CD-ROM shows how our drinking water resources are under siege from nature and our activities at home, work, and play. Gives tips for conserving water, using pesticides wisely, and recycling water for further use. **674M. Free.**

NONTRADITIONAL EDUCATION: ALTERNATIVE WAYS TO EARN YOUR CREDENTIALS
Get high school or college credit through the GED program, the National External Diploma program, correspondence and distance study, and standardized tests. 13 pp. **101 M. $3.00.**

SMART SAVING FOR COLLEGE-BETTER BUY DEGREES
Provides information to help you save and invest wisely for college expenses. Explains 529 Plans, Coverdell Education Savings Accounts, Savings Bonds, and more. 23 pp. **511 M. Free.**

WALK ON THE WILD SIDE: EXPLORE YOUR PUBLIC LANDS ACTIVITY BOOK
Go wild with fun activities designed to help children in grades 3-5 learn more about the fish, wildlife, and plants that inhabit America's public lands. 37 pp. **545M. Free.**

EMPLOYMENT

APPRENTICESHIPS: CAREER TRAINING, CREDENTIALS-AND A PAYCHECK IN YOUR POCKET
Apprenticeships are available in more than 850 occupations. Learn how they work, how to find them, and how to choose the best program for you. 20 pp. **102M.** $3.75.

EMPLOYMENT INTERVIEWING
Gives useful advice on what to do before, during, and after a job interview. Includes tips about job fairs. 9 pp. **103M.** $1.75.

How to Get a Job in the Federal Government
Offers a step-by-step plan for finding and applying for federal jobs. Detailed information on finding openings, understanding vacancy announcements, developing your rbsum6, and more. 24 pp, **128M.** $3.00.

Long-Term Disability Income Insurance
Outlines features and costs, with tips and a checklist on buying the policy that's right for you. 24 pp. **333M.** $1.00.

Resumes, Applications, and Cover Letters
Use this helpful guide's samples to prepare a winning cover letter and r6sumb. 15 pp. **108M.** $2.00.

Tips for Finding the Right Job
Assess your skills and interests, create a r6sum6, write cover letters, and prepare for a job interview. 27 pp. **104M.** $3.00.

Top 10 Ways to Make Your Health Benefits Work for You
Use these easy-tofollow tips to help you understand and choose your health benefits. 2 pp. **525M. Free.**

Catch the Spirit: A Student's Guide to Community Service
Ideas and information on how young people can help make their community a better place. 15 pp. **501 M. Free.**

Citizens' Preparedness Guide
Simple, but vital, steps you should take to prepare and protect yourself and your family in a variety of different places and circumstances. 26 pp. **644M. Free.**

Fun Play, Safe Play
Discover the importance of play in your child's learning and development. Suggests toys for different ages. 17 pp. **503M. Free.**

Handbook on Child Support Enforcement
A "how to" guide for getting the payments owed to you and your children. Lists state and federal offices to contact for more information. 61 pp. **505M. Free.**

Kids and Their Bones: A Parents' Guide
Taking care of your child's bones now can protect against later fractures and possible osteoporosis. Learn about the factors that may affect the health of your child's bones. 11 pp. **504M. Free.**

Mr. Plug's Fun Book, Kindergarten through Third Grade
Fun-filled coloring book with activities and games to help teach children about electrical safety. 12 pp. **638M. Free.**

MR. PLUG'S FUN BOOK, PRE-KINDERGARTEN
Coloring activity book geared towards preschoolers to teach them about electrical safety. 12 pp. **637M. Free.**

MY HISTORY IS AMERICA'S HISTORY
Colorful 17" x 22" poster has easy-to-follow ideas for discovering and preserving your family's history, with useful tips on recording family stories. **350M. $1.00.**

SUMMERTIME FAVORITES
Illustrated poster lists nearly 300 books published before 1960 for children of all ages. Divided into grade groups of Kindergarten-Grade 3, Grades 4-6, Grades 7-8, and Grades 9-12. 1 pp. **353M. $1.00.**

YOUR FAMILY DISASTER SUPPLIES KIT
Lists kinds of food, first aid supplies, tools, and other items you should stock for an emergency. 4 pp. **349M. 50c.**

AMERICANS WITH DISABILITIES ACT: QUESTIONS AND ANSWERS
Explains how the civil rights of persons with disabilities are protected at work and in public places. 31 pp. **513M. Free.**

CAN I GET FREE LAND FROM BLM?
Describes the Bureau of Land Management's program to sell excess undeveloped public land and why there is no more available for homesteading. 4 pp. **114M. $2.00.**

A GUIDE TO DISABILITY RIGHTS LAWS
Covers the rights of persons with disabilities regarding education, employment, fair housing, public accommodations, and telecommunications. 21 pp. **514M. Free.**

GUIDE TO FEDERAL GOVERNMENT SALES
Explains how to buy homes, cars, and other property from 20 federal sales programs. 32 pp. **115M. $3.25.**

HOW YOU CAN BUY USED FEDERAL PERSONAL PROPERTY
Describes used equipment and industrial items sold by the government, how they are sold, and where to call for more information. 5 pp. **318M. $1.00.**

NATIONAL SELLERS LIST
How to contact dealers who sell real estate and personal property forfeited to federal law enforcement agencies. 8 pp. **31 9M. $1.00.**

SOCIAL SECURITY: YOUR NUMBER AND CARD
Explains why we have Social Security numbers, when and how to get one, and more. 2 pp. **515M. Free.**

U.S. REAL PROPERTY SALES LIST
Information on government real estate properties that are sold by auction or sealed bid. 5 pp. **592M. Free.**

YOUR RIGHT TO FEDERAL RECORDS
Use the Freedom of Information Act and the Privacy Act to request federal government records. 36 pp. **320M.** $1.00.

BENEFITS

APPLY ONLINE FOR SOCIAL SECURITY BENEFITS
How to fill out an online application, how your personal information is protected, who can apply, and more. **517M. Free.**

FACTS ABOUT MEDICARE PRESCRIPTION DRUG PLANS
Find out how to apply for this insurance program, with details on eligibility, compatibility with other health plans, and more. 2 pp. **673M. Free.**

FACTS ABOUT MEDICARE'S NEW PREVENTIVE BENEFITS
Learn more about coverage for cardiovascular and diabetes screenings, and a free one-time physical exam for new enrollees. 2 pp. **672M. Free.**

FEDERAL BENEFITS FOR VETERANS AND DEPENDENTS
Explains disability, pension, health care, education and housing loans, and other programs for veterans and their families. 120 pp. **113M.** $7.00.

REQUEST FOR SOCIAL SECURITY STATEMENT
Complete this form and return it to Social Security to get your earnings history and an estimate of future benefits. 3 pp. **516M. Free.**

SOCIAL SECURITY: UNDERSTANDING THE BENEFITS
Provides details on retirement, disability, survivor's benefits, Medicare coverage, Supplemental Security Income, and more. 21 pp. **518M. Free.**

FOOD

CAN YOUR KITCHEN PASS THE FOOD SAFETY TEST?
Take the 10-point quiz on food storage, handling, and cooking to protect your family from food-borne illnesses. 4 pp. **622M. Free.**

COOKING FOR GROUPS: A VOLUNTEER'S GUIDE TO FOOD SAFETY
Whether its a family reunion or community cookout, learn how to cook and serve food safely to avoid food-borne illness. 40 pp. **621M. Free.**

DIABETES RECIPES
Five tasty and easy-tofollow recipes for people with diabetes. Nutrition facts for each dish help you keep track of what you are eating. 5 pp. **565M. Free.**

FABULOUS FRUITS ... VERSATILE VEGETABLES
Get tips on new ways to serve them, the importance of variety, and how to make eating fruits and vegetables both convenient and fun. 6 pp. **117M. $2.50.**

FIGHT BAC: FOUR SIMPLE STEPS TO FOOD SAFETY
Advice on how to handle food safely so you, your family, and friends don't become ill. 5 pp. **625M. Free.**

HOW MUCH ARE YOU EATING?
Use the helpful charts to determine how much you need daily from each food group and to compare what you eat with what is recommended so that you don't overeat. 6 pp. **121M. $2.25.**

PREVENTING FOOD-BORNE ILLNESS
Tips on handling food safely. Use the storage guidelines chart to know when to throw away leftovers. 8 pp. **624M.** Free.

RECIPES AND TIPS FOR HEALTHY, THRIFTY MEALS
How to create healthy and budgetfriendly meals-with tips on planning meals, a sample 2-week menu, shopping lists, and 40 great recipes. 76 pp. **119M. $5.50.**

THERMY: USE A FOOD THERMOMETER
Get the right thermometer and use this handy temperature chart for safe, delicious food. 4 pp. **623M.** Free.

BE AN ACTIVE MEMBER OF YOUR HEALTH CARE TEAM
Tips to protect yourself and get the most benefit from prescription and overthe-counter drugs. Includes a list of questions to ask your doctor, nurse, or pharmacist. 4 pp. **524M.** Free.

GUIDE TO HEALTH INSURANCE
Get answers to the most frequently asked questions and use the checklist in this guide to compare costs and services of health insurance plans. 23 pp. **328M. $1.00.**

GUIDE TO LONG-TERM CARE INSURANCE
Check out the costs, limitations and exclusions, and coverage options you need for this type of insurance, which covers services needed by those with chronic illness or disability. 20 pp. **669M.** Free.

How to Find Medical Information
How to use your local library, the federal government, and the Internet to get information on an illness or disorder. 24 pp. **528M.** Free.

How to Keep Your Heart Healthy
Over one million people have heart attacks each year Learn to recognize heart attack symptoms and make lifestyle changes to reduce your risk, 7 pp. **552M.** Free.

How Well Are You Sleeping?
Discusses the causes and treatments for the most common sleep problems- insomnia, excessive daytime sleepiness, snoring, and sleep apnea-and gives tips on how to get better sleep. 6 pp. **649M.** Free.

Mammography Today
How to tell if you are getting a high-quality mammograrn, what to do if you need to change mammogram facilities, and more. 6 pp. **627M.** Free.

A Primer on Summer Safety
Helpful information on how to avoid or treat typical summer injuries and illnesses such as sunburn, mosquito and tick bites, bee stings, heat illness, burns, food-borne illness, poison ivy, and poisoning in children. 8 pp. **650M.** Free.

Protect Your Drinking Water
Learn where your water comes from, the factors that affect its quality, and how to prevent pollution. 7 pp. **547M.** Free.

Staying Healthy at 50+.
Covers everything from cholesterol levels, various cancers, weight control, and checkups, with helpful charts to keep track of your medications, shots, and screening test results. 64 pp. **120M.** $3.00.

DRUGS & HEALTH AIDS

Botox
Why it is used, how it works, what its side effects are, and what to consider before trying. 2 pp. **652M.** Free.

Buying Contact Lenses Online or by Mail
Tips to follow when ordering contact lenses online or through the mail, including prescription information required and what to watch out for. 2 pp. **653M.** Free.

Buying Prescription Medicines Online: A Consumer Safety Guide
Here's a helpful list of do's and don'ts when shopping for medications over the Internet. 5 pp. **526M.** Free.

DIETARY SUPPLEMENTS
Questions to ask before taking dietary supplements, including risks and where to find more information. 2 pp. **522M.** Free.

DRUG INTERACTIONS
What You Should Know. Protect yourself and your family from potentially dangerous interactions of prescription drugs, over-the-counter drugs, food, and medical conditions. 8 pp. **527M.** Free.

GENERIC DRUGS
Covers effectiveness, appearance, safety, and how they save you money. 2 pp. **654M.** Free.

KNOW WHEN ANTIBIOTICS WORK
Answers common questions about antibiotics, including when they won't help and why to be careful about their use. 4 pp. **560M.** Free.

LASIK LASER EYE SURGERY
What to know before having laser eye surgery, including cost, health risks, lifestyle considerations, and more. 2 pp. **655M.** Free.

MENOPAUSE & HORMONES: FACT SHEET
Explains the benefits and risks of treating symptoms of menopause with hormone therapy. 2 pp **629M.** Free.

MENOPAUSE & HORMONES: PURSE GUIDE
Questions to ask your doctor concerning hormone therapy for symptoms of menopause. 2 pp. **628M.** Free.

MY MEDICINES
Take care of yourself with this easy-to-follow guide that features questions to ask your doctor and a simple chart to keep track of your medications. 6 pp. **556M.** Free.

NEW OVER-THE-COUNTER MEDICINE LABEL ... TAKE A LOOK!
Medicine labels are now easier to understand and compare. View a sample label and the standard information you'll find on it. 5 pp, **557M.** Free.

THINK IT THROUGH: A GUIDE TO MANAGING THE BENEFITS AND RISKS OF MEDICINES
Before you start a new medication, know the right questions to ask your doctor, read your medication labels, avoid harmful interactions, and more. 4 pp. **559M.** Free.

WHOLE-BODY CT SCREENING
Discusses the risks, limitations, and benefits of this procedure. 2 pp. **656M.** Free.

You Know the Questions That Go Through Your Mind When You Take Your Generic Drug?
Find out what generic drugs are, how they differ from brand name drugs, and what is done to ensure their safety and effectiveness. 3 pp, **558M**. Free.

Exercise & Diet

Fitness and Exercise.
Get fit and feel better with daily activities that fit the weather, your lifestyle, and your schedule. 12 pp. **555M**. Free.

Handout on Health: Sports Injury
Especially if you're not a pro athlete, you need to have the facts about sports injuries. Learn what kinds of activities are most likely to cause injuries, how to prevent them, and recent treatment advances. 16 pp. **502M**. Free.

Losing Weight: More Than Counting Calories
Use this guide to learn whether you're overweight, develop healthier eating habits, increase your physical activity, and create a successful weight loss plan. 6 pp. **523M**. Free.

Questions & Answers About Arthritis and Exercise
Suggestions on the best exercises to include in an exercise program to help treat arthritis. 18 pp. **529M**. Free.

MEDICAL PROBLEMS

Allergies
Discusses the symptoms, tests, and treatments. Also provides a comparison chart to help you distinguish between allergy and cold symptoms. 1 pp. **643M**. Free.

Alzheimer's: Searching for a Cure
Learn how Alzheimer's is diagnosed, its symptoms, current drug treatments, and lifestyle advice to help prolong mental health. 6 pp. **613M**. Free.

Arthritis and Rheumatic Diseases
Basic facts about these conditions, including examples of rheumatic diseases, symptoms, causes, diagnosis, and treatments. 34 pp. **543M**. Free.

Atopic Dermatitis
Find out more about the symptoms and treatments for this disease, which causes extremely itchy, inflamed skin. 37 pp. **509M**. Free.

Boning Up on Osteoporosis
Learn the risk factors, diagnosis, and treatment options for preventing, minimizing, and even building back bone mass. 6 pp. **537M.** Free.

Breathing Better
Control your asthma with an action plan to recognize your triggers, track your symptoms, monitor your breathing and know when to take medication. 8 pp. **566M.** Free.

Diabetes
Many people who have diabetes are unaware they have it. Find out more about diabetes, its risk factors, the warning signs, and treatments available. 6 pp. **564M.** Free.

Do I Have Lupus?
Lupus is a disease in which the immune system attacks the body's healthy cells and tissues. Learn about the three main types, their symptoms, who is affected and how lupus is diagnosed and treated. 50 pp. **562M.** Free.

Eating Disorders.
Recognize the symptoms of different eating disorders, who is most likely to be affected, and various treatment options. 8 pp. **521M.** Free.

Fibroids
Explains symptoms and treatments, and answers common questions about fibroids. 2 pp. **657M.** Free.

The Flu
The flu is different than a cold and usually appears without warning signs. Know the symptoms, types of vaccines available, who is at risk, and more. 2 pp. **561M.** Free.

Heart Disease
Heart disease is a leading cause of death in the U.S. Learn the signs of heart disease, including the "silent" symptoms, and get tips on how to lower your risk. 2 pp. **553M.** Free.

Lung Cancer.
Describes how it is diagnosed, the types and stages of lung cancer, warning signs, and more. 2 pp. **567M.** Free.

Lupus.
Discover more about lupus, including warning signs and available treatments. 33 pp. **563M.** Free.

Osteoarthritis
Explains symptoms, treatments, and helpful exercises for the most common type of arthritis. 36 pp. **541M.** Free.

PREVENTING STROKE
Learn about the most common cause of adult disability and estimate your risk with the informative strokerisk chart. 8 pp. **329M**. $1.00.

QUESTIONS & ANSWERS ABOUT ACNE
Find out how acne develops, what treatments will and won't work, and how to care for your skin. 12 pp. **507M**. Free.

QUESTIONS & ANSWERS ABOUT FIBROMYALGIA
Explains causes, treatments, and latest research efforts on this chronic disorder, which causes widespread pain and tenderness in your muscles and soft tissue. 26 pp. **538M**. Free.

QUESTIONS & ANSWERS ABOUT GOUT
Here are the details on this painful type of arthritis, including symptoms, treatments, and more. 11 pp. **531M**. Free.

QUESTIONS & ANSWERS ABOUT HIP REPLACEMENT
Who is a likely candidate, alternatives available, possible complications, and what to expect during recovery and rehabilitation. 15 pp. **533M**. Free.

QUESTIONS & ANSWERS ABOUT KNEE PROBLEMS
Causes, symptoms, diagnosis, and treatment of specific knee conditions. 30 pp. **534M**. Free.

QUESTIONS & ANSWERS ABOUT PSORIASIS
This chronic skin disorder causes scaling and inflammation. Learn about its causes, symptoms, types, diagnosis, and treatments. 17 pp. **508M**. Free.

QUESTIONS & ANSWERS ABOUT ROSACEA
This chronic disease affects the skin and causes redness and pimples. Find out about its causes, treatments, and how to minimize flare-ups. 10 pp. **532M**. Free.

REACTIVE ARTHRITIS
This form of arthritis occurs as a reaction to an infection in another part of the body. This helpful guide details its causes, symptoms, diagnosis, treatments, and more. 17 pp. **536M**. Free.

RHEUMATOID ARTHRITIS
Discusses diagnosis and treatments, with a medication chart for drug benefits and side effects. 44 pp. **539M**. Free.

STROKES
Facts about the 3 types of strokes, warning signs to look for, and how to lower your risk. 2 pp, **554M**. Free.

URINARY TRACT INFECTIONS IN ADULTS
Learn more about its causes, symptoms, and treatments available. 8 pp. **330M**. $1.00.

WEST NILE VIRUS
Learn the facts on how this virus is contracted through mosquito bites, its symptoms, who is most at risk, and ways to protect yourself. 2 pp. **658M**. Free.

MENTAL HEALTH

DEPRESSION
Outlines the three main types of depression, causes, symptoms, and how to find out more information. 2 pp. **618M**. Free.

LET'S TALK ABOUT DEPRESSION
Helps teenagers learn the symptoms of depression and where to get help. 3 pp. **614M**. Free.

WHAT TO DO WHEN A FRIEND IS DEPRESSED
Depression is a serious disease that affects people of all ages, even teenagers. This guide helps teens understand the myths about depression and find out where to get help. 3 pp. **615M**. Free.

FINANCING & SALES

100 QUESTIONS AND ANSWERS ABOUT BUYING A NEW HOME
This great guide focuses on finances-from how much home you can afford, to various mortgage loan programs, insurance, taxes, and more. 40 pp. **594M**. Free.

BORROWER'S GUIDE TO HOME LOANS
Here's how to find the best loan when shopping for home equity loans and reverse mortgages. 16 pp. **595M**. Free.

DON'T BE A VICTIM OF LOAN FRAUD
Be a smart consumer when buying or refinancing a home. Use these 11 tips to learn more about predatory lending, recognize tactics that predators use, identify warning signs of fraud, and more. 5 pp **609M**. Free.

HOW TO AVOID FORECLOSURE.
Explains how homeowners with FHA-insured mortgages can avoid losing their homes and ruining their credit because of missed payments. 5 pp. **601M**. Free.

How to Buy a Home With a Low Down Payment
Describes how to qualify for a low down payment mortgage, determine what you can afford, and how mortgage insurance works. 9 pp. **597M.** Free.

How to Buy a Manufactured (Mobile) Home
Tips on selection and placement, warranties, site preparation, transportation, installation, and more. 14 pp. **304M.** $1.00.

HUD Home Buying Guide
Step-by-step instructions for finding and financing a HUD home. Includes charts to help you estimate mortgage payments. 14 pp. **647M.** Free.

Looking for the Best Mortgage-Shop, Compare, Negotiate
Use these 3 steps to save money on a mortgage or home loan. Includes a mortgage shopping worksheet. 7 pp. **334M.** $1.00.

Tips for a Successful Interstate Move
Helpful information when you move across state lines. Includes what you should know before choosing a mover, as well as tips on what to do if there is a problem. 7 pp. **602M.** Free.

Twelve Ways to Lower Your Homeowners Insurance Costs
Practical tips and phone numbers of state insurance departments for more information. 4 pp. **335M.** $1.00.

HOME MAINTENANCE

Am I Covered?
Answers 15 common questions regarding homeowners insurance and explains what is covered in a standard policy. 9 pp. **336M.** $1.00.

Cooling Your Home Naturally
Ways to save electricity and keep your home cool with landscaping, roof treatments, shading, and windows. 8 pp. **127M.** $2.00.

Drinking Water From Household Wells
Families with their own wells are responsible for maintaining them and making sure that the water is safe to drink. Here's the facts on sources of pollution and how to keep your water safe. 16 pp. **548M.** Free.

Energy Savers: Tips on Saving Energy & Money at Home
Reduce your home energy use with tips on insulation, weatherization, heating, and more. 36 pp. **337M.** $1.00.

ENERGY-EFFICIENT AIR CONDITIONING
Explains how air conditioners work, what different types are available, and how to troubleshoot and maintain your air conditioners. 8 pp. **125M**. $1.50.

THE GREAT AMERICAN HOME SAFETY CHECK
Gives important tips to prevent fire and burns, slips and falls, and poisoning-the leading causes of home safety issues in the U.S. 4 pp. **603M**. Free.

HEALTHY LAWN, HEALTHY ENVIRONMENT
Tips on lawn care, including soil preparation, watering, mowing, pesticides, and choosing a lawn care service. 17 pp. **355M**. $1.00.

INDOOR AIR HAZARDS EVERY HOMEOWNER SHOULD KNOW ABOUT
How to get rid of molds, carbon monoxide, radon, asbestos, lead, tobacco smoke, and other pollutants. 16 pp. **593M**. Free.

INDOOR ELECTRICAL SAFETY CHECK
Quick and easy tips to make your home safe from electrical hazards. 21 pp. **604M**. Free.

NATIONAL FLOOD INSURANCE GUIDE
Property owners can purchase insurance against flooding losses. Learn the requirements, questions to ask, and more. 20 pp. **596M**. Free.

OUTDOOR ELECTRICAL SAFETY CHECK
Detailed guide to preventing outdoor electrical hazards that can cause fires and dangerous shocks. 33 pp. **605M**. Free.

SELECTING A NEW WATER HEATER
Describes how different types of water heaters work and important features to consider when buying. 6 pp. **124M**. $1.25.

WATER ON TAP: WHAT YOU NEED TO KNOW
Explains where it comes from and how it's treated, what contaminants are, and what to do in case of a problem with either your public or private water supply. 27 pp. **549M**. Free.

CONSUMER GUIDE TO CHECK 21 AND SUBSTITUTE CHECKS
A new law, Check 21, allows banks to send you "substitute checks" in place of your original cancelled checks. Find out your rights. 2 pp. **338M**. $1.00.

ELECTRONIC BANKING
Learn more about electronic transactions, such as debit cards and online account access, including how transactions are processed, their timing, security, and legal protections. 15 pp. **345M**. $1.00.

ESTABLISHING A TRUST FUND
Learn what different kinds of trusts can and can't do, their benefits, the role of a trustee, and more. 10 pp. **574M.** Free.

LIVING TRUST OFFERS
Find out if living trusts are right for you and how to protect yourself from scams when planning your estate. 2 pp. **322M.** $1.00.

PERSONAL FINANCIAL CHOICES
Explains the basics of Chapter 7 bankruptcy, how to set up a sound financial plan, how to rebuild your credit, and much more. 98 pp. **571M.** Free.

PLANNING YOUR ESTATE
Information on how to estimate the size of your estate, minimize taxes, and provide for your heirs. 10 pp. **577M.** Free.

PROTECTING YOURSELF FROM OVERDRAFT AND BOUNCED CHECK FEES
Find out how much overdraft and bounced check fees can cost you and learn how to avoid these fees. 2 pp. **340M.** $1.00.

THERE'S A LOT TO LEARN ABOUT MONEY
Simple tips to help you set goals, develop a budget, and manage your credit. 6 pp. **344M.** $1.00.

WHAT YOU SHOULD KNOW ABOUT BUYING LIFE INSURANCE
Describes various types with tips on choosing a company, an agent, and a policy that meets your needs. 23 pp. **332M.** $1.00.

WHEN IS YOUR CHECK NOT A CHECK?
Merchants can use the information from your checks to withdraw money directly from your bank account. Learn about your rights when it comes to electronic check conversion and what to do if you have a problem. 2 pp. **339M.** $1.00.

CREDIT

BUILDING A BETTER CREDIT RECORD
Learn how to legally improve your credit report, how to deal with debt, how to spot creditrelated scams, and more. 16 pp. **311M.** $1.00.

CHOOSING A CREDIT CARD
Compare the features and costs, and learn your liability limits when using a credit card. Covers what to do if there is a billing error or other problem with your card. 20 pp. **356M.** $1.00.

CONSUMER HANDBOOK TO CREDIT PROTECTION LAWS
This guide explains how consumer credit laws can help you shop for credit, apply for it, keep up your credit standing, and more. 44 pp. **310M.** $1.00.

CREDIT MATTERS
How to qualify for credit, keep a good credit history, protect your credit once you have it, and more. 2 pp. **312M.** $1.00.

ID THEFT: WHAT'S IT ALL ABOUT?
Thieves can steal your personal information and use it to commit fraud for long periods without your knowledge. Here's how to protect yourself, and what to do if you are a victim. 18 pp. **341M.** $1.00.

IDENTITY THEFT AND YOUR SOCIAL SECURITY NUMBER
Someone illegally using your Social Security number can steal your financial identity and your money, Find out how to prevent identify theft, how to report it if you suspect it, and how to get a new Social Security number if you are a victim. 8 pp. **675M.** Free.

YOUR CREDIT SCORES
Learn why your credit score matters, what good and bad scores are, the elements of your FICO credit score, and how you can raise your score. 5 pp. **671M.** Free.

INVESTING & SAVING

66 WAYS TO SAVE MONEY
Practical ways to cut everyday costs on transportation, insurance, banking, credit, housing, utilities, food, and more. 10 pp. **342M.** 500.

BUILDING FINANCIAL FREEDOM
Features a worksheet to help track your spending, tips on creating a financial plan, and an investor's checklist. 12 pp. **579M.** Free.

CERTIFICATES OF DEPOSIT: TIPS FOR INVESTORS
Learn how CDs work, how to purchase them, and questions to ask before buying. 6 pp. **606M.** Free.

THE CONSUMER'S ALMANAC
Organize your expenses, save for the future, and manage your credit with monthly calendars and worksheets. 32 pp. **343M.** $1.00.

GET THE FACTS ON SAVING AND INVESTING
Use this guide's helpful tips and worksheets for calculating net worth, income, and expenses. 18 pp. **610M.** Free.

HANDS ON BANKING
Interactive CD-ROM helps you build the money skills you need

for life. Four separate programs from 4th grade through adult, in English and Spanish, cover budgeting, saving, investing, buying a home, and more. **641M.** Free.

How SIPC Protects You
If your brokerage firm closes due to bankruptcy or other financial difficulties, the Securities Investor Protection Corporation (SIPC) works to return your assets. Find out what SIPC does and does not cover. 10 pp. **570M.** Free.

Insuring Your Deposits
Find out if your bank or savings institution is insured, what types of accounts are covered, and how much of your money is protected. 2 pp. **612M.** Free.

Introduction to Mutual Funds
Details on what they are, how to compare them, what to consider before investing, and how to avoid common pitfalls. 36 pp. **611M.** Free.

Investors' Bill of Rights
What you should know about investments and what information you are entitled to before investing. 7 pp. **578M.** Free.

Questions You Should Ask About Your Investments
The secret to investing wisely is knowing what to ask about investment products, your broker's history, your investment's performance, and how to handle problems. 8 pp. **608M.** Free.

Ten Questions to Ask When Choosing a Financial Planner
Covers credentials, costs, services, an interview checklist, and resources to contact for more information. 12 pp. **580M.** Free.

What You Should Know About Financial Planning
Discusses the benefits of financial planning for life-changing events, such as buying a home or retirement. 13 pp. **581M.** Free.

Your Rights as a Financial Planning Client
Here's a checklist of your rights, what to expect from your financial planner, and what to do if you have a problem. 5 pp. **572M.** Free.

RETIREMENT PLANNING

401 (k) Plans
Explains what these plans are, what happens when you change employers, and what to do if you need the money before retirement. 14 pp. **583M.** Free.

ANNUITIES
Learn the different types of annuities and take a helpful quiz to see if annuities are right for you. 11 pp. **584M.** Free.

SAVINGS FITNESS: A GUIDE TO YOUR MONEY AND YOUR FINANCIAL FUTURE
Create your personal savings plan and prepare for retirement with this step-by-step guide. 20 pp. **585M.** Free.

TOP 10 WAYS TO PREPARE FOR RETIREMENT
Gives practical tips to build your retirement savings and lists resources for more information. 2 pp. **586M.** Free.

VARIABLE ANNUITIES: WHAT YOU SHOULD KNOW
Explains what they are, how they work, what you have to pay, and questions to ask before you invest. 20 pp. **607M.** Free.

WOMEN AND RETIREMENT SAVINGS
What women need to know about retirement benefits, including plan type, eligibility, penalties, spousal benefits, and more. 6 pp. **587M.** Free.

YOUR GUARANTEED PENSION
Frequentlyasked questions about the security of private pension plans, including benefits and plan termination. 12 pp. **582M.** Free.

SMALL BUSINESS

COPYRIGHT BASICS
Provides details on what a copyright is, what can be copyrighted, who can apply, how to register, what fees are involved, what forms to use, and more. 12 pp. **313M.** $1.00.

EMPLOYMENT LAW GUIDE
Comprehensive guide covers laws and regulations regarding wages and hours of work, safety and health standards, pension and benefit plans, federal contracts, and more. 110 pp. **576M.** Free.

A GUIDE TO BUSINESS CREDIT FOR WOMEN, MINORITIES, AND SMALL BUSINESSES
Learn more about what loans are available, the credit approval process, and your legal rights. 12 pp. **317M.** $1.00.

INTRODUCTION TO FEDERAL TAXES FOR SMALL BUSINESS/SELF- EMPLOYED
This helpful CDROM explains what you need to document expenses and deductions and file federal taxes. **314M.** $1.00.

SMALL BUSINESS RESOURCE GUIDE 2004
CD-ROM containing tax forms, instructions, and publications, plus help on preparing a business plan, financing your business, and more. **316M.** $1.00.

GET MORE HELP FOR YOUR SMALL BUSINESS AT WWWBUSINESS.GOV.

VIRTUAL SMALL BUSINESS WORKSHOP
This user-friendly CD-ROM covers a variety of small business tax issues, including payroll taxes, electronic filing, and recordkeeping. **315M.** $1.00.

NATIONAL PARK SYSTEM MAP AND GUIDE
This newly revised full-color map lists activities at more than 300 parks, monuments, and historic sites. **129M.** $2.50.

PASSPORTS: APPLYING FOR THEM THE EASY WAY
How, when, and where to apply for U.S. passports. Includes information on fees. 12 pp. **324M.** $1.00.

WASHINGTON: THE NATION'S CAPITAL
Use this full-color map to learn more about our country's heritage by exploring Washington, D.C. **112M.** $2.50.

AND MORE.....

2005 CONSUMER ACTION HANDBOOK
Use this updated guide to get help with consumer problems and complaints. Find consumer contacts at hundreds of companies and trade associations, local, state, and federal government agencies, national consumer organizations, and more. 172 pp. **568M.** Free.

THE CIVIL WAR AT A GLANCE
This full-color map illustrates and briefly describes major Civil War battle campaigns. **111M.** $2.00.

CONSERVING THE NATURE OF AMERICA
Beautiful photos show how fish, wildlife, and plants are protected in more than 500 National Wildlife Refuges. Also gives details on volunteer and recreational opportunities. 24 pp. **550M.** Free.

THE CONSTITUTION OF THE UNITED STATES AND THE DECLARATION OF INDEPENDENCE
Learn about the foundations of our country's freedom with the

full text of both historic documents. 48 pp. **110M.** $2.75.

FISHING IS FUN FOR EVERYONE
Find out what equipment you'll need, what kind of bait to use, how to cast and tie knots, and where to get more information. 11 pp. **544M.** Free.

FOR THE BIRDS
How to attract different species of birds, feed them, and select suitable homes. 50 pp. **351M**. $1.00.

FUNERALS: A CONSUMER GUIDE
Know your rights as a consumer and what to keep in mind when making funeral arrangements. 29 pp. **321M**. $1.00.

GOING WIRELESS: A CONSUMER GUIDE TO CHOOSING CELLULAR SERVICE
How to select the right service and calling plans, understand your contract, avoid fraud, and more. 8 pp. **589M.** Free.

LISTA DE PUBLICACIONES FEDERALES EN ESPANOL PARA EL CONSUMIDOR
Lists 200 free publications in Spanish available from various federal agencies. Bulk copies of this publication are available. 16 pp. **801M.** Free.

OUR FLAG
Are you familiar with the U.S. flag's history and customs? Here is everything you want to know about the flag. 52 pp. **109M.** $4.50.

WHERE TO WRITE FOR VITAL RECORDS
Listing of state offices to contact for birth, death, marriage, and divorce certificates, with guidelines to follow when submitting a request. 50 pp. **107M.** $4.25.

ORDERING INFORMATION

You'll notice that some booklets have a price and others are entirely free. The small price that may be charged helps the government pay a part of the cost to print and distribute these useful booklets.

However, all of these booklets can be viewed, downloaded and printed free by going to the following web site: www.pueblo.gsa.gov

HOW TO ORDER

Select the publications you would like to order. At the end of each listing there is a item number followed by either a price or the word 'Free' (for example, 'INTERNET AUCTIONS: A GUIDE FOR BUYERS AND SELLERS' booklet has the item number and price .... **347M**. $1.00 Write down the item number and include a check, money order or charge card information (including expiration date and your signature) with your order and send it to:

FCIC - 05C
PO Box 100
Pueblo, CO 81002

While there is no charge for individual free publications, there is a $2.00 service fee to help defray program costs. For that $2.00, you may order up to 25 different free booklets. Payment can be made by check or money order made payable to the "Superintendent of Documents" or charged to your VISA, MasterCard or Discover card (include expiration date & signature.) Priority handling is available when orders are placed by phone at an extra charge.

If you would like you can also order by phone using your credit card. Call: **1-888-878-3256**

Get answers from Uncle Sam

Find out how to apply for government benefits and grants, renew your driver's license, get a passport, buy government surplus property and much much more. It's easy., it's fast and best of all...it's FREE. Yes, if you have a government question... any question no matter how big or small... now you can get answers by calling **1-800 FED-INFO** (that's 1-800-333-4636) any time Monday thru Friday from 8am to 8pm ET. If you prefer you can visit them anytime on the internet or email your questions to them at **FirstGov.gov**

Free Help For Seniors From Your State's Office of The Aging

Every state in the nation has an agency dedicated to providing seniors with a full range of services they may need. These services will vary from state to state but they include:

- Food Stamps
- Home delivered meals
- Transportation to and from doctor's offices
- In-Home care and assistance where needed
- Job Training programs for older workers wanting to get back into the workforce
- Health insurance counseling & assistance programs to help the elderly get all the health care they need.
- Free prescription drug programs

To find out exactly what services are available to you, contact your state's office of the aging directly. Here is a directory of the offices of the aging for all 50 states plus the District of Columbia, Puerto Rico and the Pacific Islands

National Offices

Administration on Aging -
Washington D.C.
U.S. Administration on Aging Office
of Management and Policy
330 Independence Avenue, S.W.
Washington, DC 20201
1-800-677-1116
www.aoa.dhhs.gov

National Association of Area
Agencies on Aging
1112 16th Street N.W., Suite 100
Washington, DC 20036-4823
202-296-8130
www.n4a.org

State Offices

Alabama
Alabama Commission on Aging
770 Washington Avenue
Montgomery, AL 36104-3816
334-242-5743
www.adss.state.al.us

Alaska
Alaska Commission on Aging
P.O. Box 110209
Juneau, AK 99811-0209
907-465-3250
www.alaskaaging.org

Arizona
Arizona Aging and Adult
Administration
1789 W. Jefferson, #950A
Phoenix, AZ 85007
602-542-4446
www.de.state.az.us

Arkansas
Arkansas Division of Aging and Adult
Services
7th and Main Street
P.O. Box 1437, Slot 1412
Little Rock, AR 72203-1412
501-682-2441
www.state.ar.us/dhs

California
California Department on Aging
1600 K Street
Sacramento, CA 95814
916-324-5290
916-322-3887
www.aging.state.ca.us

Colorado
Colorado Division of Aging and Adult
Services
1525 sherman St.
Denver, CO 80203
303-866-2800
www.state.co.us

Connecticut
Connecticut Dept. of Social
Services
25 Sigourney Street, 10th floor
Hartford, CT 06106-5033
1800-842-1508
www.dss.state.ct.us

Delaware
Delaware Division of Services for
Aging & Adults
1901 N. Dupont Highway
New Castle, DE 19720
1-800-223-9074
www.dsaapd.com

District of Columbia
District of Columbia Office on Aging
441 4th Street N.W., Suite 900
Washington, DC 20001
202-724-5622
www.dcoa.dc.gov

Florida
Florida Department of Elder Affairs
4040 Esplanade Way
Tallahassee, FL 32399-0700
850-414-2000
elderaffairs.state.fl.us

Georgia
Georgia Office of Aging
2 Peachtree Street N.W., Suite 18-
403
Atlanta, GA 30303-3176
404-657-5258
www.state.ga.us

Hawaii
Hawaii Executive Office on Aging
250 South Hotel Street, Room 109
Honolulu, HI 96813
808-586-0100

Idaho
Idaho State Office on Aging
Statehouse, Room 108
Boise, ID 83720
208-334-3833
www.state.id.us/icoa

Illinois
Illinois Dept. on Aging
421 E. Capital Avenue, #100
Springfield, IL 62701-1789
217-785-3356
www.state.il.us/aging

Indiana
Indiana Family & Social Services
Administration
10 W. Market St Suite 600
Indianapolis, IN 46204
317-233-2010
www.ai.org/fssa/elderly/index.html

Iowa
Iowa Department of Elder Affairs
200 Tenth St., 3rd Floor
Des Moines, IA 50309
515-242-3333
www.state.ia.us/elderaffairs

Kansas
Kansas Dept. on Aging
503 S. Kansas Ave.
Topeka, KS 66603
785-296-4986
www.k4s.org/kdoa

Kentucky
Kentucky Division of Aging Services
275 E. Main Street, 5W-A
Frankfort, KY 40601
502-564-6930
www.state.ky.us/aging

Louisiana
Louisiana Governor's Office of
Elderly Affairs
412 North 4th Street
Baton Rouge, LA 70802
225-342-7100
www.laaging.org

Maine
Maine Bureau of Elder & Adult Services
35 Anthony Avenue
State House, Station #11
Augusta, ME 04333
207-624-5335
www.state.me.us/dhs/beas

Maryland
Maryland Office on Aging
301 W. Preston Street, 10th floor
Baltimore, MD 21201
410-767-1116
www.mdoa.state.md.us

Massachusetts
Massachusetts Executive Office of
Elder Affairs
1 Ashburton Place, 5th floor
Boston, MA 02108
617-727-7750
www.800ageinfo.com

Michigan
Michigan Office of Services to the
Aging
Ottawa Building 3rd floor
P.O. Box 30676

Lansing, MI 48909
517-373-8230
www.miseniors.net

Minnesota
Minnesota Board on Aging
444 Lafayette Road
St. Paul, MN 55155-3843
651-296-2770
www.mnaging.org

Mississippi
Mississippi Council on Aging
750 N. State Street
Jackson, MS 39202
601-359-4925
www.state.ms.us

Missouri
Missouri Division on Aging
615 Howerton Court
P.O. Box 1337
Jefferson City, MO 65102
573-751-3082
www.health.state.mo.us

Montana
Montana Senior & Long Term Care
Div
111 North Sanders Room 210
Helena, MT 59604
406-444-4077
www.dphhs.state.mt.us/sltc

Nebraska
Nebraska Division on Aging
P.O. Box 95044
Lincoln, NE 68509-5044
402-471-2306
www.state.ne.us

Nevada
Nevada Division for Aging Services
3100 West Sahara Ave Suite 103
Las Vegas, NV 89102
702-486-3545
www.nvaging.net

New Hampshire
New Hampshire Division of Elderly
Services

129 Pleasant St.
Concord, NH 03301
603-271-4680
www.dhhs.state.nh.us

New Jersey
New Jersey Division of Senior Affairs
PO Box 807
Trenton, NJ 08625-0807
609-943-3437
www.state.nj.us

New Mexico
New Mexico State Agency on Aging
228 E. Palace Avenue
Santa Fe, NM 87501
505-827-7640
www.nmaging.state.nm.us

New York
New York Office for the Aging
Agency Building #2
Albany, NY 12223
800-342-9871
www.aging.state.ny.us
Elderly Prescription Insurance
Coverage (EPIC) Hotline:
1-800-332-3742

North Carolina
North Carolina Division of Aging
2101 Mail Service Center
Raleigh, NC 27699
919-733-3983
www.state.nc.us

North Dakota
North Dakota Aging Services
Division
600 South Second Street, Suite 1C
Bismarck, ND 58504
701-328-8910
http://discovernd.com

Ohio
Ohio Department of Aging
50 W. Broad Street, 9th floor
Columbus, OH 43215
614-466-5500
www.state.oh.us/age

Oklahoma
Oklahoma Aging Services Division
312 N.E. 28th Street
P.O. BOx 25352
Oklahoma City, OK 73125
405-521-2327
www.okdhs.org/aging

Oregon
Oregon Senior & Disabled Services
Division
500 Summer Street N.E., 2nd floor
Salem, OR 97310-1015
503-945-5811
www.sdsd.hr.state.or.us

Pennsylvania
Pennsylvania Department of Aging
555 Walnut Street, Fifth floor
Harrisburg, PA 17101-1919
717-783-1550
www.aging.state.pa.us

Pacific Islands-Agana
Guam Division of Senior Citizens
P.O. Box 2816
Agana, GU 96910
(011) 671-475-0263

Puerto Rico
Governor's Office for Elderly Affairs
Corbian Plaza Stop 23
Ponce deLeon Ave. # 1603
UM Office C
San Ture, PR 00908
809-721-5710

Rhode Island
Rhode Island Dept. of Elderly Affairs
160 Pine Street
Providence, RI 02903-3708
401-222-2858
www.dea.state.ri.us

South Carolina
South Carolina Division on Aging
PO Box 8206
Columbia, SC 29202
803-898-2500
www.myscgov.com

South Dakota
South Dakota Office of Adult Services and Aging
700 Governors Drive
Pierre, SD 57501
605-773-3656
www.state.sd.us/social/asa

Tennessee
Tennessee Commission on Aging
500 Deaderick Street, 9th Floor
Nashville, TN 37243-0860
615-741-2056
www.state.tn.us/comaging

Texas
Texas Department on Aging
4900 North Lamar 4th Floor
P.O. Box 12786
Austin, TX 78711
512-424-6845
www.state.tx.us

Utah
Utah Division of Aging and Adult Services
120 North 200 West, Room 401
Salt Lake City, UT 84103
801-538-3910
www.hsdaas.state.ut.us/srvag.htm

Vermont
Vermont Dept. of Aging and Disabilities
103 S. Main Street
Waterbury, VT 05671-2301
802-241-2400
www.dad.state.vt.us

Virginia
Virginia Department For The Aging
1600 Forest Avenue, Suite 102
Richmond, VA 23229
804-662-9333
www.aging.state.va.us

Washington
Washington Aging & Adult Services Administration
P.O. Box 45050
Olympia, WA 98504-5050
360-725-2300
www.aasa.dshs.wa.gov

West Virginia
West Virginia Office of Aging
Holly Grove-Building 10,
1900 Kanawha Blvd. E.
Charleston, WV 25305-0160
304-558-3317
www.state.wv.us/seniorservices

Wisconsin
Wisconsin Bureau of Aging
1 W Wilson Street Room 450
Madison, WI 53707
608-266-2536
www.dhfs.state.wi.us/aging

Wyoming
Wyoming Department of Health, Division on Aging
6101 Yellowstone Road Room 259B
Cheyenne, WY 82002
307-777-7986
www.state.wy.us/

State Pharmaceutical Programs

Free Medication For Seniors

If you're a senior living on a fixed income in one of the following eleven states and you do not have Medicare or private insurance, you could be getting all of your prescription drugs free or for as little as a dollar or two. All you do is make a phone call to your state's office at the numbers listed. If you live in a state not listed here, check with your state's *Office Of The Aging* listed in a directory at the back of this book. Also check out the *Directory of Free Prescription Drugs Programs* that follows the listings below.

Alabama

The state of Alabama Department of Senior Services has introduced a program to help seniors take advantage of free and low cost pharmaceutical programs. For more information call toll-free:
1-800-243-5463

Connecticut

CONN PACE Program
PO Box 5011
Hartford, CT 06102
860-832-9265
800-423-5026 (in CT)
• State resident for at least 6 months
• Must be 65 or older or receive Social Security
• Income must not exceed $15,100 (single) or $18,100 (married)
• No Medicaid or private insurance that covers medications
You pay a one time fee of $25 to register. You pay $12 for each prescription and must use generic drugs wherever available unless your physician writes 'brand drug only'.

Delaware

IN WILMINGTON COUNTY
Nemours Health Clinic Program
1801 Rockland Road
Wilmington, DE 19803
302-651-4400   800-292-9538 (in DE only)

IN KENT OR SUFFEX COUNTIES
Nemours Health Clinic Program
915 N. Dupont Blvd.
Milford, DE 19963
302-424-5420   800-763-9326 (in DE only)
• For Delaware residents only
• Age 65 or older
• Can not earn more than 12,500 if single or $17,125 if married
This privately funded prgram covers four areas of health needs: dental, eye, hearing and medicines. In the Kent & Suffex office the coverage is for eye and hearing problems only.

Illinois

Pharmaceutical Assistance Program
PO Box 19022
Springfield, IL 62794
217-524-0435   800-624-2459 (IL only)
Internet site: www.revenue.state.il.us (click on 'circuit breaker")
• Must be a resident of Illinois
• Must be 65or older or over 16 and totally disabled or a
  widow or widower who turned 63 before spouses death
• Income of $21,218 or less for a one person household. Or
  $28,480 for two people; $35,740 for a 3 person household
• You must purchase a Pharmaceutical Assistance card that
  will cost you either $5 or $25 per year depending upon
  income.
• You must use a generic brand where available unless you
  are willing to pay the difference.
• Covers medications for your heart, blood pressure, diabetes
  or arthritis.

Maine

Elderly Low-Cost Drug Program
State House Station 24
Augusta, ME 04332
207-626-8475
www.state.me.us/revenue

- Must be a Maine resident
- Must be 62 or older or if disabled, 19 or older
- Your income must not exceed $15,448 (single person)
- Drug will cost you $2.00 or 20% of the price allowed by the Department of Human Services whichever is greater.

Maryland

Maryland Pharmacy Assistance Program
PO Box 386
Baltimore, MD 21203
410-767-5397   800-492-1974

- Must be a Maryland resident
- Program is for anyone in the state who can not afford their medications. Call for income requirements.

Michigan

Michigan Elder Prescription Insurance Coverage (EPIC)
PO Box 27586
Richmond, VA 23261
1-866-747-5844
www.miepic.com

- Must be a resident of Michigan
- You must be 65 or older
- You must earn no more than 150% of the federal poverty guidelines
- Must spend 10% or more of your monthly income on drugs
- Must use generic drugs unless your doctor specifies otherwise

Here are other programs you will want to check out if you are a Michigan resident.

Medicare and Medicaid Assistance Progam, call: 1-800-803-7174

Michigan Legal Hotline For Seniors, call: 1-800-347-5297

The Michigan Dental Association has a dental program for seniors. For information, call them toll-free at: 1-800-255-7543

New Jersey

Pharmaceutical Assistance to the Aged and Disabled (PAAD)
Special Benefit Programs
PO Box 715
Trenton, NJ 08625
609-588-7049   800-792-9745

- Must be New Jersey resident and purchase the medications in the state.

- Must be 65 or older; if on social Security disability you may be as young as 18
- Must earn no more than $19,238 if single or $23,589 if married. Partial assistance is available for those who earn up to $10,000 over the income restriction.
- Copay of $5 per prescription. PAAD will collect payments on your behalf from any insurance or other program you may have that covers prescription drugs.

New York

New York State Elderly Pharmaceutical Insurance Coverage (EPIC)
PO Box 15018
Albany, NY 12212
518-452-3773   800-332-3742
www.health.state.ny.us/nysdoh/epic/faq.htm

- Must be New York State resident
- Must be 65 or older
- Your income must not exceed $35,000 if single or $50,000 if married.
- You must not be eligible for Medicaid benefits
- There are two EPIC plans. You can qualify right away by paying an annual fee that will range from $8 to $300 depending upon your income. There is also the EPIC Deductible plan where you pay no fee but you pay full price for the medications until the deductible amount of $530 to $650 is reached. As income increases so does the deductible.

Pennsylvania

Pennsylvania Pharmaceutical Assistance Contract For The Elderly
555 Walnut Street 5th Floor
Harrisburg, PA 17101
717-787-7313   800-225-7223
www.aging.state.pa.us

- Must be a state resident for at least 90 days and purchase the medications in the state.
- Must be 65 or older
- Your income can not exceed $14,000 if single or $17,200 if married. You pay a $6.00 co-payment
- There is also the PACE NET program that allows you to earn more and still qualify. With this program there is a $500 prescription deductible each year.
- The copayment for PACE NET is $15.00 or $8.00 for generic drugs.

Rhode Island

Rhode Island Pharmaceutical Assistance To The Elderly (RIPAE)
Rhode Island Department of Elderly Affairs
160 Pine St
Providence, RI 02903
401-222-2880
www.dea.state.ri.us

- You must be a Rhode Island resident
- Must be 65 or older
- Must have no other prescription drug doverage
- Your income must not exceed $15,000 if single or $41,000 if married
- You pay 60%, 30% or 15% copay depending upon income.
- Program covers drugs needed for the following illnesses: high blood pressure; heart disease; cholesterol; asthma; cancer; Parkinson; glaucoma; diabetes; Alzheimers; and circulatory insufficiency

Vermont

VSCRIPT Program
State Pharmaceutical Assistance Program For Elderly & Disabled
103 S. Main St
Waterbury, VT 05671
802-241-2880   800-250-8427
www.dsw.state.vt.us

- Must be a Vermont resident
- Must be 65 or older
- Your income can not exceed $1,253 per month if single.
- You may not be in a health insurance plan that pays all or part of your prescription drugs.
- You have a copay of $1 for drugs costing up to $30 and $2.00 for drugs costing over $30.

Other Discount Programs

A number of pharmaceutal companies offer special senior discount cards to help with the growing problem of drug affordability. Here are a few:

Glaxo Smith Kline Orange Card
Call 1-888-672-6436
or on the web: www.pharma.us.novartis.com

Lilly Answers Card
1-877-795-4559
www.lillyanswerscard.com

Directory Of Free Prescription Drugs Programs

It's a little known fact but the pharmaceutical industry has had a long tradition of providing prescription medicines free of charge to people who might not otherwise be able to afford to have medicines they need. This directory lists the drug companies with programs that provide prescription medicine for those people. The programs are listed alphabetically by company. Check with the individual manufacturer for the specific requirements to qualify for their free prescription drug program.

Common Questions
Q. I need medication but can not afford to pay for it. Why hasn't my doctor told me about these programs?
A. Believe it or not even many doctors themselves don't know about these programs until you mention it to them.
Q. What are the steps I should take if I need a medication and can't afford it?
A. First, find out from your doctor the name of the drug you need and the manufacturer. Next, go through this directory and find the listing for the manufacturer. If they list the medication you need as one that they offer free for needy patients, have your physician contact the company and request any forms needed to enroll you in their program. As a general rule, the application for free medication must be filled out and returned by your doctor.
Q. Who determines whether a medication is covered?
A. The individual pharmaceutical company determines which drugs are covered.

Q. Who is eligible for the program? How do you apply?
A. Once again each company makes the determination as to
who is eligible for its program. Often they will rely on the
doctor's opinion as to whether he/she feels you are needy
enough to qualify for free medication.

Just because you don't see a drug company listed here doesn't
mean they don't have a program that covers the medicine
you need. For numbers of companies not listed here, ask your
doctor to consult a Physician's Desk Reference (PDR) for the
company's phone number.

Abbott Laboratories

Contact:
Patient Assistance Program
200 Abbott Park Road D31C, J23
Abbott Park, IL 60064
1-800-222-6885 option 1
Product(s) Covered By Program
Isoptin® SRm Mavik, Rythmol®, Synthroid® Tablets, Tarka.
Other Information:
Physician must document the patient's indigence to the
company. A mazimum of three month's supply will be shipped
on any one request.

Alza Pharmaceuticals

Contact:
Indigent Patient Assistance Program
c/o Documedics
1250 Bayhill Dr., Suite 300
San Bruno, CA 94066
(800) 577-3788
Product(s) Covered By Program
Bicitra, Concerta, Ditropan, Ditropan XL, Elmiron, Flexeril,
Mycelex, Neutra-Phos, Neutra-Phos-K Ocusert, PolyCitra,
PolyCitra-K, Progestasert, Testoderm, Urispas.
Other Information:
Eligibility if based on patient's income level and insurance
status. Physician must request the application from Alza

American Pharmaceutical Partners

Contact:
NebuPent® Indigent Drug Program
American Pharmaceutical Partners
1101 Perimeter Drive Suite 300
Schaumberg, IL 60173
1-888-391-6300
Product(s) Covered By Program: NebuPent®
Provided to help AIDS patients who could otherwise not afford the drug.

Amgen, Inc.

NAME OF PROGRAM
Amgen SAFETY NET Program for EPOGEN®
Contact: (800) 272-9376
www.amgen.com
Product Covered By Program: EP0GEN®
Other Information:
The program for dialysis patients who are uninsured or underinsured and is based on patient's income level. Phone-in or written applications are acceptable.

NAME OF PROGRAM
Amgen SAFETY NET® Program for Neupogen®
Contact: (800) 272-9376
Product Covered By Program: Neopogen® (Filgrastim)
Other Information:
For medically indigent patients. To enroll a patient, provider should call 1-800-272-9376

Anzemet

Contact:
Anzemet Hotline
1-800-996-6626
Other Information:
This program is designed for patients who do not have health care insurance outpatient drug benefits but who have been denied coverage for ANZEMET by their insurer.

Astra U.S.A., Inc.

NAME OF PROGRAM
Foscavir@ Assistance and Information on Reimbursement (FA.I.R.)
Contact:
Parexel
5870 Trinity Parkway Suite 600
Centerville, VA 20120
1-800-488-3247
(703) 310-2526 (fax)
Product Covered By Program: Foscavir® Injection
Other Information:
If the patient is not covered by private insurance or public coverage and has an income below a level selected by the company, medication will be provided. Patient does not have to be poor but retail drug purchase would cause financial hardship. Company determines eligibility based upon income information provided by the physician.

AstraZeneca Pharmaceuticals

Contact:
AstraZeneca Foundation Patient Assistance Program
1800 Concord Pike
Box 15437
Wilmington, DE 19850
1-800-424-3727
Product(s) Covered By Program:
Accolate®, Arimidex®, Atacand®, Casodex®, Emla Cream®, Lexxel®, Nexium™, Nolvadex®, Plendil®, Prilosec®, Pulmicort Respules®, Seroquel®, Sorbitrate®, Sular™, Tenoretic®, Tenormin®, Tonocard®, Toprol-XL®, Zestoretic®, Zestril®, Zoladex®, Zomig™

Athena Neurosciences, Inc.

Contact:
Athena Indigent Patient Program
Athena Neurosciences, Inc.
800 Gateway Boulevard South
San Francisco, California 94080
Product(s) Covered By Program
Permax®, Zanaflex®, Diastat®
Other Information:

Patient must have a net worth of less than $30,000 and no third party insurance coverage to qualify. Physician must provide patient's financial information to the company along with a request for the medication on his/her letterhead. Upon approval, three month's supply of the medication will be sent to physician's office

Bayer Corporation
Pharmaceutical Division

Contact:
Bayer Indigent Program
PO. Box 29209 Phoenix
Arizona 85038-9209
(800) 998-9180
Product(s) Covered By Program
Most Bayer pharmaceutical prescription medications used as recommended in prescribing information
Other Information:
Patient must be a U.S. resident, not covered by insurance and have an income below the federal poverty-level guidelines. Physician must monitor medication usage throughout the therapy. Patient/physician can qualify over the phone with approval or denial given immediately.

Biogen, Inc.

Contact:
Avonex Support Line
(800) 456-2255
Product Covered By Program: Avonex®
Other Information:
Eligiblity is based on patient's insurance status and income.

Boehringer Ingelheim
Pharmaceuticals, Inc.

Contact::
Partners in Health
Boehringer Ingelheim Pharmaceuticals, Inc. (BIPI)
P.O. Box 66555
St. Louis, MO 63166

(800) 556-8317 (for information and form)
Product(s) Covered By Program
Aggrenox®, Atrovent®; Catapres-TTS; Combivent®; Flomax®;
Micardis®, Mobic, OramorphSR® tablets, Roxanol™,
Roxicodone.
Other Information:
Patient must be a U.S. citizen who meets established financial
criteria who is ineligible for prescription assistance from
public or private sources. A maximum of 3 months supply of
medication will be supplied per request.

Bristol-Myers Squibb Company

Contact:
Bristol-Myers Squibb
Patient Assistance Program
P.O. Box 4500
Princeton, New Jersey 08543-4500
Mailcode P25-31
(800) 332-2056;
Fax: (609) 897-6859
Product(s) Covered By Program
Many Bristol-Myers Squibb pharmaceutical products
Other Information:
Medications will be supplied free of charge to patients with a
financial hardship and without prescription coverage from
other sources.

Ciba Pharmaceuticals

(See Novartis Pharmaceuticals)

Dupont Pharmaceutical Company

Contact:
DuPont Merck Pharmaceutical Company
Patient Assistance Program
Chestnut Run Plaza Hickory Run Bldg.
974 Center Road
Wilmington, Delaware 19805
(800) 474-2762 Ext 5
Product(s) Covered By Program

All marketed non-controlled prescription products
Other Information:
Physician should request the application by calling the toll-free number above. Patient must have a financial need and have exhausted all third party insurance and other available programs. Patient and physician must complete the application which will be supplied by the company.

Eisai, Inc.

Contact:
The Aricept® Patient Assistance Program
(800) 226-2072
Product(s) Covered By Program: Aricept®
Other Information:
Eisai, Inc. and Pfizer, Inc. have developed this program for U.S. residents with no insurance or other coverage and whose income falls within predetermined guidelines. Patient must have been diagnosed by the physician as having mild or moderate demential of the Alzheimer's type.

Fujisawa U.S.A., Inc.

NAME OF PROGRAM
Prograf™ Patient Assistance Program
Fujisawa Reimbursement Hotline
PO Box 221644
Chantilly, VA 20153
(800) 4-PROGRAF
(800) 477-6472, or
(202) 393-5563 in the Washington, DC area
Product(s) Covered By Program:
Prograf™ capsules
Eligibility
Please call the **Prograf™ Reimbursement Hotline (800-4-PROGRAF)** for an application or for information about eligibility. Once you describe the patient's insurance and financial situation a member of the program staff can determine whether patient is likely to quality.

Genentech, Inc.

Contact
Uninsured Patient Assistance Program

Genentech, Inc.
1 DNA Way
S. San Francisco, CA 94080
(800) 879-4747, (415) 225-1366 (fax)
Product(s) Covered By Program
Actimmune®, Activase®, Protropin®, Nutropin®, Nutropin AQ™, Rituxan™
Other Information:
An application must be submitted with patient's medical, financial and insurance information. To be eligible, patient must have an annual income of less than $25,000 and must not be eligible for public or private insurance reimbursement. Medication will be sent to physician's office.

Genetics Institute, Inc.

NAME OF PROGRAM
The BENEFIX Reimbursement and Information Program
Contact: (888) 999-2349
Product(s) Covered By Program:
Benefix™ Coagulation Factor IX (recombinant)
Other Information:
This program is designed to provide temporary assistance to patients who meet the financial and insurance criteria. Patients must reapply every 90 days. Application forms must be signed by the patient and physician prior to returning to the program at:
1101 King Street, Suite 600
Alexandria, VA 22314.

NAME OF PROGRAM
The Neumega ® Access Program
(888)-NEUMEGA (638-6342)
Product Covered By Program: Neumega®
Other Information:
This program is for uninsured and underinsured patients with limited financial resources.

Genzyme Corp.

NAME OF PROGRAM
Ceredase®/Cerezyme ® Access Program (CAP Program)

Contact:
Wytske Kingma, M.D.
Medical Affairs
Genzyme Corp.
One Kendall Square
Cambridge, MA 01239-1562
(800) 745-4447, ext. 7808
Product(s) Covered By Program
Ceredase®, Cerexyme®
Other Information:
Eligibility is based on financial and medical need. The patient
must be uninsured and lack the financial means to purchase
the drug. In order to maintain eligibility, patient is expected to
continue to explore alternative funding options with the
Genzyme Case Management Specialist.

Gilead Sciences, Inc.

Contact:
Gilead Sciences Support Services
1-800-Gilead 5 (445-3235)
or fax 1-713-760-0049
(9:00 a.m. to 5:30 p.m. EST)
Product Covered By Program:: VISTIDE ®, for the
treatment of cytomegalovirus (CMV) retinitis in patients with
AIDS
Other Information:
To determine eligibility, the patient or physician may request
a Patient Assistance Program application and mail or fax the
completed application to Gilead Sciences Support Services.

Glaxo Wellcome, Inc.

Contact:
Glaxo Wellcome Inc.
Patient Assistance Program
PO Box 52185
Phoenix, Arizona 85072-2185
(800) 722-9294
(800) 750-9832 (fax)
Additional information can be found at: www.Helix.com
Program materials may also be ordered by health
professionals through this website.
Product(s) Covered By Program:

All marketed Glaxo Wellcome prescription products
Other Information:
Glaxo Wellcome is dedicated to assuring that no one is denied
access to their prescription drugs as a result of their inability
to pay. This program is designed for financial disadvantaged
patients who do not qualify for or have drug benefits through
private or government-funded programs. Income eligibility is
based on multiples of the poverty level which is then adjusted
for household size. The program is available only to patients
treated in an outpatient setting.

Hoechst Marion Roussel, Inc.

Contact:
Indigent Patient Program
Hoechst Marion Roussel, Inc.
PO Box 9950
Kansas City, Missouri 64134-0950
(800) 221-4025
Product(s) Covered By Program:
All prescription products manufactured by Hoechst Marion
Roussel, except Rifadin, Rifamate, Rifater, Tenuate
Other Information:
Eligibility is determined by the physician based on the
patient's income level and lack of insurance. Physicians are
encouraged to participate in the spirit of the program by also
providing their services without charge.

NAME OF PROGRAM
Anzement Patient Assistance Program
c/o Comprehensive Reimbursement Consultants (CRC)
8990 Springbrook Drive, Suite 200
Minneapolis, Minnesota 55433
(888) 259-2219
Product(s) Covered By Program: Anzement

Janssen Pharmaceutica

Contact:
Janssen Patient Assistance Program
1800 Robert Fulton Drive

Reston, Virginia 22091-4346
(800) 544-2987
Product(s) Covered By Program:
Janssen's medical prescription products including Duragesic®,
Ergamisol®, Hismanal®, Imodium®, Nizoral® Cream,
Nizoral® Shampoo, Nizoral® Tablet, Propulsid®, Sporanox®,
Vermox®
Other Information:
Medications will be provided free of charge to patients who
lack the financial resources and third-party insurance
necessary to obtain treatment. Janssen requests that
physician not charge patients beyond insurance coverage for
their professional services.

NAME OF PROGRAM
Janssen Cares
The Risperdal Patient Assistance Program
4828 Parkway Plaza Blvd., Suite 120
Charlotte, North Carolina 28217-1969
(800) 652-6227, Monday through Friday
(9:00 a.m. to 5:00 p.m. E.T.)
Fax: (704) 357-0036
Product(s) Covered By Program:
Risperda®
Other Program Information:
Reimbursement specialists will determine eligibility based
upon medical criteria and financial resources. Janssen
requests that physicians not charge patients beyond insurance
coverage for professional services. The Risperdal
Reimbursement Support Program is designed to answer
physicians' and patients' questions and solve problems related
to Risperdal reimbursement as efficiently and quickly as
possible.

Knoll Pharmaceutical Company

Contact:
Knoll Indigent Patient Program
Knoll Pharmaceutical Company
3000 Continental Drive, North
Mount Olive, New Jersey 07828-1234
Attn: Telemarketing
Product(s) Covered By Program

Isoptin ® SR, Mavik, Rythmol®, Collagenase Santyl, Synthroid® Tablets, Tarka
Other Program Information:
Physician must submit documentation proving patient's indigence to the company. A maximum of three month's supply will be supplied on any one request.

Lederle Laboratories

NAME OF PROGRAM
Lederle PARTNERS IN PATIENT CARE™ Assistance Program
(see Wyeth-Ayerst Laboratories Indigent Patient Program)

Eli Lilly And Company

Contact:
Lilly Cares Program Administrator
Eli Lilly and Company
P. O. Box 25768
Alexandria, Virginia 22313
(800) 545-6962
Product(s) Covered By Program:
Most Lilly prescription products and insulins (except controlled substances) are covered by this program. Gemzar® is covered under a separate program.
Other Program Information:
Patients must be U.S. residents. Eligibility is determined on a case-by-case basis based upon patients inability to pay and lack of third-party drug payment assistance. Medications will be provided directly to the physician for dispensing to the patient. Application forms will be provided to the physician to complete and return. Subsequent requests requires another prescription and restatement of medical and financial need.

NAME OF PROGRAM
Gemzar® Patient Assistance Program
Contact:
Gemzar ® Reimbursement Hotline
(888) 4-GEMZAR (888-443-6927)
Product Covered By Program: Gemzar®
Other Program Information:
Applications for the program are available by calling the

Gemzar Hotline. Applicants will be approved on the basis their low income and of their not having medical insurance and being ineligible for any programs with a drug benefit including Medicare and Medicaid and third-party coverage.

The Liposome Company, Inc.

Contact:
Financial Assistance Program for ABELCET®
The Liposome Company, Inc.
One Research Way
Princeton, New Jersey 08540-6619
(800) 335-5476
Product Covered By Program: Abelcet®
Other Program Information:
Eligibility for this program is based upon the patient's financial need and the lack of coverage for any third-party reimbursement program. The company will determine eligibility based upon medical and financial information supplied by the hospital or physician.. Application forms must be completed and signed by a physician.

Merck & Company, Inc.

Contact:
The Merck Patient Assistance Program
Health care professionals with prescribing privileges may call: (800) 994-2111
Product(s) Covered By Program:
Most Merck products are covered. Requests for vaccines and injectables are not accepted with the exception of requests for anti-cancer injectable products.
Other Program Information:
The Merck Patient Assistance Program is designed to provide temporary assistance to patients who truly are unable to afford prescription medications and who have no access to any insurance coverage. Eligibility is determined on a case-by-case basis upon receipt of a completed application signed by both the physician and the patient and accompanied by a prescription. Once the application is approved a three month supply of medication will be sent to the physician for distribution to the patient.

NAME OF PROGRAM
SUPPORT™

Reimbursement Support and Patient
Assistance Services for Crixivan®
Contact: Health care professionals or patients may call (800)
850-3430
Product Covered By Program: Crixivan®

Novartis Pharmaceuticals

Contact:
Novartis Pharmaceuticals
Patient Assistance Program
P. O. Box 52052
Phoenix, Arizona 85072-9170
(800) 257-3273
Product(s) Covered By Program:
Certain single source and/or life-sustaining products.
Controlled substances are not included.
Other Program Information:
The Patient Assistance Program provides temporary
assistance to patients who are experiencing financial hardship
and who have no prescription drug insurance. Patient must
complete the application along with their physician and
return it for evaluation.

Ortho Biotech, Inc.

Contact:
The Ortho Biotech FAP™ Program
1800 Robert Fulton Drive, Suite 300
Reston, Virginia 20191-4346
(800) 553-3851
Product(s) Covered By Program:
Procrit® for non-dialysis use, Leustatin® Injection
Other Program Information:
A reimbursement specialist will determine eligibility for a
patient who meets specific medical criteria and who lack the
financial resources and third-party insurance necessary to
obtain treatment. Ortho Biotech requests that physicians not
charge FAP patients for professional services.

Ortho Dermatological

Contact:

Ortho-McNeil Patient Assistance Program
1800 Robert Fulton Drive, Suite 300
Reston, Virginia 20191-4346
(800) 797-7737
Product(s) Covered By Program:
Prescription products prescribed according to approved
labeled indications and dosage regimens.
Other Program Information:
To be eligible for this program patient should not be eligible
for other sources of drug coverage. They should also have
applied for and been denied for coverage under public sector
programs. Patient's income level should be below poverty level
and retail purchase would cause hardship. Health care
practitioner should request an application form.

Ortho-McNeil Pharmaceutical, Inc.

Contact:
Ortho-McNeil Patient Assistance Program
1800 Robert Fulton Drive, Suite 300
Reston, Virginia 20191-4346
(800) 797-7737
Product(s) Covered By Program:
Prescription products prescribed according to approved
labeled indications and dosage regimens.
Other Program Information:
The program is for indigent patients who lack other sources of
drug coverage including having applied for and been denied
assistance from public sector programs.

Parke-Davis

Division of Warner-Lambert Company
Contact:
The Parke-Davis Patient Assistance Program
P. O. Box 1058
Somerville, New Jersey 08876
(908) 725-1247
Product(s) Covered By Program:
Accupril, Cognex, Dilantin, Loestrin, Neurontin, Rezulin, and
Zarontin
Other Program Information:
The physician should request an application from their sales

representative. Patient must be deemed financially eligible based on company guidelines and the physician's certification and patient's lack of insurance coverage. Up to a three month supply of medication will be supplied to the physician for dispensing.

NAME OF PROGRAM
The Lipitor Patient Assistance Program
P. O. Box 1058
Somerville, New Jersey 08876
(908) 218-0120
Product Covered By Program: Lipitor
Other Program Information:
To be eligible for this program, the patient must not be eligible for other sources of drug coverage and must be deemed financially eligible based on company guidelines and physician certification. Physician should request an application from their Parke-Davis or Pfizer sales representative.

Pasteurmerieux Connaught

NAME OF PROGRAM
Indigent Patient Program
Contact:
Customer Account Management
Pasteur Merieux Connaught
Route 611, PO Box 187
Swiftwater, Pennsylvania 18370-0187
(800) 822-2463
Product(s) Covered By Program:
Imovax® Rabies, rabies vaccine; Imogam ® Rabies-HT, rabies immune globulin (human); TheraCys ® BCG live intravesical (Note: Imovax ® and Imogam® Rabies-HT are provided on a post-exposure basis)
Other Program Information:
Patient must be identified as indigent, uninsured and ineligible for Medicare or Medicaid. Physician must waive all fees and certify that the product will not be sold, traded or used for any other purpose than to treat the patient. Physician needs to specify the quantity of Imogam® Rabies need for patient (in mL) as well as the number of doses of Imovax® Rabies needed.

Pfizer, Inc.

Contact:
Pfizer Prescription Assistance
PO Box 25457
Alexandria, Virginia 22313-5457
(800) 646-4455

Product(s) Covered By Program:
Most Pfizer outpatient products with chronic indications are covered by this program. Diflucan® and Zithromax® are covered by a separate program.

Other Program Information:
Any patient that a physician is treating as indigent is eligible. Patients must have incomes below $12,000 (single) or $15,000 (family). Patient must not be eligible for third-party or Medicaid reimbursement for medications. No copayment or cost-sharing is required by the patient.

Specific forms are not required. The physician must write on his/her letterhead to Pfizer stating that the patient meets the income criteria and is uninsured for prescription drugs. A prescription for the needed medication must also be enclosed. It may take up to 4 weeks to receive the product.

NAME OF PROGRAM
Diflucan® and Zithromax® Patient Assistance Program
(800) 869-9979

Product(s) Covered By Program:
Difucan® and Zithromax®

Other Program Information:
Patient must not have insurance or other third-party coverage including Medicaid and must not be eligible for a state's AIDS drug assistance program. Patient must have an income of less than $25,000 a year without dependents or less than $40,000 a year with dependents.

Physician should call the Program and explain the patient's situation to the Patient Assistance Specialist. The specialist will then send a short qualifying form that requests insurance status, income information and the amount of Diflucan® or Zithromax® the patient will need. Upon receipt of the completed form, the specialist will make the determination of eligibility the same day it is received.

NAME OF PROGRAM
Sharing the Care

Pfizer Inc.
235 E. 42nd Street
New York, New York 10017-5755
(800) 984-1500
Product(s) Covered By Program:
Certain Pfizer single-source products
Eligibility
The program, a joint effort of Pfizer, the National Governors'
Association, and the National Association of Community
Health Centers, works solely through community, migrant,
and homeless health centers that are funded under Section
330 of the Public Health Service Act and that have an in-
house pharmacy. The program includes the participation of
more than 340 health centers throughout the United States.
To be eligible to participate in Sharing the Care, the patient
must be registered at a participating health center, must not
be covered by any private insurance or public assistance
covering pharmaceuticals, must not be Medicaid-enrolled, and
must have a family income that is equal to or below the
federal poverty level.

NAME OF PROGRAM
Aricept® Patient Assistance Program
(See Eisai Inc.)

NAME OF PROGRAM
Lipitor Patient Assistance Program
(Please see Parke-Davis)

NAME OF PROGRAM
A Participant in the Arkansas Health Care Access Program
Contact:
Program Director
Arkansas Health Care Access Foundation
P. O. Box 56248
Little Rock, Arkansas 72215
(800) 950-8233, (501) 221-3033
Product(s) Covered By Program:
Most Pfizer prescription products are covered
Other Program Information:
Must be an Arkansas resident to qualify. Eligible individuals
are certified by the Arkansas Local County Department of
Human Services as being Arkansas residents below the

poverty level who do not have third-party insurance overage for medications. No co-payments is required. Physician must waive his/her fee for the initial visit. This program does not apply to individuals during hospital inpatient stays.

NAME OF PROGRAM
A Participant in the Kentucky Health Care Access Program
Contact:
Program Director
Kentucky Health Care Access Foundation
12700 Shelbyville Road, Suite 1000
Louisville, Kentucky 40243
(800) 633-8100, (502) 244-4214
(502) 244-4209 (fax)
Product(s) Covered By Program
Most Pfizer prescription products are covered
Other Program Information:
Must be a Kentucky resident to qualify. Patient must be certified by the Kentucky Cabinet for Human Resources as Kentuckians below the federal poverty standards without third-party health insurance coverage. No copayment is required from the patient.

NAME OF PROGRAM
A Participant in Commun-I-Care
Contact:
Ms. Parker Sparrow, Director
Commun-I-Care
PO Box 12054
Columbia, South Carolina 29211
(800) 763-0059, (803) 779-4875
(803) 254-0320 (fax)
Product(s) Covered By Program
Most Pfizer prescription products are covered
Other Program Information:
Eligible individuals must be South Carolina residents.
Patients are first certified by Commun-I-Care as below the federal poverty line and not covered by any government entitlement programs. No copayment is required from the patient. Physician must waive his/her fee.

Pharmacia & Upjohn, Inc.

Contact:
Rx MAP Prescription Medication Assistance Program
P. O. Box 29043
Phoenix, Arizona 85038
(800) 242-7014
Product(s) Covered By Program:
Numerous products
Other Program Information:
Eligibility is based on federal poverty level and no prescription drug coverage. All inquiries should be go to RxMAP at 1-800-242-7014.

Proctor & Gamble Pharmaceuticals, Inc.

Contact:
Proctor & Gamble Pharmaceuticals, Inc.
P. O. Box 231
Norwich, New York 13815
Attn: Customer Service Department
(800) 448-4878
Product(s) Covered By Program:
Alora, Asacol, Dantrium Capsules, Didronel, Helidac, Macrodantin, Macrobid
Other Program Information:
The company relies on the physician's assessment of need to determine need. To qualify, patients should not have insurance coverage for prescription medicines or Medicaid reimbursement. The program is intended for patients who fall below the federal poverty level and have no other means of health care coverage.
The amount of product supplied depends on the diagnosis and need but generally one month's supply is provided for chronic medication. Refills require a new prescription and application form from the physician. Medication is sent to the physician who provides it to the patient.

Rhone-Poulen Rorer, Inc.

Contact:
Medical Affairs/Patient Assistance Program
Rhone - Poulenc Rorer Inc.
P. O. Box 5094, 500 Arcola Road

Mailstop #4C29
Collegeville, Pennsylvania 19426-0998
(610) 454-8110, (610) 454-2102 (fax)
Product(s) Covered By Program:
All products are included, with some limitations
Other Program Information:
A patient is eligible for this program if there is a medical and
financial need for assistance as identified by the physician,
social agent or agency and if the effort to obtain assistance
from all third-parties has been exhausted. Application forms
are obtained from the company and completed by the
physician and sent to the company along with a prescription.
Medication will be sent to the physician for dispensing.

Roche Laboratories, Inc.

A Division of Hoffmann-La Roche Inc.
Contact:
Roche Medical Needs Program
Roche Laboratories, Inc.
340 Kingsland Street
Nutley, New Jersey 07110
(800) 285-4484
Product(s) Covered By Program:
Roche product line with some exceptions
Other Program Information:
This program is designed for patients who are unable to afford
to purchase the medication and who have no third-party
medication coverage. It is for individual outpatients and is
offered through physicians. It is not intended for clinics,
hospitals or other institutions.
Applications are provided only to licensed practitioners and a
new application must be completed for refills. Up to a 3 month
supply of the medication will be supplied directly to the
physician within two to three weeks of acceptance to the
program.

NAME OF PROGRAM
Roche Medical Needs Program for CellCept®,
Cytovene®, and Cytovene® -IV
Contact:
Roche Transplant Reimbursement Hotline
(800) 772-5790

Product(s) Covered By Program:
CellCept® , Cytovene®; Cytovene ®-IV; Cytovene products for use with transplant patients

NAME OF PROGRAM
Roche Medical Needs Program for Fortovase™; Invirase®; Cytovene®; Cytovene®-IV, and HIVID®
Contact:
Roche HIV Therapy Assistance Program
(800) 282-7780
Product(s) Covered By Program
Fortovase™; Invirase®; Cytovene®
Cytovene ® -IV, and HIVID®; Cytovene products for use with HIV/AIDS patients

NAME OF PROGRAM
Roche Medical Needs Program for Roferon® -A, Vesanoid®, and Fluorouracil Injection
Contact:
Oncoline™/Hepline™ Reimbursement Hotline
(800) 443-6676 (press 2 or 3)
Product(s) Covered By Program
Roferon® -A, Vesanoid®, and Fluorouracil Injection

Roxane Laboratories, Inc.

Contact:
Nexus Healthcare Patient Assistance Program
4161 Arlingate Plaza
Columbus, Ohio 43228
(800) 274-8651
Product(s) Covered By Program:
Duraclon; Marinol®; Oramorph SR® Tablets; Roxanol™ ; Roxicodone Tablets; Roxicodone Intensol™; Viramune®
Other Program Information:
Medication will be provided free of charge through the patient's pharmacist, provided the patient is uninsured and meets annual income requirements.
The physician should call the toll-free number to discuss their patient's eligibility with a program representative.

Sandoz Pharmaceuticals Corporation

(See Novartis Pharmaceuticals).

Sanofi Pharmaceuticals

Contact:
Sanofi Pharmaceuticals
Needy Patient Program
c/o Product Information Department
90 Park Avenue
New York, New York 10016
(800) 446-6267
Product(s) Covered By Program
Aralen®, Breonesin®, Danocrine®, Drisdol®, Hytakerol®, Mytelase®, NegGram®, pHisoHex® , Plaquenil® , Primaquine®, Skelid® Photofrin®, Primacor®.
Other Program Information:
Eligibility determined on financial need on a case-by-case basis. Physician can obtain an application from the Sanofi Pharmaceuticals Product Information Department. Once the application is approved by the company, a three month supply of the medication will be sent directly to the physician in roughly four to six weeks. Each physician is allowed to enroll six patients per year.

Schering Laboratories/Key Pharmaceuticals

NAME OF PROGRAM
Commitment to Care
Contact:
For Intron A/Eulexin call: (800) 521-7157
For Other Products:
Schering Laboratories/Key Pharmaceuticals
Patient Assistance Program
PO Box 52122
Phoenix, Arizona 85072
(800) 656-9485
Product(s) Covered By Program:
Most Schering/Key prescription drugs
Other Program Information:
This program is designed to help patients who are truly in

need - who are not eligible for private or public insurance reimbursement and cannot afford treatment.
Physician and patient complete an application form which will be reviewed on a case-by-case basis.

Searle

Contact:
Administrator
Searle Patients in Need® Foundation
5200 Old Orchard Road
Skokie, Illinois 60077
(800) 542-2526
Fax: (1-847) 470-6633
or Local Searle Sales Representative
Product(s) Covered By Program:
Antihypertensives: Aldactazide®, Aldactone®, Calan® SR sustained-release, Kerl one® Antihypertensive/Anti-Anginal/ Antiarrhythmic: Calan®, Covera-HS™
Antiarrhythmics: Norpace®, Norpace® CR extended-release
Prevention of NSAID-induced gastric ulcers: Cytotec®
Other Program Information:
The physician is the sole determinant of a patient's eligibility for this program based on the patient's medical and financial need. Searle provides guidelines for physicians to consider but they are not requirements. Searle does not review documentation for eligibility.
The guidelines suggest that: patient has a medical need for the Searle Patients In Need® medication; does not qualify for third-party medication coverage and that the patient's income falls below a level suggested by Searle.
Once approved Searle will send the physician certificates for free medications. The physician gives the certificate to the patient who takes the prescription and certificate to a pharmacy of their choosing. The pharmacy supplies the medication free of charge and is then reimbursed by Searle.

Serono Laboratories, Inc.

NAME OF PROGRAM
Patient Assistance Programs
Contact:
Executive Director, Corporate Communications

Serono Laboratories, Inc.
100 Longwater Circle
Norwell, Massachusetts 02061
(617) 982-9000, (617) 982-1369 (fax)
Product(s) Covered By Program:
Saizen® for injection for treatment of pediatric growth
hormone deficiency
Serostim™ for treatment of AIDS

NAME OF PROGRAM
Serono Laboratories' Helping Hands Program
Contact:
Helping Hands Program
Serono Laboratories, Inc.
100 Longwater Circle
Norwell, Massachusetts 02061
(617) 982-9000 ext. 5522,
(617) 982-1369 (fax)
Product(s) Covered By Program:
Fertinex™, Gonal-F for treatment of infertility

Sigma-Tau Pharmaceuticals, Inc.
NAME OF PROGRAM
NORD/Sigma-Tau Carnitor®
Drug Assistance (CDA) Program
c/o NORD
P. O. Box 8923
New Fairfield, Connecticut 06812-8923
(800) 999-NORD
Product(s) Covered By Program:
Carnitor®
Other Program Information:
Usually a patient over the age of 18 may submit his/her own
application. If the patient is a minor his/her parent or
guardian must submit the application.
To be eligible, patient must be a resident of U.S. with a legal
prescription for Carnitor®. They must show that they have
financial need above and beyond any third-party insurance or
family resources.

SmithKline Beecham Pharmaceuticals

Contact:
SB Access to Care Program
SmithKline Beecham
One Franklin Plaza-FPl320
Philadelphia, Pennsylvania 19101
(800) 546-0420

Product(s) Covered By Program:
Most SmithKline Beecham outpatient prescription products
are covered. Controlled substances and vaccines are not.
Kytril, Hycamtin and Paxil are covered under separate Access
to Care programs. (See listings below.)

Other Program Information:
To be eligible, patient's annual household income must be less
than $25,000. They must not have medical insurance or
coverage under any private of government program that
covers prescriptions. Physician must submit the application on
an original (not photocopied) SB Access To Care form supplied
by the company. The physician and patient must certify that
the program guidelines are being observed. Medication will be
sent to the physician for dispensing.

NAME OF PROGRAM
The Oncology Access to Care Hotline
(800) 699-3806
Product(s) Covered By Program: Kytril and Hycamtin

NAME OF PROGRAM
Access to Care Paxil Certificate Program
Contact: (800) 729-4544
Product(s) Covered By Program: Paxil®

Solvay Pharmaceuticals, Inc.

NAME OF PROGRAM
Patient Assistance Program
Solvay Pharmaceuticals, Inc.
c/o Phoenix Marketing Group
One Phoenix Drive
Lincoln Park, New Jersey 07035
(800) 788-9277

Product(s) Covered By Program:
Creon® 5, 10 or 20 Minimicrospheres™ Delayed-Release
Capsules; Dexone™ tablets; Estrata B®; Estratest® &

Estratest® HS Tablets; Lithobid® Slow- Release Tablets; Lithonate®; Lithotabs®; Luvox® Tablets; Orasone™ Tablets; Amantadine HCl Capsules; Advanced Formula Zenate® Prenatal Multivitamin/ Mineral Supplement Tablets.
Other Program Information:
The patient's eligibility is determined in consultation with the physician and is based on the patient's inability to pay, lack of insurance and ineligibility for Medicaid. The physician is encouraged to waive their fee.
The physician must apply on behalf of the patient by submitting completing a request form obtained by call Solvay's Patient Assistance Program Message Center at 1-800-788-9277.

3M Pharmaceuticals

NAME OF PROGRAM
Indigent Patient Pharmaceutical Program
Contact:
Medical Services Department
275-2E-13, 3M Center
PO Box 33275
St. Paul, Minnesota 55133-3275
(800) 328-0255, (612) 733-6068 (fax)
Product(s) Covered By Program:
Most drug products sold by 3M Pharmaceuticals in the U.S.
Other Program Information:
Patients whose financial and insurance circumstances prevent them from obtaining 3M Pharmaceuticals drug products considered necessary by their physicians. Consideration is on a case-by-case basis.

Wyeth-Ayerst Laboratories

Contact:
The Norplant Foundation
P. O. Box 25223
Alexandria, VA 22314
(703) 706-5933
Product Covered By Program: The Norplant® five-year contraceptive system
Eligibility
Determined on a case-by-case basis and limited to individuals who cannot afford the product and who are ineligible for coverage under private and public sector programs .
Other Program Information:

Eligibility is on a case-by-case basis and is limited to individuals who cannot afford the product and who are ineligible for coverage under private and public sector programs.

NAME OF PROGRAM
Wyeth-Ayerst Laboratories Indigent Patient Program
555 E. Lancaster Avenue
St. Davids, Pennsylvania 19087
Product(s) Covered By Program:
Various products (not including schedule II, III, or IV products)
Eligibility
Limited to individuals, on a case-by-case basis, who have been identified by their physicians as "indigent," meaning: low or no income or not covered by any third-party agency
Other Program Information:
A three-month supply of specific products is provided directly to the physician for dispensing to the patient. The patient's signature is required on the application form.

Free Legal Services

Free Legal Help

If you have a legal problem and can't afford to pay a small fortune for an attorney, you can now get free legal assistance thanks to funding from the U.S. Government. To help you get the kind of legal help you need but can not afford, Congress has given close to 300 million dollars to The Legal Services Corporation. They in turn provide funds for 262 local Legal Services offices throughout the U.S. to give you legal assistance. The funding is used to help over 4 million low-income individuals in civil cases. To find out about the free Legal Services in your area check the listings below or contact Legal Services Corporation directly.

LEGAL SERVICES CORPORATION
750 FIRST ST., N.E.
WASHINGTON, DC 20002
(202) 336-8800

You can also get the information you need about local Legal Services programs in your area by visiting their Internet site at:
www.lsc.gov

In addition to the legal services funded by the federal government, there are hundreds of what are called 'pro bono' (in other words ... 'free') programs which are staffed by attorneys who volunteer their time and services to insure that you get the legal representation you deserve. The following is a listing of these programs. Simply call the program closest to your home for legal assistance.

Alabama
**Alabama State Bar Volunteer
Lawyers Program**
415 Dexter Ave.
Montgomery, AL 36105
Phone: 334-269-1515

**Legal Services Corporation of
Alabama**
500 Bell Building
207 Montgomery St.
Montgomery, AL 36104-3534
(334) 264-1471

**Legal Services of North-Central
Alabama**
2000-C Vernon St.
P.O. Box 2465
Huntsville, AL 35804-2465
(205) 536-9645

**Legal Services of Metro
Birmingham**
1820 Seventh Ave., North
P.O. Box 11765
Birmingham, AL 35202-1765
(205) 328-3540

Alaska
**Alaska Legal Services
Corporation**
1016 West Sixth Ave., Suite 200
Anchorage, AK 99501-6206
(907) 276-6282

Alaska Pro Bono Program
1016 W. 6th Ave.
Suite 200
Anchorage, AK 99501
Phone: 901-272-9431

Arizona
**Pinal & Gila Counties Legal Aid
Society**
343 West Central Ave.
Coolidge, AZ 85228
(520) 723-5326

Community Legal Services
305 South Second Ave.
P.O. Box 21538
Phoenix, AZ 85036-1538
(602) 258-3434 x 230

Papago Legal Services
Main St. & Education St.
P.O. Box 246
Sells, AZ 85634-0246
(520) 383-2420

Southern Arizona Legal Aid
64 East Broadway Boulevard
Tucson, AZ 85701-1720
(520) 623-9465

DNA-People's Legal Services
Route 12, Highway 264
P.O. Box 306
Window Rock, AZ 86515-0306
(520) 871-4151

**Affordable Housing Law
Program**
Arizona Commnunity Service Legal
Assistance
111 W. Monroe, Ste. 1800
Phoenix, AZ 85003
Phone: 602-340-7372

Disability Claim Service
Disability Advocacy Project
1314 N. 3rd St., Suite 116
Phoenix, AZ 85004-1749
Phone: 602-256-9673

Arkansas
**Arkansas Volunteer Lawyers for
the Elderly**
2020 W. 3rd St., Suite 620
Little Rock, AR 72201
Phone: 501-376-9263

Ozark Legal Services
26 East Center St.
Fayetteville, AR 72701
(501) 442-0600

Legal Services of Northeast Arkansas
202 Walnut St.
Newport, AR 72112
(870) 523-9892

Western Arkansas Legal Services
100 North Sixth St., Suite 107
Fort Smith, AR 72901-2197
(501) 785-5211

East Arkansas Legal Services
500 East Broadway
P.O. Box 1149
West Memphis, AR 72303-1149
(870) 732-6370

Center for Arkansas Legal Services
209 West Capitol Ave., Suite 36
Little Rock, AR 72201-3678
(501) 376-3423

California

California Indian Legal Services
510 16th St., Suite 301
Oakland, CA 94612-1500
(510) 835-0284

Greater Bakersfield Legal Assistance
615 California Ave.
Bakersfield, CA 93304
(805) 325-5943

Central California Legal Services
2014 Tulare St., Suite 600
Fresno, CA 93721
(209) 441-1611

Legal Aid Foundation of Long Beach
Security Pacific Bank Building
110 Pine Ave., Suite 420
Long Beach, CA 90802-4421
(562) 435-3501

Legal Aid Foundation of Los Angeles
1102 South Crenshaw Boulevard
Los Angeles, CA 90019
(213) 801-7990

Legal Aid Society of Alameda County
510 16th St., Suite 560
Oakland, CA 94612
(510) 451-9261

Channel Counties Legal Services Association
132 South A St.
P.O. Box 1228
Oxnard, CA 93032-1228
(805) 487-6531

San Fernando Valley Neighborhood Legal Services
13327 Van Nuys Boulevard
Pacoima, CA 91331-3099
(818) 834-7509

Legal Services Program for Pasadena and San Gabriel-Pomona Valley
243 East Mission Boulevard
Pomona, CA 91766
(909) 620-5547

Legal Aid Society of San Mateo County
298 Fuller St.
Redwood City, CA 94063
(415) 365-8411

Contra Costa Legal Services Foundation
1017 MacDonald Ave.
P.O. Box 2289
Richmond, CA 94802-2289
(510) 233-9954

Inland Counties Legal Services
1120 Palmyrita Ave., Suite 210
Riverside, CA 92507
(909) 683-5841 x429

Legal Services of Northern California Inc.
517 12th St.
Sacramento, CA 95814
(916) 551-2150

Legal Aid Society of San Diego
110 South Euclid Ave.
San Diego, CA 92114
(619) 262-5557 x320

California Rural Legal Assistance
631 Howard St., Suite 300
San Francisco, CA 94105-3907
(415) 777-2752

San Francisco Neighborhood Legal Assistance Foundation
225 Bush St., 7th Floor
San Francisco, CA 94104
(415) 982-1300

Legal Aid of Marin
30 North San Pedro Rd., Suite 245
San Rafael, CA 94903
(415) 492-0230

Community Legal Services
2 West Santa Clara St., 8th Floor
P.O. Box 1840
San José, CA 95109-1840
(408) 283-3844

Legal Aid Society of Orange County
902 North Main St.
Santa Ana, CA 92701
(714) 571-5233

Legal Aid Society of the Central Coast
21 Carr St.
Watsonville, CA 95076
(408) 724-2253

Redwood Legal Assistance
123 Third St.
P.O. Box 1017
Eureka, CA 95502
(707) 445-0866

The State Bar of California
Office of Legal Services
555 Franklin St.
San Francisco, CA 94102

Disability Rights Education and Defense Fund
2212 Sixth St.
Berkeley, CA 94710
Phone: 510-644-2555

Colorado
Pikes Peak/Arkansas River Legal Aid
617 South Nevada Ave.
Colorado Springs, CO 80903-4089
(719) 471-0380

Colorado Rural Legal Services
655 Broadway, Suite 450
Denver, CO 80203
(303) 534-5702

Legal Aid Society of Metropolitan Denver
1905 Sherman St., Suite 400
Denver, CO 80203-1181
(303) 866-9399

Colorado Bar Association Pro Bono Project
1900 Grant St., 9th Floor
Denver, CO 80203
Phone: 303-860-1115

Connecticut
Statewide Legal Services of Connecticut
425 Main St.
Middletown, CT 06457
Phone: 860-344-8096 ext. 3003

Connecticut Bar Association Law
Works for People
101 Corporate Place
Rocky Hill, CT 06067-1894
Phone: 800-722-8811

AIDS Legal Network for Connecticut (ALN)
80 Jefferson St.
Hartford, CT 06106
Phone: 860-541-5000

Delaware
Legal Services Corporation of Delaware
100 West 10th St., Suite 203
Wilmington, DE 19801
(302) 575-0408

Delaware Volunteer Legal Services
Widener University School of Law,
Concord Pike
P.O. Box 7306
Wilmington, DE 19803
Phone: 302-478-8680

District of Columbia
Neighborhood Legal Services Program of the District of Columbia
701 Fourth St., N.W.
Washington, DC 20001
(202) 682-2720

American Association of Retired Persons
601 E St., N.W.
Building A, 4th Floor
Washington, DC 20049
Phone: 202-434-2120

Archdiocesan Legal Network
Catholic Charities of Washington, D.C.
1221 Massachusetts Ave., N.W.
Washington, DC 20005
Phone: 202-628-4265

Asylum & Refugee Rights Law Project
of Washington Lawyers' Committee for Civil Rights
1300 19th St., NW, Suite 500
Washington, DC 20005
Phone: 202-835-0031

DC Bar Public Services Activities Corporation
1250 H St., NW
Sixth Floor
Washington, DC 20005-3908
Phone: 202-737-4700 ext. 290

Florida
Central Florida Legal Services
128-A Orange Ave.
Daytona Beach, FL 32114-4310
(904) 255-6573

Legal Aid Society of Broward County
609 S.W. Firth Ave.
Fort Lauderdale, FL 33301
(954) 764-8957 x223

Florida Rural Legal Services
963 East Memorial Boulevard
P.O. Box 24688
Lakeland, FL 33802-4688
(941) 688-7376

Jacksonville Area Legal Aid
126 West Adams St.
Jacksonville, FL 32202-3849
(904) 356-8371

Legal Services of Greater Miami
3000 Biscayne Boulevard
Miami, FL 33137
(305) 576-0080 x501

Legal Services of North Florida
2119 Delta Boulevard
Tallahassee, FL 32303-4209
(904) 385-9007

Greater Orlando Area Legal Services
1036 West Amelia St.
Orlando, FL 32805
(407) 841-7777

Bay Area Legal Services
Riverbrook Professional Center, 2nd Floor
829 West Dr. Martin Luther King Jr. Boulevard
Tampa, FL 33603
(813) 232-1222 x137

Withlacoochee Area Legal Services
20 South Magnolia Ave.
Ocala, FL 32671-2037
(352) 629-0105

Three Rivers Legal Services
111 Southwest First St.
Gainesville, FL 32601
(352) 372-0519

Northwest Florida Legal Services
24 West Government St., Suite 205
P.O. Box 1551
Pensacola, FL 32597-1551
(850) 432-1750

Gulfcoast Legal Services
641 First St. South
St. Petersburg, FL 33701-5003
(813) 821-0726

Florida Association for Community Action
901 Northwest 8th Ave.
Suite A-2
Gainesville, FL 32601
Phone: 352-378-6517

Georgia
Atlanta Legal Aid Society
151 Spring St., N.W.
Atlanta, GA 30303-2097
(404) 614-3990

Georgia Legal Services Program
1100 Spring St., Suite 200-A
Atlanta, GA 30309-2848
(404) 206-5175

Guam
Guam Legal Services Corporation
113 Bradley Place
Agana, GU 96910
011-671-477-9811

The Pro Bono Project of the State Bar of Georgia
The Hurt Building
50 Hurt Plaza
Atlanta, GA 30303
Phone: 404-527-8762

Hawaii
Native Hawaiian Legal Corporation
1164 Bishop St., Suite 1205
Honolulu, HI 96813-2826
(808) 521-2302

Legal Aid Society of Hawaii
1108 Nuuanu Ave.
P.O. Box 37375
Honolulu, HI 96837-0375
(808) 536-4302

Hawaii Lawyers Care
1040 Richards St.
Suite 301
Honolulu, HI 96813
Phone: 808-528-7046

Idaho
Idaho Legal Aid Services
Contract Program
310 North Fifth St.
P.O. Box 913
Boise, ID 83701
Phone: 208-336-8980

Idaho Volunteer Lawyers Program
P.O. Box 895
Boise, ID 83701-0895
Phone: 208-334-4510

Illinois
Cook County Legal Assistance Foundation
1146 Westgate, Suite LL3
Oak Park, IL 60301-1055
(708) 524-2600

Legal Assistance Foundation of Chicago
111 West Jackson Boulevard, 3rd Floor
Chicago, IL 60604-3502
(312) 341-1070

Land of Lincoln Legal Assistance Foundation
2420 Bloomer Drive
Alton, IL 62002-4809
(618) 462-0036 x13

975 North Main St.
Rockford, IL 61103-7064
(815) 965-2134

West Central Illinois Legal Assistance
1614 East Knox St.
P.O. Box 1232
Galesburgh, IL 61402-1232
(309) 343-2141

Illinois Pro Bono Center
C-U Depot
116 N. Chestnut, Suite 220
Champaign, IL 61820
Phone: 217-359-6811

Lawyers for the Creative Arts
213 W. Institute Place
Suite 411
Chicago, IL 60610-3125
Phone: 312-944-2787

Indiana
Legal Services of Maumee Valley
203 West Wayne St., Suite 410
Fort Wayne, IN 46802
(219) 422-8070

Legal Services of Northwest Indiana
504 North Broadway, Suite 301
Gary, IN 46402-1921
(219) 886-3161

Legal Services Organization of Indiana
Market Square Center, Suite 1640
151 North Delaware St.
Indianapolis, IN 46204-2517
(317) 631-9410

Legal Services Program of Northern Indiana
105 East Jefferson Boulevard, Suite 600
South Bend, IN 46601-1915
(219) 234-8121

Iowa
Legal Services Corporation of Iowa
1111 Ninth St., Suite 230
Des Moines, IA 50314-2527
(515) 243-2151

Legal Aid Society of Polk County
Human Service Campus
1111 Ninth St., Suite 380
Des Moines, IA 50314-2527
(515) 282-8375

Iowa State Bar Association
Volunteer Lawyers Project
521 E. Locust
Suite 302
Des Moines, IA 50309
Phone: 515-244-8617

Kansas
Kansas Bar Foundation
1200 Harrison
Topeka, KS 66612
Phone: 913-234-5696

Kentucky
Access to Justice Foundation
209 E. High St.
Lexington, KY 40508
Phone: 606-255-9913

Louisiana
Louisiana Bar Association
Access to Justice Foundation
601 St. Charles Ave.
New Orleans, LA 70130
Phone: 504-566-1600

**Eighth Coast Guard District
Legal Office**
Room 1311 Hale Boggs Federal
Building
501 Magazine St.
New Orleans, LA 70130
Phone: 504-589-6188

Maine
Maine Volunteer Lawyers Project
66 Federal St.
Portland, ME 04101
Phone: 207-828-2300

Maryland
Advocates for Children & Youth
School House Legal Services
34 Market Place, Suite 500
Baltimore, MD 21202
Phone: 410-547-9200

Massachusetts
**American Civil Liberties Union
of Massachusetts**
99 Chauncy St.
Boston, MA 02111
Phone: 617-482-3170

Michigan
**Legal Services of Southeastern
Michigan**
420 North Fourth Ave.
Ann Arbor, MI 48104-1197
(734) 665-6181

**Legal Services Organization of
Southcentral Michigan**
70 East Michigan Ave., 2nd Floor
Battle Creek, MI 49017
(616) 965-3951

**Wayne County Neighborhood
Legal Services**
3400 Cadillac Tower Building, Ste 1
Detroit, MI 48226
(313) 962-0466

**Legal Services of Eastern
Michigan**
547 South Saginaw St.
Flint, MI 48502
(810) 234-2621

Legal Aid of Central Michigan
300 North Washington Square, Suite
311
Lansing, MI 48933-1223
(517) 485-5418 x235

Lakeshore Legal Services
Robert A. Verkuilen Building
21885 Dunham Road, Suite 4
Clinton Township, MI 48036
(810) 469-5185

Oakland Livingston Legal Aid
35 West Huron St., 5th Floor
Pontiac, MI 48342-2125
(248) 456-8888

**Berrien County Legal Services
Bureau**
901 Port St.
P.O. Box E
St. Joseph, MI 49085-0904
(616) 983-6363

**Legal Services of Northern
Michigan**
446 East Mitchell St.

Petoskey, MI 49770
(616) 347-8115

Legal Aid of Western Michigan
Cornerstone Building, Suite 400
89 Ionia Ave., N.W.
Grand Rapids, MI 49503
(616) 774-0672

Legal Aid Bureau of Southwestern Michigan
308 Kalamazoo County
Administration Building
201 West Kalamazoo Ave.
Kalamazoo, MI 49007-3777

Michigan Indian Legal Services
160 East State St., Suite 102
Traverse City, MI 49684-2572
(616) 947-0122

State Bar of Michigan
Access to Justice
306 Townsend St.
Lansing, MI 48933-2083
Phone: 517-372-9030 ext. 6317

Micronesia
Micronesian Legal Services Corporation
P.O. Box 269
Saipan, MP 96950-0269
011-670-234-6471

Minnesota
Legal Aid Service of Northeastern Minnesota
302 Ordean Building
424 West Superior St.
Duluth, MN 55802
(218) 726-4800

Judicare of Anoka County
1201 89th Ave., N.E., Suite 310
Blaine, MN 55434
(612) 783-4970

Central Minnesota Legal Services
430 First Ave. North, Suite 359
Minneapolis, MN 55401-1780

(612) 332-8151

Legal Services of Northwest Minnesota Corporation
403 Center Ave., Suite 403
P.O. Box 714
Moorhead, MN 56561-0714
(218) 233-8585

Southern Minnesota Regional Legal Services
700 Minnesota Building
46 East Fourth St.
St. Paul, MN 55101-1112
(612) 228-9823

Anishinabe Legal Services
411 First St., N.W.
P.O. Box 157
Cass Lake, MN 56633-0157
(218) 335-2223

Minnesota Volunteer Attorney Program
Minnesota State Bar Association
Minnesota Law Center
514 Nicollet Mall, Suite 300
Minneapolis, MN 55402
Phone: 612-673-6331

Mississippi
Central Mississippi Legal Services
414 South State St., 3rd Floor
P.O. Box 951
Jackson, MS 39205-0951
(601) 948-6752

North Mississippi Rural Legal Services
2134 West Jackson Ave.
P.O. Box 767
Oxford, MS 38655-0767
(601) 234-8731

South Mississippi Legal Services Corporation
202 Fountain Square Building
P.O. Box 1386
Biloxi, MS 39533-1386
(228) 374-4160

East Mississippi Legal Services Corporation
2305 Fifth St., 2nd Floor
P.O. Box 1931
Meridian, MS 39302
(601) 693-5470

Southeast Mississippi Legal Services Corporation
111 East Front St.
P.O. Drawer 1728
Hattiesburg, MS 39403-1728
(601) 545-2950

Southwest Mississippi Legal Services Corporation
221 Main St.
P.O. Box 1242
McComb, MS 39649-1242
(601) 684-0578

Mississippi Volunteer Lawyers Project
P.O. Box 2168
Jackson, MS 39225-2168
Phone: 601-948-4476

Missouri
Southwest Missouri Legal Services
116 North Main St.
P.O. Box 349
Charleston, MO 63834-0309
(573) 683-3783

Meramec Area Legal Aid Corporation
1412 Highway 72 East
P.O. Box 135
Rolla, MO 65401-0135
(573) 341-3655

Legal Aid of Western Missouri
Lathrop Building
1005 Grand Ave., Suite 600
Kansas City, MO 64106-2216
(816) 474-6750

Legal Services of Eastern Missouri
4232 Forest Park Ave.
St. Louis, MO 63108
(314) 534-4200

Mid-Missouri Legal Services Corporation
205 East Forest Ave.
Columbia, MO 65201
(573) 442-0116

Legal Aid of Southwest Missouri
Woodruff Building
333 Park Central East, Suite 426
Springfield, MO 65806-2227
(417) 862-1100

Paralegal Farm Project
P.O. Box 1086
St. Joseph, MO 64502-1086
Phone: 816-364-2325

Montana
Montana Legal Services Association
801 North Last Chance Gulch
Helena, MT 59601
(406) 442-9830

State Bar of Montana Pro Bono Project
2442 1st Ave. No.
Billings, MT 59101
Phone: 406-252-6351

Nebraska
Legal Services of Southeast Nebraska
Terminal Building, Suite 825
941 O St.
Lincoln, NE 68508
(402) 435-2161

Legal Aid Society
500 South 18th St., 3rd Floor
Omaha, NE 68102-2588
(402) 348-1060

Western Nebraska Legal Services
1423 First Ave.
P.O. Box 1365
Scottsbluff, NE 69363-1365
(308) 632-4734

Nebraska State Bar Association
Volunteer Lawyers Project
635 S. 14th St., Ste. 200
Lincoln, NE 68501
Phone: 402-475-7091

Nevada
Nevada Legal Services
701 East Bridger Ave., Suite 101
Las Vegas, NV 89101
(702) 386-1070

New Hampshire
New Hampshire Legal Services
33 North Main St., 2nd Floor
P.O. Box 4147
Concord, NH 03302-4147
(603) 224-5723

The Pro Bono Referral of the New Hampshire Bar Association
112 Pleasant St.
Concord, NH 03301
Phone: 603-224-6942

New Jersey
Cape-Atlantic Legal Services
One So. South Carolina Ave.
Atlantic City, NJ 08401
(609) 348-4200

Warren County Legal Services
91 Front St.
P.O. Box 65
Belvidere, NJ 07823-0065
(908) 475-2010

Camden Regional Legal Services
745 Market St.
Camden, NJ 08102-1117
(609) 964-2010 x233

Union County Legal Services Corporation
60 Prince St.
Elizabeth, NJ 07208
(908) 354-4340

Hunterdon County Legal Service Corporation
82 Park Ave.
Flemington, NJ 08822-1170
(908) 782-7979

Bergen County Legal Services
47 Essex St.
Hackensack, NJ 07601
(201) 487-2166

Hudson County Legal Services Corporation
574 Newark Ave.
Jersey City, NJ 07306-2377
(201) 792-6363

Essex-Newark Legal Services Project
106 Halsey St.
Newark, NJ 07102
(973) 624-4500

Middlesex County Legal Services Corporation
78 New St., 3rd Floor
New Brunswick, NJ 08901-2584
(732) 249-7600

Passaic County Legal Aid Society
175 Market St., 4th Floor
Paterson, NJ 07505
(973) 345-7171

Somerset-Sussex Legal Services Corporation
78 Grove St.
Somerville, NJ 08876
(908) 231-0840

Ocean-Monmouth Legal Services
9 Robbins St., Suite 2A
Toms River, NJ 08753
(732) 341-2727

Legal Aid Society of Mercer County
16-18 West Lafayette St.
Trenton, NJ 08608-2088
(609) 695-6249

Legal Aid Society of Morris County
30 Schuyler Place, 2nd Floor
P.O. Box 900
Morristown, NJ 07963-0900
(973) 285-6911

New Mexico
Legal Aid Society of Albuquerque
Springer Square Building
121 Tijeras Ave., N.E., Suite 3100
Albuquerque, NM 87102
(505) 243-7871

Southern New Mexico Legal Services
300 North Downtown Mall
Las Cruces, NM 88001-1216
(505) 541-4800

Northern New Mexico Legal Services
805 Early St., Building F
P.O. Box 5175
Santa Fe, NM 87502-5175
(505) 982-2504

Indian Pueblo Legal Services
7 Eagle Road, Santa Ana Pueblo
P.O. Box 817
Bernalillo, NM 87004-0817
(505) 867-3391

Lawyers Care Pro Bono Project
State Bar of New Mexico
Special Projects
5121 Masthead NE
Albuquerque, NM 87109
Phone: 505-797-1640

New York
Legal Aid Society of Northeastern New York
55 Columbia St.
Albany, NY 12207
(518) 462-1672 x304

Legal Aid for Broome and Chenango
30 Fayette St.
P.O. Box 2011
Binghamton, NY 13902-2011
(607) 723-7966

Neighborhood Legal Services
Ellicott Square Building, Room 495
295 Main St.
Buffalo, NY 14203-2473
(716) 847-0650

Chautauqua County Legal Services
7 West Third St., 2nd Floor
Jamestown, NY 14701-5103
(716) 483-2116

Chemung County Neighborhood Legal Services
318 Madison Ave.
Elmire, NY 14901-2889
(607) 734-1647

Nassau/Suffolk Law Services Committee
One Helen Keller Way, 5th Floor
Hempstead, NY 11550
(516) 292-8100

Legal Aid Society of Rockland County
2 Congers Road
New City, NY 10956-0314
(914) 634-3627

Legal Services for New York City
350 Broadway, 6th Floor
New York, NY 10013-9998
(212) 431-7200

Niagara County Legal Aid Society
775 Third St.

P.O. Box 844
Niagara Falls, NY 14302-0844
(716) 284-8831

Monroe County Legal Assistance Corporation
80 St. Paul St., Suite 700
Rochester, NY 14604-1350
(716) 325-2520

Legal Services of Central New York
472 South Salina St., Suite 300
Syracuse, NY 13202
(315) 475-3127

Legal Aid Society of Mid-New York
255 Genesee St., 2nd Floor
Utica, NY 13501-3405
(315) 732-2131

Westchester/Putnam Legal Services
4 Cromwell Place
White Plains, NY 10601
(914) 949-1305

North County Legal Services
100 Court St.
P.O. Box 989
Plattsburgh, NY 12901-0989
(518) 563-4022

Southern Tier Legal Services
104 East Steuben St.
Bath, NY 14810
(607) 776-4126

Asian American Legal Defense and Education Fund (AALDEF)
99 Hudson St., 12th Floor
New York, NY 10013
Phone: 212-966-5932

Covenant House
Legal Services Office
460 West 41st St., Suite 715
New York, NY 10036

American Civil Liberties Union
125 Broad St., 18th Fl.

New York, NY 10036
Phone: 212-549-2500

Department of Pro Bono Affairs
One Elk St.
Albany, NY 12207
Phone: 518-487-5641

The Door's Legal Services Center
121 6th Ave.
New York, NY 10013
Phone: 212-941-9090 ext. 233

Prisoners' Legal Services of New York
105 Chambers St.
New York, NY 10007
Phone: 212-513-7373

United States Court of Appeals for the Second Circuit Pro Bono Panel
United States Courthouse
40 Centre St.
New York, NY 10007
Phone: 212-857-8800

Volunteer Lawyers for the Arts
1 E. 53rd St., 6th Flr.
New York, NY 10022
Phone: 212-319-2787

North Carolina

Legal Services of North Carolina
224 South Dawson St.
P.O. Box 26087
Raleigh, NC 27611-6087
(919) 856-2564

Legal Services of Southern Piedmont
1431 Elizabeth Ave.
Charlotte, NC 28204
(704) 376-1600

North Central Legal Assistance Program
301 West Main St., 5th Floor
P.O. Box 2101
Durham, NC 27702-2101
(919) 688-6396

Legal Aid Society of Northwest North Carolina
Patten Building
216 West Fourth St.
Winston-Salem, NC 27101-2824
(336) 725-9166

North Carolina Bar Foundation
Pro Bono Project
8000 Weston Parkway
Cary, NC 27513
Phone: 919-677-0561

Land Loss Prevention Project
P.O. Box 179
Durham, NC 27702
Phone: 919-682-5969

North Dakota
Legal Assistance of North Dakota
1025 Third St. North
P.O. Box 1893
Bismarck, ND 58502-1893
(701) 222-2110

North Dakota Legal Services
Main St.
P.O. Box 217
New Town, ND 58763-0217
(701) 627-4719

North Dakota State Bar Association LRS
515 1/2 E. Broadway, Suite 101
Bismarck, ND 58501
Phone: 701/255-1404

Ohio
Western Region Legal Services
265 South Main St., 3rd Floor
Akron, OH 44308-1223
(330) 535-4191

Stark County Legal Aid Society
306 Market Ave. North, Suite 730
Canton, OH 44702-1423

Legal Aid Society of Cincinnati
901 Elm St.
Cincinnati, OH 45202-1016
(513) 241-9400

The Legal Aid Society of Cleveland
1223 West Sixth St., 4th Floor
Cleveland, OH 44113-1301
(216) 687-1900

The Legal Aid Society of Columbus
40 West Gay St.
Columbus, OH 43215-2896
(614) 224-8374

Ohio State Legal Services
861 North High St.
Columbus, OH 43215-1427
(614) 299-2114

Legal Aid Society of Dayton
33 West First St., Suite 500
Dayton, OH 45402-3031
(937) 228-8088

Legal Aid Society of Lorain County
382 West Broad St.
Elyria, OH 44035
(440) 323-8240

Butler-Warren Legal Assistance Association
Society Bank Building, Suite 501
6 South Second St.
Hamilton, OH 45011-2808
(513) 894-7664

Allen County-Blackhoof Area Legal Services Association
311 Building, Suite 307
311 East Market St.
Lima, OH 45801-4565
(419) 224-9070

Advocates for Basic Legal Equality
Spitzer Building
520 Madison Ave., Suite 740
Toledo, OH 43604-1305
(419) 255-0814

The Toledo Legal Aid Society
One Stranahan Square, Suite 342
Toledo, OH 43604-1459
(419) 244-8345

Wooster-Wayne Legal Aid Society
121 West North St.
Suite 100
Wooster, OH 44691
(330) 264-9454

Northeast Ohio Legal Services
Metropolitan Tower, 7th Floor
11 Federal Plaza Central
Youngstown, OH 44503-1589
(330) 744-3196

Rural Legal Aid Society of West Central Ohio
31 East High St.
Springfield, OH 45502-1234
(937) 325-2809

Ohio Legal Assistance Foundation
42 East Gay St.
Suite 900
Columbus, OH 43215-2914
Phone: 614-752-8919

Oklahoma
Oklahoma Indian Legal Services
Founders Tower, Suite 610
5900 Mosteller Drive
Oklahoma City, OK 73112
(415) 840-5255

Legal Services of Eastern Oklahoma
115 West Third St., Suite 701
P.O. Box 8110
Tulsa, OK 74101-8110
(918) 584-3211

Legal Aid of Western Oklahoma
2901 Classen Blvd., Suite 112
110 Cameron Building
Oklahoma City, OK 73106
Phone: 405-521-1302

Oregon
Oregon Legal Services Corporation
700 S.W. Taylor St., Suite 310
Portland, OR 97205
(503) 224-4094

Lane County Legal Aid Service
376 East 11th Ave.
Eugene, OR 97401-3246
(541) 342-6056

Multnomah County Legal Aid Service
United Carriage Building
700 S.W. Taylor St., Suite 300
Portland, OR 97205
(503) 224-4086

Marion-Polk Legal Aid Service
1655 State St.
Salem, OR 97301-4258
(503) 581-5265

Oregon State Bar Foundation
Referral and Information Services
6200 SW Meadows Road
Lake Oswego, OR 97035
Phone: 503-620-0222, x323

Pennsylvania
Philadelphia Legal Assistance Center
1424 Chestnut Street, 2nd Floor
Philadelphia, PA 19102
(215) 981-3800

Legal Services
432 South Washington St.
Gettysburg, PA 17325
(717) 334-7623

Delaware County Legal Assistance Association
410 Welsh St.
Chester, PA 19013
(610) 874-8421

Bucks County Legal Aid Society
1290 New Rodgers Road
Box 809
Bristol, PA 19007
(215) 781-1111

Laurel Legal Services
306 South Pennsylvania Ave.
Greensburg, PA 15601-3066
(724) 836-2211

Southern Alleghenys Legal Aid
Suite 400, Franklin Center
225-227 Franklin St.
Johnstown, PA 15901-2524
(814) 536-8917

Central Pennsylvania Legal Services
213 North Front St., 3rd Floor
Harrisburg, PA 17101-1406
(717) 236-8932

Neighborhood Legal Services Association
928 Penn Ave.
Pittsburgh, PA 15222-3799
(412) 644-7450

Northern Pennsylvania Legal Services
12th Floor - SNB Plaza
108 North Washington Ave.
Scranton, PA 18503
(717) 342-0184

Keystone Legal Services
2054 East College Ave.
State College, PA 16801-7201
(814) 234-6231

Southwestern Pennsylvania Legal Aid Society
16 West Cherry Ave.
Washington, PA 15301
(724) 225-6170

Legal Aid of Chester County
112 West Gay St.
West Chester, PA 19380-2914
(610) 436-9150

Legal Services of Northeastern Pennsylvania,
Bicentennial Building, Suite 410
15 Public Square
Wilkes-Barre, PA 18701-1797
(717) 825-8567

Susqeuhanna Legal Services
329 Market St.
Williamsport, PA 17701-6306
(717) 323-8741

Northwestern Legal Services
Renaissance Centre, Suite 1200
1001 State St.
Erie, PA 16501-1833
(814) 452-6949

Lehigh Valley Legal Services
65 East Elizabeth Ave., Suite 903
Bethlehem, PA 18018
(610) 317-8757

Montgomery County Legal Aid Service
317 Swede St.
Norristown, PA 19401-4801
(610) 275-5400

Pennsylvania Bar Association
100 South St.
Harrisburg, PA 17108
Phone: 717-238-6807

Puerto Rico
Community Law Office
P.O. Box 8389
Fernández Juncos Station
San Juan, PR 00910
(787) 751-1600

Puerto Rico Legal Services
Ave. Ponce de Leon Num. 1859
Stop 26 Box 9134
Santurce, PR 00907-9134
(787) 728-9561

Rhode Island
Rhode Island Legal Services
56 Pine St., 4th Floor
Providence, RI 02903
(401) 274-2652

Legal Information & Referral Service for the Elderly Pro Bono Program
115 Cedar St.
Providence, RI 02903
Phone: 401-421-7758

South Carolina
Neighborhood Legal Assistance Program
438 King St.
Charleston, SC 29403-6283
(803) 722-0107

Palmetto Legal Services
2109 Bull St.
P.O. Box 2267
Columbia, SC 29202-2267
(803) 799-9668

Carolina Regional Legal Aid Services Corporation
279 West Evans St.
P.O. Box 479
Florence, SC 29503-0479
(803) 667-1896

Legal Services Agency of Western Carolina
1 Pendleton St.
Greenville, SC 29601
(864) 467-3248

Piedmont Legal Services
148 East Main St.
Spartanburg, SC 29306
(864) 582-0369

South Carolina Bar Pro Bono Program
P.O. Box 608
950 Taylor St.
Columbia, SC 29202-0608
Phone: 803-799-4015

South Dakota
Black Hills Legal Services
621 Sixth St., Suite 205
P.O. Box 1500
Rapid City, SD 57709-1500
(605) 342-7171

East River Legal Services
335 North Main Ave., Suite 300
Sioux Falls, SD 57102-0305
(605) 336-9230

Dakota Plains Legal Services
160 Second St.
P.O. Box 727
Mission, SD 57555-0727
(605) 856-4444

Southeast Tennessee Legal Services
414 McCallie Ave.
Chattanooga, TN 37402
(423) 756-4013

Legal Services of Upper East Tennessee
311 West Walnut St.
P.O. Drawer 360
Johnson City, TN 37605-0360
(423) 928-8311

Knoxville Legal Aid Society
502 South Gay St., Suite 404
Knoxville, TN 37902-1502
(423) 637-0484

Memphis Area Legal Services
Claridge House, 2nd Floor
109 North Main St.
Memphis, TN 38103-5013
(901) 523-8822

Legal Aid Society of Middle Tennessee
211 Union St., Suite 800
Nashville, TN 37201-1504
(615) 780-7123

Rural Legal Services of Tennessee
226 Broadway, Jackson Square
P.O. Box 5209
Oak Ridge, TN 37831-5209
(423) 483-8454

West Tennessee Legal Services
210 West Main St.
P.O. Box 2066
Jackson, TN 38302-2066
(901) 423-0616

Legal Services of South Central Tennessee
104 West Seventh St.
P.O. Box 1256
Columbia, TN 38402-1256
(931) 381-5533

Texas
Legal Aid of Central Texas
205 West Ninth St., Suite 200
Austin, TX 78701-2306
(512) 476-7244

Coastal Bend Legal Services
Pueblo Building
102 Pueblo St.
Corpus Christi, TX 78405
(512) 883-3667 x143

Legal Services of North Texas
1515 Main St.
Dallas, TX 75201-4803
(214) 748-1234

El Paso Legal Assistance Society
1220 North Stanton
El Paso, TX 79902
(915) 544-3022

West Texas Legal Services
600 East Weatherford St.
Fort Worth, TX 76102
(817) 877-0609

Gulf Coast Legal Foundation
1415 Fannin Ave., 3rd Floor
Houston, TX 77002
(713) 652-0077

Bexar County Legal Aid Association
434 South Main Ave., Suite 300
San Antonio, TX 78204
(210) 227-0111

Heart of Texas Legal Services Corporation
900 Austin Ave., 7th Floor
P.O. Box 527
Waco, TX 76703
(254) 756-7944

Texas Rural Legal Aid
259 South Texas Boulevard
Weslaco, TX 78596
(956) 968-6574

East Texas Legal Services
414 East Pillar St.
P.O. Box 631070
Nacogdoches, TX 75963-1070
(409) 560-1850

AIDS Legal Resource Project
Texas Human Rights Foundation
P.O. Box 1626
Austin, TX 78767
Phone: 512-479-8473

Next Lawfirm Pro Bono Project
140 E. Tyler St., Suite 150
Longview, TX 75601
Phone: 903-758-9123

Pro BAR
301 E. Madison Ave.
Harlingen, TX 78550-4907
Phone: 210-425-9231

Women's Advocacy Project
P.O. Box 833
Austin, TX 78767-0833
Phone: 512-476-5377

Utah
Utah Legal Aid Services
254 West 400 South, 2nd Floor
Salt Lake City, UT 84101
(801) 328-8891

Utah State Bar Association
Pro Bono Project
645 South 200 East
Salt Lake City, UT 84111
Phone: 801-531-9077

Vermont
Vermont Volunteer Lawyer's Project
Legal Services Law Line of Vermont
264 North Winooski Ave.
Burlington, VT 05401
Phone: 802-863-7153

Virgin Island

Legal Services of the Virgin Islands
3017 Orange Grove
Christiansted
St. Croix, VI 00820-4375
(340) 773-2626

Virginia

Legal Services of Northern Virginia
6400 Arlington Boulevard, Ste 630
Falls Church, VA 22042
(703) 534-4343

Rappahannock Legal Services
910 Princess Anne St., Suite 216
Fredericksburg, VA 22401
(540) 371-1105

Southwest Virginia Legal Aid Society
227 West Cherry St.
Marion, VA 24354
(540) 783-6576

Peninsula Legal Aid Center
2013 Cunningham Drive, Suite 336
P.O. Box 7502
Hampton, VA 23666
(757) 827-5078

Central Virginia Legal Aid Society
101 West Broad St., Suite 101
P.O. Box 12206
Richmond, VA 23241-2206
(804) 648-1012

Legal Aid Society of New River Valley
155 Arrowhead Trail
Christianburg, VA 24073
(540) 382-6157

Legal Aid Society of Roanoke Valley
416 Campbell Ave., S.W.
Roanoke, VA 24016-3627
(540) 344-2088

Tidewater Legal Aid Society
125 St. Paul's Boulevard, Suite 400
Norfolk, VA 23510
(757) 627-5423

Virginia Legal Aid Society
513 Church St.
P.O. Box 6058
Lynchburg, VA 24505-6058
(804) 528-4722

Southside Virginia Legal Services
10A Bollingbrook St.
Petersburg, VA 23803-4549
(804) 862-1100

Blue Ridge Legal Services
204 North High St.
P.O. Box 551
Harrisonburg, VA 22801-0551
(540) 433-1830

Client Centered Legal Services of Southwest Virginia
County Road 811 off Alternative Route 58
Castlewood, VA 24224-0147
(540) 762-5501

Piedmont Legal Services
416 East Main St., Suite 201
Charlottesville, VA 22902
(804) 296-8851

Virginia State Bar
Eighth & Main Building
707 E. Main St., Ste. 1500
Richmond, VA 23219
Phone: 804-775-0522

Washington

Northwest Justice Project
401 Second Ave. South, Suite 407
Seattle, WA 98104
(206) 464-1519
Outside county call: (888) 201-1014

West Virginia
West Virginia Legal Services Plan
922 Quarrier St., Suite 550
Charleston, WV 25301

**Appalachian Research &
Defense Fund**
Private Bar Involvement Project
922 Quarrier St., Suite 500
Charleston, WV 25301
Phone: 304-344-9687

**Pro Bono Referral Project
Legal Aid Society of
Charlestown**
922 Quarrier St., Suite 400
Charlestown, WV 25301
Phone: 304-343-4481
(304) 343-3013 x28

Wisconsin
Legal Action of Wisconsin
230 West Wells St., Room 800
Milwaukee, WI 53203-1866
(414) 278-7777

Wisconsin Judicare
300 Third St., Suite 210
P.O. Box 6100
Wausau, WI 54402-6100
(715) 842-1681

**Legal Services of Northeastern
Wisconsin**
417 Pine St.
Green Bay, WI 54301-5101
(920) 432-4645

**Western Wisconsin Legal
Services**
202 North Main
P.O. Box 101
Dodgeville, WI 53533-0101
(608) 935-2741

State Bar of Wisconsin
Delivery of Legal Services Program
402 W. Wilson St.
Madison, WI 53703
Phone: 608-250-6177

Wyoming
Wind River Legal Services
Highway 287
P.O. Box 247
Ft. Washakie, WY 82514-0247
(307) 332-6626

Nationwide Directory Of Consumer Protection Offices

Check Out A Company Before Doing Business With Them

It is always smart before doing business with any company you have questions about to check with your local Better Business Bureau. They will be able to tell you whether other consumers have reported any problems they have had with this company.

Usually you can find the address and phone number of the Bureau nearest you in your local phone book but some of the Better Business Bureaus are serviced by bureaus in adjoining states. To locate the bureau nearest you, you can also check with the U.S. National Headquarters listed below or use the zip code search or state directory at: **http://www.bbb.org/bureaus/index.html.**

UNITED STATES-NATIONAL HEADQUARTERS
Council of Better Business Bureaus
4200 WILSON BLVD., SUITE 800
ARLINGTON, VA 22203
703-276-0100
http://www.bbb.org

Don't Be The Victim Of Consumer Fraud

As a general rule, once it's clear that you are not going to get satisfaction directly from the company you are having a dispute with, the first place to call for help with a consumer problem is your local consumer protection office. It is their job to protect you, the consumer against unfair and illegal business practices.

Listed here are consumer protection offices throughout the country. If you have a complaint, check this directory for your state, city or county and call the office nearest you.

If you are having a problem with a business outside your state, however, contact the consumer office in the state in which you made the purchase.

When you call the consumer protection or Attorney General's office, simply ask to be connected to the person in charge of consumer complaints.

Alabama
Consumer Protection   In Alabama call: 800-392-5658
                        or nationwide: 334-242-7334

Alaska
Attorney General's Office Faair Practice Section   907-269-5100

Arizona-State Offices
For Arizona residents: 800-352-8431
Phoenix Consumer Protection / 800-352-8431
Tucson Consumer Protection / 602-628-6504

Arizona-County Offices
Apache County / 602-337-4364
Cochise County / 602-432-9377
Coconino County / 602-779-6518
Gila County / 602-425-3231
Graham County / 602-428-3620
Greenlee County / 602-865-3842
La Paz County / 602-669-6118
Mohave County / 602-753-0719
Navajo County / 602-524-6161
Pima County / 602-740-5733
Pinal County / 602-868-5801
Santa Cruz County / 602-281-4966
Yavapai County / 602-771-3344
Yuma County / 602-329-2270

Arizona-City Office
Tucson Consumer Affairs / 602-791-4886

Arkansas-State Office
Consumer Protection / 501-682-2341

California-State Offices
California Consumer Affairs / 916-445-1254 (consumer information)
Attorney General's Office / 916-322-3360
California Bureau of Automotive Repair / 916-366-5100

California-County Offices
Alameda County / 415-530-8682
Contra Costa County / 415-646-4500
Fresno County / 209-488-3156
Kern County / 805-861-2421
Los Angeles County / 213-974-1452
Marin County / 415-499-6190
Consumer Protection / 415-499-6450
Mendocino County District / 707-463-4211
Monterey County / 408-755-5073
Napa County / 707-253-4059
Orange County / 714-541-7600
Orange County / 714-541-7600
Riverside County / 714-275-5400
Sacramento County / 916-440-6174
San Diego / 619-531-3507 (fraud complaint line)
San Francisco County / 415-552-6400 (public inquiries)
415-553-1814 (complaints)
San Joaquin County / 209-468-2419
San Luis Obispo County / 805-549-5800
San Mateo County / 415-363-4656
Santa Barbara County /805-568-2300
Santa Clara County / 408-299-7400
Santa Clara County / 408-299-4211
Santa Cruz County /408-425-2054
Solano County / 707-421-6860
Stanislaus County / 209-571-5550
Ventura County / 805-654-3110
Yolo County / 916-666-8424

California-City Offices
Los Angeles / 213-485-4515
Santa Monica / 213-458-8336

Colorado-State Offices
Consumer Protection Unit / 303-620-4500
Consumer and Food Specialist / 303-239-4114

Colorado-County Offices
Archuleta, LaPlata, and San Juan Counties / 303-247-8850

Boulder County / 303-441-3700
Denver County / 303-640-3555 (inquiries) / 303-640-3557 (complaints)
El Paso and Teller Counties / 719-520-6002
Pueblo County / 719-546-6030
Weld County / 303-356-4000 ext. 4735

Connecticut-State Offices
Department of Consumer Protection / 203-566-4999 / 800-538-2277 (CT only)
Antitrust/Consumer Protection / 203-566-5374 / 800-538-2277 (CT only)

Connecticut-City Office
Middletown / 203-344-3492

Delaware-State Offices
Division of Consumer Affairs / 800-443-2179
Office of Attorney General / 800-736-4000

District of Columbia
Consumer Affairs / 202-727-7000

Florida-State Offices
Division of Consumer Services / 904-488-2226 / 800-327-3382 (FL only)
Consumer Litigation Section / 904-488-9105
Office of the Attorney General / 305-985-4780

Florida-County Offices
Broward County / 305-357-6030
Metropolitan Dade County Consumer Protection / 305-375-4222
Dade County / 305-324-3030
Hillsborough County / 813-272-6750
Orange County / 407-836-2490
Palm Beach County / 407-355-3560
Palm Beach County / 407-355-2670
Pasco County / 813-847-8110
Pinellas County / 813-530-6200
Seminole County / 407-322-7534
Titusville Consumer Fraud Unit / 407-264-5230

Florida-City Offices
City of Jacksonville / 904-630-3667
Lauderhill / 305-321-2450
Tamarac / 305-722-5900

Georgia-State Office
Governors Office of Consumer Affairs / 404-651-8600 / 800-869-1123 (toll-free in GA only)

Hawaii-State Offices
Office of Consumer Protection / 808-586-2630
Hilo Office of Consumer Protection / 808-933-4433
Lihue Office of Consumer Protection / 808-241-3365
Honolulu Office of Consumer Protection / 808-586-2630

Idaho-State Office
Consumer Protection Unit / 208-334-2424 / 800-432-3545 (ID only)

Illinois-State Offices
Governors Office of Citizens Assistance / 217-782-0244 / 800-252-8666 (IL only)
Chicago Consumer Protection / 312-814-3580
Springfield Consumer Protection / 217-782-9011 / 800-252-8666 (IL only)
Chicago Department of Citizen Rights / 312-814-3289

Illinois-Regional Offices
Carbondale Regional Office / 618-457-3505
Champaign Regional Office / 217-333-7691 (voice/TDD)
East St. Louis Regional Office / 618-398-1006
Granite City Regional Office / 618-877-0404
Kankakee Regional Office / 815-935-8500
LaSalle Regional Office / 815-224-4861
Mount Vernon Regional Office / 618-242-8200 (voice/TDD)
Peoria Regional Office / 309-671-3191
Quincy Regional Office / 217-223-2221 (voice/TDD)
Rockford Regional Office / 815-987-7580
Rock Island Regional Office / 309-793-0950
Waukegan Regional Office / 708-336-2207
West Frankfort Regional Office / 618-937-6453
West Chicago Regional Office / 708-653-5060 (voice/TDD)

Illinois-County Offices
Cook County / 312-443-4600
Madison County / 618-692-6280
Rock Island County / 309-786-4451, ext. 229

Illinois-City Offices
Wheeling Township / 708-259-7730 (Wed. only)
Chicago Department of Consumer Services / 312-744-4090
Des Plaines Consumer Protection / 708-391-5363

Indiana-State Office
Consumer Protection / 317-232-6330 / 800-382-5516 (IN only)

Indiana-County Offices
Consumer Protection / 219-755-3720
Marion County / 317-236-3522
Vanderburgh County / 812-426-5150

Indiana-City Office
Gary Office of Consumer Affairs / 219-886-0145

Iowa-State Office
Consumer Protection / 515-281-5926

Kansas-State Office
Consumer Protection / 913-296-3751 / 800-432-2310 (KS only)

Kansas-County Offices
Johnson County / 913-782-5000
Sedgwick County / 316-268-7921
Shawnee County / 913-291-4330

Kansas-City Office
Topeka Consumer Protection / 913-295-3883

Kentucky-State Offices
Consumer Protection / 502-564-2200 / 800-432-9257 (KY only)
Louisville Consumer Protection / 502-588-3262 / 800-432-9257 (KY only)

Louisiana-State Office
Consumer Protection / 504-342-7373

Louisiana-County Office
Consumer Protection / 504-364-3644

Maine-State Offices
Consumer Credit Protection / 207-582-8718 / 800-332-8529
Office of the Attorney General / 207-289-3716

Maryland-State offices
Consumer Protection / 301-528-8662 / 800-969-5766
Motor Vehicle Administration / 301-768-7420
Consumer Affairs Specialist
Office of the Attorney General / 301-543-6620
Western Maryland / 301-791-4780

Maryland-County Offices
Howard County / 301-313-7220

Montgomery County / 301-217-7373
Prince Georges County / 301-925-5100

Massachusetts-State Offices
Consumer Protection / 617-727-8400
Executive Office of Consumer Affairs / 617-727-7780
Western Massachusetts Consumer Protection / 413-784-1240

Massachusetts-County Offices
Franklin County / 413-774-5102
Hampshire County / 413-586-9225
Worcester County / 508-754-7420

Massachusetts-City Offices
Boston Mayor's Office of Consumer Affairs / 617-725-3320
Springfield Action Commission / 413-737-4376 (Hampton and Hampshire counties)

Michigan-State Offices
Consumer Protection / 517-373-1140
Michigan Consumers Council / 517-373-0947
Bureau of Automotive Regulation / 517-373-7858 / 800-292-4204 (Michigan only)

Michigan-County Offices
Bay County / 517-893-3594
Macomb County / 313-469-5350
Washtenaw County / 313-971-6054

Michigan-City Office
Detroit Department of Consumer Affairs / 313-224-3508

Minnesota-State Offices
Office of Consumer Services / 612-296-2331
Duluth Consumer Services / 218-723-4891

Minnesota-County Office
Hennepin County / 612-348-4528

Minnesota-City Office
Minneapolis Consumer Services / 612-348-2080

Mississippi -State Offices
Consumer Protection / 601-354-6018

Department of Agriculture & Commerce / 601-354-7063
Gulf Coast Regional Office / 601-436-6000

Missouri-State Offices
Office of the Attorney General / 314-751-3321 / 800-392-8222 (MO only)
Office of the Attorney General-Trade Offense Division / 314-751-3321 /
800-392-8222 ((toll-free in MO only)

Montana-State Office
Consumer Affairs / 406-444-4312 / 800-332-2272

Nebraska-State Office
Consumer Protection / 402-471-2682

Nebraska-County Office
Douglas County / 402-444-7040

Nevada-State Offices
Las Vegas Commissioner of Consumer Affairs / 702-486-7355 /
800-992-0900 ((toll-free in NV only)
Reno Consumer Affairs / 702-688-1800 / 800-992-0900 (Nevada only)

Nevada-County Office
Washoe County / 702-328-3456

New Hampshire-State Office
Consumer Protection / 603-271-3641

New Jersey-State Offices
Consumer Affairs / 932-648-4010 / 800-242-5846
Department of the Public Advocate / 609-292-7087 / 800-792-8600 (toll-
free in NJ only)
New Jersey Division of Law / 973-648-7579 / 800-242-5846

New Jersey-County Offices
Atlantic County / 609-345-6700
Bergen County / 201-646-2650
Burlington County / 609-265-5054
Camden County / 609-757-8397
Cape May County / 609-463-6475
Cumberland County / 609-453-2202
Essex County / 973-678-8071/8928
Gloucester County / 609-853-3349
Hudson County / 201-795-6295
Hunterdon County / 908-236-2249
Mercer County / 609-989-6671
Middlesex County / 732-324-4600

Monmouth County / 732-431-7900
Morris County / 973-285-6070
Parsippany Consumer Affairs / 973-263-7011
Perth Amboy / 732-826-0290, ext. 61
Plainfield Action Services / 908-753-3519
Secaucus Consumer Affairs / 201-330-2019
Union Township / 908-688-6763
Wayne Township / 973-694-1800
Weehawken Consumer Affairs / 201-319-6005
West New York Consumer Affairs / 201-861-2522

New Mexico-State Office
Consumer Protection / 505-827-6000 / 800-432-2070 (in New Mexico only)

New York-State Offices
New York State Consumer Protection / 518-474-8583
Bureau of Consumer Frauds & Protection / 518-474-5481
NY State Consumer Protection Board / 212-417-4908 (complaints) / 212-417-4482 (main office)
Bureau of Consumer Frauds & Protection / 212-341-2345

New York-Regional Offices
Binghamton Regional Office / 607-773-7877
Buffalo Regional Office / 716-847-7184
Plattsburgh Regional Office / 518-563-8012
Poughkeepsie Regional Office / 914-485-3920
Rochester Regional Office / 716-546-7430
Suffolk Regional Office / 516-231-2400
Syracuse Regional Office / 315-448-4848
Utica Regional Office / 315-793-2225

New York-County Offices
Broome County / 607-778-2168
Dutchess County / 914-471-6322
Eric County / 716-858-2424
Nassau County / 516-535-2600
Orange County / 914-294-5151
Orange County / 914-294-5471
Putnam County / 914-621-2317
Rockland County / 914-638-5282
Steuben County / 607-776-9631 (voice andTDD)
Suffolk County / 516-360-4600
Ulster County / 914-339-5680
Westchester County Fraud Bureau / 914-285-3303
Westchester Consumer Affairs / 914-285-2155

New York-City Offices
Babylon Consumer Protection Board / 516-422-7636

Town of Colonie Consumer Protection / 518-783-2790
Mt. Vernon Consumer Affairs / 914-665-2433
New York City Consumer Affairs / 212-487-4444
Bronx Consumer Affairs / 718-579-6766
Brooklyn Consumer Affairs / 718-636-7092
Queens Consumer Affairs / 718-261-2922
Staten Island Consumer Affairs / 718-390-5154
Oswego Consumer Affairs / 315-342-8150
Ramapo Consumer Protection / 914-357-5100
Schenectady Consumer Protection / 518-382-5061
White Plains Dept. of Weights & Measures / 914-422-6359
Yonkers Consumer Protection / 914-377-6807

North Carolina-State Office
Consumer Protection / 919-733-7741

North Dakota-State Offices
Office of the Attorney General / 800-472-2600 (toll-free in ND only)

North Dakota-County Office
Quad County / 701-746-5431

Ohio-State Offices
Consumer Frauds and Crimes Section / 614-466-4986 (complaints) /
800-282-0515 ((toll-free in OH only)
Office of Consumers' Counsel / 614-466-9605 (voice/TDD) / 800-282-9448
((toll-free in OH only)

Ohio-County Offices
Franklin County / 614-462-3555
Lake County / 800-899-5253 (Ohio only)
Montgomery County / 513-225-5757
Portage County / 216-296-4593
Summit County / 216-379-2800

Ohio-City Offices
Cincinnati Office of Consumer Services / 513-352-3971
Youngstown Consumer Affairs / 216-742-8884

Oklahoma-State Offices
Attorney General / 405-521-4274
Department of Consumer Credit / 405-521-3653

Oregon-State Office
Financial Fraud / 503-378-4320

Pennsylvania-State Offices
Consumer Protection / 717-787-9707 / 800-441-2555 (PA only)
Consumer Advocate-(Utilities Only) / 717-783-5048
Pennsylvania Public Utility Commission / 717-787-4970 / 800-782-1110 ((toll-free in PA only)

Pennsylvania- Branch Offices
Allentown Consumer Protection / 215-821-6690
Erie Consumer Protection / 814-871-4371
Harrisburg Consumer Protection / 717-787-7109 / 800-441-2555 (PA only)
Ebensburg Bureau of Consumer Protection / 814-949-7900
Philadelphia Consumer Protection / 215-560-2414 / 800-441-2555 (PA only)
Pittsburg Consumer Protection / 412-565-5394
Scranton Consumer Protection / 717-963-4913

Pennsylvania-County Offices
Beaver County / 412-728-7267
Bucks County / 215-348-7442
Chester County / 215-344-6150
Cumberland County / 717-240-6180
Delaware County / 215-891-4865
Montgomery County / 215-278-3565
Philadelphia District Attorney / 215-686-8750

Rhode Island-State Offices
Consumer Protection / 401-277-2104 / 800-852-7776 (RI only)
Rhode Island Consumers' Council / 401-277-2764

South Carolina-State Offices
Consumer Protection Office / 803-734-9452 / 800-922-1594 (in SC only)
State Ombudsman / 803-734-0457

South Dakota-State Office
Consumer Affairs / 605-773-4400

Tennessee-State Offices
Consumer Protection / 615-741-2672
Consumer Affairs / 615-741-4737 / 800-342-8385 ((toll-free in TN only)

Texas-State Offices
Dallas Consumer Protection / 214-742-8944
El Paso Consumer Protection / 915-772-9476

Houston Consumer Protection / 713-223-5886
Lubbock Consumer Protection / 806-747-5238
McAllen Consumer Protection / 512-682-4547
San Antonio Consumer Protection / 512-225-4191
Austin Consumer Protection / 512-322-4143

Texas-County Offices
Dallas County / 214-653-3820
Harris County / 713-221-5836

Texas-City Office
Dallas Dept. of Environmental & Health Services / 214-670-5216

Utah-State Offices
Consumer Protection / 801-530-6601
Assistant Attorney General for Consumer Affairs / 801-538-1331

Vermont-State Offices
Office of the Attorney General / 802-828-3171
Consumer Assurance / 802-828-2436

Virginia-State Offices
Richmond Branch of Consumer Affairs / 804-786-2042 / 800-552-9963 ((toll-free in VA only)
Northern Virginia Branch of Consumer Affairs / 703-532-1613

Virginia-County Offices
Arlington County / 703-358-3260
Fairfax County / 703-246-5949
Prince William County / 703-792-7370

Virginia-City Offices
Alexandria Citizens Assistance / 703-838-4350
Norfolk Consumer Affairs / 804-441-2821
Roanoke Consumer Protection / 703-981-2583
Virginia Beach Consumer Affairs / 757-426-5836

Washington-State Offices
Seattle Consumer Services / 206-464-6431 / 800-551-4636 (WA only)
Spokane Office of the Attorney General / 509-456-3123
Tacoma Office of the Attorney General / 206-593-2904

Washington-City Offices
Department of Weights and Measures / 206-259-8810
Seattle Prosecuting Attorney / 206-296-9010
Seattle Department of Licenses & Consumer Affairs / 206-684-8484

West Virginia-State Offices
Consumer Protection / 304-348-8986 / 800-368-8808 ((toll-free in WV only)
Division of Weights and Measures / 304-348-7890

West Virginia-City Office
Charleston Consumer Protection / 304-348-8172

Wisconsin-State Offices
Madison Consumer Protection / 608-266-9836 / 800-422-7129 (in WI only)
Altoona Consumer Protection / 715-839-3848 / 800-422-7128 (in WI only)
Green Bay Consumer Protection / 414-448-5111 / 800-422-7128 (in WI only)
Milwaukee Consumer Protection / 414-257-8956
Madison Department of Justice / 608-266-1952 / 800-362-8189
Milwaukee Department of Justice / 414-227-4948 / 800-362- 8189

Wisconsin-County offices
Marathon County / 715-847-5555
Milwaukee County / 414-278-4792
Racine County / 414-636-3125

Wyoming-State Office
Office of Attorney General / 307-777-7874

American Samoa
Consumer Protection / 011-684-633-4163/64

Puerto Rico
Secretary of Consumer Affairs / 809-721-0940
Department Of Justice / 809-721-2900

Virgin Islands
Commissioner & Consumer Affairs / 809-774-3130

NOTES:

free & Low Cost Dental Programs

Throughout the U.S. professional dental care is available to senior citizens living on a limited budget at a reduced rate or even absolutely free depending upon their income and circumstances. This care is offered through a wide variety of programs including dental clinics, dental colleges, and through dentists who volunteer their time and service without charge or at a greatly reduced rate. You will get the finest professional dental care from licensed dentists with many years of experience.

To get free or low cost dental care, check the listing below for your state. Call the phone number listed for each of the organizations listed and explain that you are a senior citizen looking for a low cost dental program. In some instances you will be referred to an agency in your local area that will assist you in getting the dental care you need. If the organization you call does not have the particular kind of care you need, always ask them to refer you to another organization that does provide the care.

In addition to the listings below, be sure to check with your STATE'S OFFICE OF THE AGING (also listed in the back of this book). They often will have access to special programs not available anywhere else.

Alabama
Alabama Dental Association
836 Washington St.
Montgomery, AL 36104
334-265-1684
800-489-2532

University of Alabama
School of Dentistry
1919 Seventh Avenue, S.
Birmingham, AL 35294
205-934-2700

Alaska
Alaska Dental Society
3305 Arctic Blvd., Suite 102
Anchorage, AK 99503-4975
907-563-3009

Anchorage Neigthborhood Health Center
1217 East 10th Ave.
Anchorage, AZ 99501
907-257-4600

Senior Citizen Discounts
Anchorage Dental Society
3400 Spenard Rd., Suite 10
Anchorage, AK 99503
907-279-9144

Arizona
Arizona Dental Association
4131 N. 36th St.
Phoenix, AZ 85018
602-957-4777
800-866-2732

Department of Health Services
Office of Dental Health
1740 West Adams St.
Phoenix, AZ 85007
602-542-1866

Arkansas
Arkansas State Dental Association
2501 Crestwood Drive, Suite 205
North Little Rock, AR 72116
501-771-7650

California
Senior Dent Program
California Dental Association
P.O. Box 13749
1201 "K" Street
Sacramento, CA 95853-4749
916-443-0505
800-736-8702

Loma Linda University
School of Dentistry
11092 Anderson St.
Loma Linda, CA 92350
909-824-4675

University of California at Los Angeles
School of Dentistry
10833 LeConte Ave.
Los Angeles, CA 90095-1668
310-206-3904

University of Southern California
School of Dentistry Rm. 203
University Park, MC 0641
Los Angeles, CA 90089-0641
213-740-2800

University of California
School of Dentistry
513 Parnassus Ave., S-630
San Francisco, CA 94143
415-476-1891

University of the Pacific
School of Dentistry
2155 Webster Street
San Francisco, CA 94115
415-929-6400

Colorado
Colorado Dental Association
3690 S. Yosemite, Suite 100
Denver, CO 80237
303-740-6900
800-343-3010
Ask for Senior Discount referrals

State Health Dept.
Oral Health Department
4300 Cherry Creek Dr. South
Denver, CO 80246
303-692-2360

University of Colorado Medical
School of Dentistry
4200 East 9th Ave., Box A095
Denver, CO 80262
303-270-8751

Connecticut
Connecticut State Dental Association
62 Russ Street
Hartford, CT 06106
860-278-5550

The University of Connecticut
School of Dental Medicine
263 Farmington Avenue
Farmington, CT 06032
203-679-3400

Delaware
Delaware State Dental Society
1925 Lovering Ave.
Wilmington, DE 19806
302-654-4335

Division of Public Health
Department of Dentistry
501 W. 14th Street
Wilmington, DE 19801
302-428-4850

Nemours Health Clinic
1801 Rockland Rd
Wilmington, DE 19803
800-292-9538
302-651-4400

Ministry of Caring Dental Program
1410 N. Claymont St
Wilmington, DE 19802
302-594-9476

District Of Columbia
District of Columbia Dental Society
502 C Street N.E.
Washington, DC 20002
202-547-7613

Howard University
College of Dentistry
600 "W" Street, N.W.
Washingon, DC 20059
202-806-0100

Florida
Florida Dental Association
1111 E. Tennessee St.
Tallahassee, FL 32308
904-681-3629 / 800-877-9922

Department of Health & Rehabilitative Services
Public Health Dental Program
1317 Winewood Blvd
Tallahassee, FL 32399
850-245-4333
Ask for referral to a clinic near you

Nova Southeastern University
College of Dental Medicine
3200 S. University Drive
Fort Lauderdale, FL 33328
954-262-7500

University of Florida
College of Dentistry
P.O. Box 100405
Gainesville, FL 32610-0405
904-392-4261

Georgia
Georgia Dental Association
2801 Buford Highway, Suite T-60
Atlanta, GA 30329
404-636-7553
800-432-4357

West End Medical Center
868 York Ave
Atlanta, GA 30310
404-752-1443

Ben Massell Dental Clinic
18 7th St., NE
Atlanta, GA 30308
404-881-1858

Southeast Health Center
1039 Ridge Ave.
Atlanta, GA 30315
404-688-1350 ext 305

Medical College of Georgia
School of Dentistry
1459 Laney Walker Blvd.
Augusta, GA 30912-0200
706-721-2696

Hawaii
Hawaii Dental Association
1345 S. Beretania St. Ste. 301
Honolulu, HI 96814
808-593-7956

Department of Health
Dental Health Division
1700 Lanakila Ave. Room 202
Honolulu, HI 96817
808-832-5710

Idaho

Idaho State Dental Association
1220 W. Hays St.
Boise, ID 83702
208-343-7543
800-932-8153
Ask for a referral to your local
Community Health Center

Senior Care Program
Boise City/Ada County
3010 W. State St. Suite 120
Boise, ID 83703
208-345-7783

Illinois

Illinois State Dental Society
P.O. Box 376
Springfield, IL 62705
217-525-1406
800-475-4737

Southern Illinois University
School of Dentistry Medical Bldg 273
2800 College Avenue - Room 2300
Alton, IL 62002
618-474-7000

University of Illinois at Chicago
College of Dentistry
801 South Paulina Street
Chicago, IL 60612
312-996-7558

Northwestern University
Dental School
240 East Huron Street
Chicago, IL 60611
312-908-5950

Indiana

**Senior Smile Dental Care
Program
Indiana Dental Association**
401 W. Michigan Street
Indianapolis, IN 46206
317-634-2610
800-562-5646

Indiana University
School of Dentistry
1121 West Michigan Street
Indianaplis, IN 46202
317-274-3547

Iowa

Iowa Dental Association
505 5th Ave. #333
Des Moines, IA 50309
515-282-7250
800-828-2181

**The University of Iowa
College of Dentistry**
Dental Building
Iowa City, IA 52242
319-335-7499

Kansas

**Senior Access Program
Kansas Dental Association**
5200 SW Huntoon St.
Topeka, KS 66604
800-432-3583

Kentucky

Kentucky Dental Association
1940 Princeton Drive
Louisville, KY 40205
502-459-5373
800-292-1855

**Jefferson County Dental
Park Duval Community Health
Facility**
1817 South 34th St.
Louisville, KY 40211
502-774-4401

University of Kentucky
College of Dentistry
800 Rose Street - Medical Ctr.
Lexington, KY 40536-0084
606-323-6525

University of Louisville
School of Dentistry
Health Sciences Center
Louisville, KY 40292
502-852-5096

Louisiana
Louisiana Dental Association
7833 Office Park Blvd.
Baton Rouge, LA 70809
504-926-1986

Louisiana State University
School of Dentistry
1100 Florida Ave., Bldg. 101
New Orleans, LA 70119
504-947-9961

Maine
Senior Dent Program
Maine Dental Association
P.O. Box 215
Manchester, ME 04351
800-369-8217

Maryland
Maryland State Dental Association
6450 Dobbin Road
Columbia, MD 21045
410-964-2880
800-766-2880

University of Maryland
Baltimore College of Dental Surgery
666 West Baltimore Street
Baltimore, MD 21201
410-706-5603

Massachusetts
Massachusetts Dental Society
83 Speen Street
Natick, MA 01760
508-651-7511
800-342-8747

Boston Univsity
School of Dental Medicine
100 East Newton Street
Boston, MA 02118
617-638-4671

Harvard School of Dental Medicine
188 Longwood Avenue
Boston, MA 02115
617-432-1423

Tufts University
School of Dental Medicine
1 Kneeland Street
Boston, MA 02111
617-956-6547

Michigan
Michigan Dental Association
230 N. Washington Square #208
Lansing, MI 48933
517-372-9070
800-589-2632

The University of Michigan
School of Dentistry
1234 Dental Building
Ann Arbor, MI 48109-1078
734-763-6933

University of Detroit Mercy
School of Dentistry
8200 W. Outer Drive, PO Box 98
Detroit, MI 48219-0900
313-494-6600

Minnesota
Minnesota Dental Association
2236 Marshall Avenue
St. Paul, MN 55104
612-646-7454
800-950-3368

University of Minnesota
School of Dentistry
515 S.E. Delaware Street
Minneapolis, MN 55455
612-625-8400

In Minnesota also contact:
Neighborhood Health Care Network
612-489-2273

Senior Link Line
1-800-333-2433
"First Call For Help"
612-224-1133

Mississippi
Mississippi Dental Association
2630 Ridgewood Road
Jackson, MS 39216
601-982-0442

The University of Mississippi
School of Dentistry - Med. Ctr.
2500 North State Street
Jackson, MS 39216-4505
601-984-6155

Missouri
Missouri Dental Association
230 W. McCarty Street
Jefferson City, MO 65102
573-634-3436
800-688-1907

University of Missouri
School of Dentistry
650 East 25th Street
Kansas City, MO 64108
816-235-2100

Montana
Montana Dental Association
P.O. Box 1154
Helena, MT 59624
406-443-2061 / 800-257-4988

Donated Dental Services
PO Box 1154
Helena, MT 59624
406-449-9670

Cooperative Health Dental Clinic
1930 Ninth Ave.
Helena, MT 59601
406-443-2584

Nebraska
Senior Dent Program
Nebraska Dental Association
3120 "O" Street
Lincoln, NE 68510
402-476-1704
800-234-3120

University of Nebraska Medical Ctr.
College of Dentistry
40th & Holdrege Street
Lincoln, NE 68583-0740
402-472-1333

Creighton University
School of Dentistry
2500 California Street
Omaha, NE 68178
402-280-2865

Nevada
Nevada Dental Association
6889 W. Charleston Blvd. #B
Las Vegas, NV 89117
702-255-4211
800-962-6710

New Hampshire
New Hampshire Dental Society
P.O. Box 2229
Concord, NH 03302
603-225-5961
800-244-5961

New Jersey
New Jersey Dental Association
One Dental Plaza
North Brunswick, NJ 08902-6020
732-821-9400

University of Medicine & Dentistry
New Jersey Dental School
110 Bergen Street
Newark, NJ 07103-2425
201-982-4300

New Mexico
New Mexico Dental Association
3736 Eubank Blvd. N.E. Suite C-1
Albuquerque, NM 87111
505-294-1368

New York

Dental Society of the State of New York
7 Elk Street
Albany, NY 12207
518-465-0044
800-255-2100

State University of New York
School of Dental Medicine
325 Squire Hall
Buffalo, NY 14214
716-829-2720

Columbia University
School of Dental & Oral Surgery
640 West 168th Street
New York, NY 10032
212-305-5665

New York University
College of Dentistry
345 E. 24th Street
New York, NY 10010
212-998-9800

State University of New York
School of Dental Medicine
South Campus
Stony Brook, NY 11794-8700
516-632-8974

North Carolina

North Carolina Dental Society
P.O. Box 4099
Cary, NC 27519
919-677-1396

University of North Carolina
School of Dentistry
104 Brauer Hall, 211 H
Chapel Hill, NC 27599-7450
919-966-1161

North Dakota

North Dakota Dental Association
Box 1332
Bismarck, ND 58502
800-795-8870

Ohio

Oral Health Access Coordinator
Bureau of Oral Health Services
246 North High St.
Columbus, OH 43266-0118
614-466-4180
In Ohio: 1-888-765-6789
Provides access to over 90 dental programs throughout the state

Ohio Dental Association
1370 Dublin Road
Columbus, OH 43215
800-MY-SMILE 1-800-69-76453)
or Options Program: 1-888-765-6789

Case Western Reserve Univ.
School of Dentistry
2123 Abington Road
Cleveland, OH 44106
216-368-3200

Ohio State University
College of Dentistry
305 West 12th Avenue
Columbus, OH 43210
614-292-2751

Oklahoma

Senior Dent/Care-Dent Programs
Oklahoma Dental Association
629 West Interstate 44, Service Rd.
Oklahoma City, OK 73118
405-848-8873
800-876-8890

University of Oklahoma Health Science Center
College of Dentistry
P.O. Box 26901
Oklahoma City, OK 73190
405-271-6056

Oregon

Oregon Dental Association
17898 S.W. McEwan Rd.
Portland, OR 97224
503-620-3230 / 800-452-5628

**Department of Health
Dental Health Division**
Community Access Programs
800 NE Oregon St.
Portland, OR 97232
503-731-4098

Senior Smile Dental Service
Multnomah Dental Society
1618 SW First Ave.
Portland, OR 97201
503-223-4738

Donated Dental Services
CDRC
PO Box 574 Room 2205
Portland, OR 97207
503-248-3816

**The Oregon Health Services
University**
School of Dentistry
Sam Jackson Park
611 S.W. Campus Drive
Portland, OR 97201
503-494-8867

Pennsylvania
Pennsylvania Dental Association
P.O. Box 3341
Harrisburg, PA 17105
717-234-5941 / 800-692-7256

Dental Care For Senior Citizens
Access To Care Program
3501 North Front St.
Harrisburg, PA 17110
717-234-5941

Temple University
School of Dentistry
3223 North Broad Street
Philadelphia, PA 19140
215-707-2900

University of Pennsylvania
School of Dental Medicine
4001 West Spruce Street
Philadelphia, PA 19104
215-898-8961

University of Pittsburgh
School of Dental Medicine
3501 Terrace Street
Pittsburgh, PA 15261
412-648-8760

Puerto Rico
Colegio de Cirujanos Dentistas
Avenida Domenech #200
Hato Rey, PR 00918
787-764-1969

University of Puerto Rico
School of Dentistry
G.P.O. Box 5067
San Juan, PR 00936
787-555-1212

Rhode Island
Rhode Island Dental Association
200 Centerville Place
Warwick, RI 02886
401-732-6833

Department of Public Health
Oral Health Division
3 Capital Hill
Providence, RI 02908
401-222-2588

South Carolina
**Senior Care Dental Program
South Carolina Dental
Association**
120 Stonemark Lane
Columbia, SC 29210
803-750-2277
800-327-2598

**Medical University of South
Carolina**
College of Dental Medicine
171 Ashley Avenue
Charleston, SC 29425
803-792-2611

South Dakota
South Dakota Dental Association
330 South Poplar
Pierre, SD 57501
605-224-9133

Tennessee
Tennessee Dental Association
2104 Sunset Place
Nashville, TN 37212
615-383-8962

Tennessee Department of Dentistry
Cordell Hull
425 Fifth Ave. North
Nashville, TN 37247
615-532-5073

University of Tennessee
College of Dentistry
875 Union Avenue
Memphis, TN 38163
901-448-6257

Meharry Medical College
School of Dentistry
1005 Dr. D.B. Todd Blvd.
Nashville, TN 37208
615-327-6669

Texas
Texas Dental Association
P.O. Box 3358
Austin, TX 78764
512-443-3675

Texas A&M University System
Baylor College of Dentistry
3302 Gaston Ave.
Dallas, TX 75266-0677
214-828-8100

The University of Texas
Health Science Center
Dental Branch
6516 John Freeman Avenue
Houston, TX 77030
713-792-4056

The University of Texas
Health Science -Dental School
7703 Floyd Curl Drive
San Antonio, TX 78284-7914
210-567-3222

Utah
Department of Health
Dental Health Division
1365 West 1000 North
Salt Lake City, UT 84116
801-328-5756

Utah Dental Association
1151 E. 3900 S., Suite B160
Salt Lake City, UT 84124
800-662-6500

Vermont
Island Pond Health Center
Dental Program
PO Box 425
Island Pond, VT 05846
802-723-4300

Vermont State Dental Society
100 Dorset Street Suite 12
South Burlington, VT 05403
802-864-0115

Virginia
Virginia Dental Association
P.O. Box 6906
Richmond, VA 23230
804-358-4927 / 800-552-3886

Health Department
Dental Division
1500 E. Main
Richmond, VA 23219
804-786-3556

Virginia Commonwealth Univ.
MCV-School of Dentistry
P.O. Box 566
Richmond, VA 23298
804-828-9095

Washington
Elderly and Disabled
Washington State Dental Assn.
2033 6th Ave., Suite 333
Seattle, WA 98121
206-448-1914
800-448-3368

University of Washington
School of Dentistry
Health Science Blvd. SC-62
Seattle, WA 98195
206-543-5830

West Virginia
West Virginia Dental Association
2003 Quarrier Street
Charleston, WV 25311
304-344-5246

West Virginia University
School of Dentistry
The Medical Center
P.O. Box 9400
Morgantown, WV 26506-9400
304-598-4810

Wisconsin
Wisconsin Dental Association
111 E. Wisconsin Avenue, Ste 1300
Milwaukee, WI 53202
414-276-4520
800-364-7646

Dane County Public Health Division
Dental Health Program
1202 Northport Drive
Madison, WI 53704
608-242-6510

Marquette University
School of Dentistry
604 North 16th Street
Milwaukee, WI 53233
414-288-6500

Wyoming
Wyoming Dental Association
P. O. Box #1123
Cheyenne, WY 82003
307-634-5878
800-244-0779

State Health Department
Dental Division
Hathaway Building, 4th Floor
Cheyenne, WY 82002
307-777-7945

Job Training Programs For Seniors

The government offers excellent programs aimed at helping seniors get back into the workforce. Listed below are the state offices you can contact for information about training programs in your area. When you call, ask about the *Senior Community Service Employment Program* (called Title V) and also *Job Training Partnership Act Programs* (JTPA). They offer job training, help with job searches and resume writing and more. They also offer financial assistance to companies who hire graduates of these programs.

Alabama Commission On Aging / 334-242-5743
      Department of Economic & Community Affairs / 334-242-5300
Alaska Older Alaskans Commissions / 907-465-3250
      Department of Community & Regional Affairs / 907-465-5545
Arizona Department of Economic Security / 602-542-4446
Arkansas Division of Aging & Adult Services / 501-682-2441
      Department of Labor - JTPA / 501-371-4487
California Department of Aging / 916-323-0217
      Employment Development - JPTA / 916-654-7110
Colorado Department of Labor & Employment / 303-620-4200
Connecticut Social Services/Elderly Services Division / 860-424-5274
Delaware Services For Aging & Adults w/ Disabilities / 302-577-4660
District Of Columbia Office On Aging / 202-724-7073
      Department of Employment Services / 202-724-7073
Florida Department of Elder Affairs / 800-96-ELDER
Georgia Department of Human Services / 404-657-5330
Hawaii Office On Aging / 808-586-0100
      Honolulu Community Action Program / 808-586-8813
Idaho Commission On Aging / 208-334-3833
Illinois Department On Aging / 1-800-252-8966
      Department of Commerce & Community Affairs / 217-782-7500
Indiana Disability/Rehabilitation & Aging Services / 317-232-7000
Iowa Department of Elder Affairs / 512-282-5187
Kansas Department of Aging / 913-296-4986
Kentucky Social Services/Aging Services Division / 502-564-6930
      JTPA Coordinator / 502-564-5360
Louisiana Office of Elderly Affairs / 504-342-7100
Maine Bureau of Elder Services / 207-624-5335
      Bureau of Employment Services (JPTA) / 207-624-6390
Maryland Office On Aging / 1-800-AGE-DIAL
Massachusetts Office Of Elder Affairs / 1-800-882-2003
Michigan Office of Services To The Aging / 517-373-8230
      Michigan Job Commission (JTPA) / 517-373-9808

Minnesota Board On Aging / 1-800-882-6262
Mississippi Division of Aging & Adult Services / 1-800-948-3090
Missouri Department Of Aging / 573-751-3082
     Division of Job Development (JPTA) / 1-800-877-8698
Montana Green Thumb Program / 406-761-4821
     Montana JTPA / 406-444-1309
Nebraska Department On Aging / 402-471-2307
Nevada AARP / 702-648-3356
     Nevada Business Services (JPTA) / 702-647-4929
New Hampshire AARP / 1-800-652-8808
     Job Training Council (JPTA) / 1-800-772-7001
New Jersey Division of Senior Affairs / 609-292-4833
     New Jersey Department Of Labor (JPTA) / 609-292-5005
New Mexico State Agency On Aging / 1-800-432-2080
     State Department of Labor (JPTA) / 505-827-6827
New York State Office For The Aging / 1-800-342-9871
North Carolina Division Of Aging / 919-733-3983
     DivisionOf Employment & Training JPTA) / 919-733-6383
North Dakota Aging Services Division (JPTA) / 701-328-8910
     Green Thumb / 701-258-8879
Ohio Department of Aging / 614-466-5500
     Employment Services (JPTA) / 614-466-3817
Oklahoma Aging Services Division / 405-521-2327
Oregon Department of Human Resources Seniors Div. / 503-945-6413
     JTPA Office / 503-373-1995
Pennsylvania Department of Aging / 717-783-1550
     Department of Labor & Industry (JTPA) / 717-783-0142
Rhode Island Department of Elderly Affairs / 401-222-2858
South Carolina Office On Aging / 803-253-6177
     JTPA Office / 803-737-2660
South Dakota Adult Services & Aging Division / 605-332-7991
Tennessee Commission On Aging / 615-741-2056
     Department of Labor - JTPA Office / 615-741-1031
Texas Senior Texans Employment Program / 254-776-7002
     Texas Workforce Commission (JPTA) / 512-936-0345
Utah Division Of Aging Services / 801-538-3910
     Economic Development & Training (JPTA) / 801-468-3246
Vermont Department Of Aging & Disabilities / 802-241-2400
     Vermont Training & Development / 802-524-3200
Virginia Department For The Aging / 804-662-9333
Washington Job Development & Training / 360-786-5586
West Virginia Bureau Of Senior Services / 304-558-3317
     JTPA Employment Services / 304-558-2664
Wisconsin Department of Workforce Development / 608-266-6886
Wyoming Senior Citizens Office / 307-635-1245

Colleges With Special Programs For Seniors

If you've been thinking how great it would be to go back to college either to finish your education or to get it started again, there is something very important you should know. There are colleges throughout the U.S. that offer special free or very low cost tuition programs for seniors. Many colleges let you take the courses for full college credit.

Others you take just for the fun of it. But one thing's for sure...you can't beat the price!

The listings below are by no means complete. Because of the increase in the 55 plus age group, more and more colleges are adding courses and special programs for seniors. If there is a particular college in your town that you might want to attend, call them and ask if they have any programs for seniors.

Alabama

Glasden State Community College
Admissions
PO Box 227
Gadsden, AL 35902-0227
Call: 1-205-549-8201
The minimum age is 60 and you must be a state resident
Tuition: free
There will be fees for books , parking, etc. Check with the registrar.
Courses can be taken for credit if you have a high school diploma, or a GED diploma

Jefferson State Community College
Admissions
2601 Carson Rd.
Birmingham, AL 35215-3098
Call: 1-205-853-1200
The minimum age is 60 and you must be a state resident
Tuition: $6 per credit hour.
Courses can be taken for credit

Alaska
University of Alaska Southeast
Admissions
11120 Glacier Hwy
Juneau, AK 99801
Call: 1-907-465-6457
Web site: www.jun.alaska.edu
E-mail: jyuas@acad1.alaska.edu
The minimum age is 60 and you must be a state resident
Tuition is waived, but you must sign up for class the first day it is offered. There are additional fees for student government and books
You can take unlimited classes for credit provided there is space.

Arkansas
Arkansas State University
Admissions
PO Box 1630
State University, AR 72467-1630
Call: 1-800-382-3030
Web site: www.astate.edu
E-mail:
admissions@chickasaw.astate.edu
The minimum age is 60 and you must be a state resident
The tuition is free and courses can be taken for credit
Basic fees depend on the amount of credit hours taken.

Arkansas State University
Beebe Branch
PO Drawer H
Beebe, AR 72012
Call: 1-501-882-6452
The minimum age is 60
The tuition is free, and courses can be taken for credit
There are basic fees for books, parking, etc.

California
California State University at Chico
First&Normal Streets
Chico, CA 95929
Call: 1-800-542-4426
Web site: www.csuchico.edu
E-mail: info@
oavax.csuchico.edu
The minimum age is 60 and you must be a state resident
They have a program for seniors aged 60+ for credit, open to all state residents
You pay $93.00 per semester
Fees for books and activities are extra.
They also have Elder College where students audit only. This is $45.00 per semester. Both programs are based on space available.

Colorado
Adams State College
Alamosa , CO 81102
Call: 1-719-589-7712
The minimum age is 65 and you must be a state resident. Classes can be taken with the permission of the professor. No credit is given.

University of Colorado, Boulder
Regent Administrative Center, Room 125
Campus Box 6
Boulder, CO 80309
Call: 1-303-492-6301
Web site: www.colorado.edu
E-mail: apply@colorado.edu
The minimum age is 55 and the tuition is free. No classes for credit.

University of Colorado at Denver
PO Box 173364
Campus Box 146
Denver, CO 80217-3364
Call: 1-303-556-2400
The minimum age is 60, and you must be a state resident, and part of a senior citizen program. No grade is given and tuition is free
Web site: www.cudenver.edu
E-mail:
admissions@castle.cudenuer.edu

Connecticut
University of Connecticut, Storrs
2131 Hillside Road, U-88
Storrs, CT 06269
Call:1-860-486-3137
Web Site: www.uconn.edu
E-mail:
beahusky@uconnvm.uconn.edu
The minimum age is 62 and you must be a state resident and the fees are waived. The tuition is $15.00 per semester and courses can be taken for non-academic credit.

University of Hartford Adult Services
200 Bloomfield Ave.
West Hartford, CT 06117-0395
Call: 1-860-768-4457
Web site:
www.hartford.edu/
uofhwelcome.html
E-mail:
admission@uhavax.hartford.edu
The minimum age 65 and you must be a state resident. You can audit one course free. Fees for books, activities, etc.

Delaware
Delaware Technical and Community College: Southern Campus
PO Box 610
Georgetown, DE 19947
Call: 1-302-856-5400
The minimum age is 60. They have an Adult Plus program with special interest courses. The tuition is free

District of Columbia
American University
c/o Institute for Learning Retirement
4400 Massachusetts Ave
Washington, DC 20016
Call: 1-202-885-6000
Web site: www.american.edu
E-mail: afa@american.edu
They offer non-credit -low cost

classes for retired people.
Seniors can take up to 3 classes per semester for $175.00

Florida
Florida Institute of Technology
150 W. University Blvd.
Melbourne, FL 32901
Call: 1-800-888-4348
Web site: www.fit.edu
E-mail: admissions@fit.edu
The minimum age is 65 and you can take a limited number of courses for free tuition.

Georgia
Augusta State University
2500 Walton Way
Augusta, GA 30910
Call: 1-706-737-1632
Web site: www. aug.edu
E-mail: lyoung@aug.edu
Seniors 62 and older can take courses free providing there is space available.
To study for credit you must apply and be accepted as a regular student

Piedmont College
PO Box 10
Demorest, GA 30535
Call:1-800-277-7020
Web site: www.piedmont.edu
E-mail:
jem.clement@gateway.piedmont.edu
Seniors can attend classes at discounted prices. They can also register to audit a class as a guest.

Hawaii
University of Hawaii at Manoa
2600 Campus Rd.
Honolulu, HI 96822
Call: 1-808956-8975
Web site: www.hawaii.edu/
welcome/manoa.html
Seniors can take courses free with the permission of the professor for no credit.

Idaho
Boise State University
1910 University Dr.
Boise, ID 83725
Call: 1-800-824-7017
Web site: www.idbsu.edu
E-mail - Admissions:
mwheelcrobsu.edu
The minimum age is 60 and you must be a state resident There is a $20.00 Registration fee and they can take the classes for credit The cost is $5.00 per credit.

College of Southern Idaho
Admissions PO Box 315 Falls Ave.
Twin Falls , ID 83303-1238
Call:1-208-733-9554
The minimum age is 60 and you must be a state resident. You can get a Gold Card from their Office On Aging to take classes for free. There is a fee for books, activities, and supplies. They also have a special program for seniors over 60 called "Getting Fit."

Illinois
Belleville Area College
2500 Carlyle Ave.
Belleville, IL 62221
Call: 1-618-235-2700
The minimum age is 60 and you must be a state resident. Seniors pay $38.50 per credit hour for credit courses.
If you earn less than $14,000.00 you can apply for free tuition.

Indiana
Ball State University
2000 University Ave.
Muncie, IN 47306
Call: 1-765-285-8300
They only have an Elderhostel program. It's worth checking out.

University of Southern Indiana
8600 University Blvd.
Evansville, IN 47712
Call: 1-812-464-1765
Web site: www.usi.edu
The minimum age is 65 and you must be a state resident. You can take one class per semester for $5.00

Indiana University-Purdue
Office of Admissions
University Fort Wayne
2101 East Coliseum Blvd.
Fort Wayne, IN 46805
Call: 1-219-481-6812
Web site: www.iupui.edu
E-mail: Apply@SES.1upui.edu
The minimim age is 60 and you must be a state resident who is not employed full time. You can take courses at 1/2 off the regular State resident fee. You must register during the final regustration (providing there is room). The couses can be taken for credit.
The only cost is for books.

Iowa
Iowa Western Community College Business
923 East Washington St.
Clarinda, IA 51632
Call:1-712-542-5117
The minimum age is 55 and you must be a state resident. You can attend classes for credit at a reduced tuition. The reduced rate would be equal to 1/3 of the regular hourly rate, and you are allowed three credit hours per semester.

Kansas
Baker University
PO Box 65
Baldwin City, KS66006
Call: 1-800-873-4282
Web site: www.bakeru.edu
AdmissionsE-mail:

jjohnson@harvey.bakeru.edu
The minimum age is 55 and you must be a state resident. You can take one course at a time for credit in the Arts and Sciences. All fees are waived except course supplies.

Bethany College
421 N. First
Lindsborg, KS 67456
Call: 1-800-826-2281
Web-site: www.bethanylib.edu
They offer a summer Elderhostel program for seniors.

Kentucky
Kentucky State University
400 East Main Street
Frankfort, KY 40601
Call: 1-800-325-1716
Web site: www.kysu.edu
Admissions E-mail:
idyson@gwmail.kysu.edu
The minimum age is 65 and you must be a state resident. Seniors can take courses for credit and all tuition and fees are waived.

Midway College
512 E. Stephens St
Midway, KY 40347
Web site: www.Midway.edu
Call: 1-800-755-0031
Web site: www.Midway.edu
The Lewis and Ann Piper Scholarship Program allows seniors age 60 plus (must be a state resident) to take academic courses with all fees waived including textbooks.
Women can take courses for credit or audit. Men through the Career Development School. You can take courses for audit or credit.

University of Kentucky
658 South Limestone
Ligon House
Lexington, KY 40506-0042
Call: 1-606-257-2000

Website www.uky.edu
The Donovan Scholars program offers seniors age 65 who are state residents free tuition for credit or non-credit. There are fees for books and supplies.

Louisiana
Louisiana State University at Alexandria
8100 Highway 71 South
Alexandria , LA 71302-9633
Call:1-318-473-6423
The minimum age for seniors is 65 and you must be a state resident. The tuition is waived. You pay for books, application fee and supplies. You can take courses for credit or audit the class.

Louisiana State University at Baton Rouge
Room 110 Thomas Boyd Hall
Baton Rough, LA 70803
Call: 1-504-388-1175
!-504-388-1175
The minimum age for seniors is 65 and you must be a state resident. The tuition is waived, you pay for books, application fee and supplies.

Maine
University of Maine-Augusta
46 University Drive
Augusta, ME 04330
Call: 1-207-621-3000
Web site: www.uma.maine.edu
Admissions E-mail:
umaar@maine.maine.edu
The minimum age for seniors is 65 and you must be a state resident. The tuition is waived. Books and supplies are extra.

University of Maine-Fort Kent
25 Pleasant St.
Fort Kent, ME 04743
Call: 1-888-879-8635

Web site:www.umfk.maine.edu
Admissions E-mail:
llmfkadm@maine.maine.edu
The minimum age for seniors is 65 and you must be a state resident. You can apply for a tuition waiver (must show financial need) and can take any course for credit or audit.

Maryland
St. Mary's College of Maryland
St. Mary's City, MD 20686
Call: 1-800-492-7181
Web site: www.smcm.edu
Admissions E-mail:
admissions@honors.smcm.edu
The minimum age for seniors is 60. You can take classes for credit or non credit. The tuition is waived. You pay for books, supplies, and parking.

McDaniel College
2 College Hill
Westminster, MD 21157
Call: 1-800-638-5005
Web site: www.wmdc.edu
Admissions E-mail:
admissions@ns1.wmc.car.md.us
The minimum age for seniors is 65 and a you must be a state resident. You pay $25.00 per class and can attend for credit or non-credit.

Massachusetts
Boston University
Evergreen Program
808 Commonwealth Ave.
Boston, MA 92215
Call: 1-617-353-9852
The minimum age for seniors is 60 and tuition is $20.00 per course but not for credit.

Michigan
Central Michigan University
Admissions Dept.
105 Warriner Hall

Mount Pleasant, MI 48859
Call: 1-517-774-3261
The minimum age is 60 and you must be a state resident. Tuition is free subject to available space.) No credit for the courses. There is a fee for books and supplies.

Spring Arbor College
106 E. Main
Spring Arbor, MI 49283
Call: 1-800-968-0011
Web site: www.arbor.edu
Admissions E-mail:
admissions@admin.arbor.edu
The minimum age is 65. The tuition is $25.00 per credit hour. You can take up to 7 hours in any semester. To audit, you pay $20.00 per credit.

Minnesota
Riverland Community College
1600 Eighth Ave., NW
Austin, MN 55912
Call: 1-507-433-0600
The minimum age is 62 and the cost is $9.35 per credit. You can take courses for credit.

Minnesota Universities-Twin Cities
150 Williamson Hall
231 Pillsbury Dr., SE
Minneapolis, MN 55455
Call: 612-625-5333
The minimum age is 62 and you must be a state resident. The tuition is $6.00 per credit hour, and you can take the course for credit.

Mississippi
Delta State University
Admissions Office
Cleveland, MS 38733
Call: 601-846-4018
The minimum age for seniors is 60, and you must be a state resident. The tuition is $10.00 for 1 course up to 3

credit hours; up to 15 credits @ 10.00 per 3 credits.

Mississippi Gulf Coast Community College:
Jackson County Campus Business Services
PO Box 100
Gautier, MS 39553
Call: 228-497-9602
The minimum age is 50 and you must be a state resident. They have a program for $50.00 a year where courses are given for non-credit, also with lunches and a trip once a month. You also can sign up free for regular courses for credit and pay only for books and activity fees.

Missouri
Crowder College
601 La Clede Ave.
Neosho, MO 64850
Call: 417-451-3223
The minimum age is 60, and you must be a state resident in the district. Tuition is free and courses can be taken for credit.

Missouri Western State College
4525 Downs Dr.
St. Joseph, MO 64507
Call: 816-271-4200
The minimum age is 60 and you must be a state resident. You can take courses for credit or non-credit at a 10% discounted price.

Montana
Montana Tech of the University of Montana
1300 West Park Street
Butte, MT 59701
Call: 406-496-4178
1-800-445-8324
Web site: www.mtech,edu
Admissions E-mail:
admissions@mtvms2.mtech.edu
The minimum age is 62 and you must be a state resident. The tuition

id $59.10 for 3 credit hours; $285.00 for 12 credit hours.

University of Montana
Missoula, MT 59812
Call: 406-243-6266
Web site: www.umt.edu
Admissions E-mail:
admiss@selway.umt.edu
The minimum age is 65, and you must be a state resident. They have the Golden College plan for seniors where you attend college for credit or non-credit for greatly reduced tuition. (You pay about 20%).

Nebraska
McCook Community College
1205 East Third Street
McCook, NE 69001
Call: 308-345-6303
The minimum age is 60 and you must be a state resident. The tuition is waived and courses are given for non-credit.

Mid-Plains Community College
601 State Farm Rd.
Morth Platte, NE 69101
Call: 308-532-8740
The minimum age is 60 and you must be a state resident. The tuition is free and the only cost to you would be books, activity fees and supplies.

Nevada
University of Nevada: Las Vegas
4505 S. Maryland Parkway
Las Vegas, NV 89154
Call: 895-3394 (continuing Ed)
Web site: www.univ.edu
The minimum age is 62, and you must be a state resident for at least one year, to take courses for credit.

Western Nevada Community College
2201 West College Pkwy.

Carson City, NV 89703
Call: 702-887-3138
The minimum age is 62, and you must be a state resident. The tuition is free and you can take courses for credit. Your only cost is books and lab fees.

New Hampshire
New Hampshire Technical College: Manchester
1066 Front Street
Manchester, NH 03102
Call: 603-668-6706
The minimum age is 65, and you must be a state resident. The tuition is 50% of the cost, and you can take courses for credit.

University of New Hampshire at Manchester
220 Hackett Hill Rd.
Manchester, NH 03102
Call: 603-668-0700
The minimum age is 65, and you must be a state resident. The tuition is free and you can take up to 2 courses per semester (subject to available space). The only cost would be a registration fee, books and supplies. You can take courses for credit or non-credit.

New Jersey
Bloomfield College
467 Franklin Street
Bloomfield, NJ 07003
Call: 1-800-848-4555
Web Site: www.bloomfield.edu
Admissions E-mail:
admissions@bloomfield.edu
The minimum age is 62 and you must be a state resident. You pay a $25.00 registration fee and $15.00 for the course (subject to available space). You can take the course for credit and the college sets aside a day just for seniors to register,.

Fairleigh Dickinson University
1000 River Rd
Teaneck, NJ 07666
Call: 1-800-338-8803
Web site: www.fdu.edu
Admissions E-mail:
boyer@hrserv.fdu.edu
The minimum age is 62 and a you must be a resident. You can take any course with permission from the professor. You pay $100. per course.

New Mexico
New Mexico State University at Almogordo
Admissions
2400 N. Scenic Dr.
Almogordo, NM 88310
Call: 505-439-3720
The minimum age is 65, and you must be a state resident. The tuition is $8.00 per credit hour. The basic fees are $10.00, a one time admission fee. Seniors can take courses for credit or non-credit.

New York
City University of New York
Hunter College
Admissions
695 Park Ave.
New York, NY 10021
Call: 212-772-4490
Web site: www.hunter.cuny.edu
The minimum age is 60 and you must be a state resident. A senior can audit any 2 classes for a fee of $70.00 per semester.

SUNY Purchase
735 Anderson Hill Road
Purchase, NY 10577
Call: (914) 251-6300
Web Site: www.purchase.edu
The minimum age is 62. Each semester there is one day seniors can register for classes. You pay

$50.00 to audit classes, provided there is room in the class. The registration for seniors is usually after full-tuition paying students have registered for their classes.

Wells College
Route 90
Aurora, NY 13026
Call: 1-800- 052-9355
Web site: www.wells.edu
Seniors can audit any course for free provided there is room in the class.

North Carolina
High Point University
University Station
Montilieu Ave
High Point, NC 27262
Call: 1-800-345-6993
Web site: www.highpoint.edu
Seniors can audit classes for 1/2 price.

Appalachian State University
Boone,NC 28608
Call: 262-2120
Web site: www.appstate.edu
The minimum age is 65 and you must be a state resident. You can take courses free for crediit or non-credit. There are fees for books, supplies, activities.

North Dakota
North Dakota State University
PO Box 5454
Fargo, ND 58105
Call: 231-7981
Web site: www.ndsu.nodak.edu
They have a"Project 65" program, where seniors age 65+ can audit classes for free. Tuition and related fees are waived, however there is a $25.00 application fee.

Ohio
Lake Erie College
391 W. Washington Street

Painesville, OH 44077
Call: 1-800-533-4996
Web site: www.lakeerie.edu
Seniors can audit any course for free (no credit), provided there is room in the class.

Bowling Green State University
Dept of Continuing Education
McFall Center
40 College Park
Bowling Green, OH 43403
Call: 372-2086
They have a program for seniors called the "Sage Program", where seniors age 60 can take any courses free (subject to available space) paying only fees for books, supplies, labs. No credit is given.

Oklahoma
Oklahoma State University
104 Whitehurse
Stillwater, OK 74078
Call: 744-6858
Web site: www.okstate.edu
The minimum age for seniors is 65. You can audit any course for free (no credit).There is a fee for books and other supplies .

Oregon
University of Oregon
1217 University of Oregon
Eugene, OR 97403
Call: 1-800-232-3825
Web site: www.uoregon.edu
The minimum age for seniors is 62, and you can audit any class for free but not for credit.

Oregon Institute of Technology
3201 Campus Drive
Klamath Falls , OR 97601
Call: 1-800-422-2017
Web site: www.oit.edu
The minimum age for seniors is 65. You can take courses for free tuition.

The classes can be for credit or non-credit. They also run an Elderhostel Program throughout the year.

Pennsylvania
University of Pennsylvania
3440 Market Street
Suite 100
Philadelphia, PA 19104
Call: 215-898-3526
The minimum age is 65 and they offer courses for seniors for a donation depending on the number of classes taken.

University of Pittsburgh-Bradford
Auxiliary Services
300 Campus Drive
Bradford, PA 16701
Call: 1-800-872-1787
Web site: www.upb.pitt.edu
Seniors are eligible to take non-credit courses for a discounted fee (call to check). They must be at least 65 and a state resident.

Rhode Island
Rhode Island College
600 Mt. Pleasant Ave.
Providence, RI 02908
Call: 401-456-8090
Seniors who are at least 60 and residents of the State, may enroll for free tuition in the 'Seniors Mean Test Program'. They must supply certain tax forms.

South Carolina
Clemson University
Business Office
105 Sikes Hall
Clemson, SC 29634-5307
Call: 864-656-5592
Web site: www.clemson.edu
The minimum age for seniors is 60 and you must be a state resident (age

must be verified). They can audit or take any course (space available) for free tuition. Books and supplies are additional.

South Dakota
Dakota Wesleyan University
1200 W. University Avenue
Mitchell, SD 57301
Call: 1-800-333-8506
Web site: www.dwu.edu
Seniors age 62 or older can enroll in their Blue and White Club program which enables them to audit any classes (subject to available space) for free tuition.

Tennessee
Tennessee State University
3500 John Merritt Boulevard
Nashville, TN 37209
Call: 615- 963-5105
Web site: www.tnstate.edu
The minimum age for seniors is 65 and they must be residents of the State. They pay$75.00 for the semester.

Texas
University of Houston
Central Campus
Financial Services
Houston, TX 77204-2160
Call: 713-743-1096
The minimum age for seniors is 65 , and they must be a State resident. The tuition is free and they can take courses for no credit.

University of North Texas
PO Box 13797
Denton, TX 76203
Call: 817-565-2165
The minimum age for seniors is 65 and they can take classes for no credit , tuition free.

Utah
Brigham Young University
BYU Evening Classes
122 Harman Bldg.
Provo, UT 84602
Call: 801- 378-2872
Web site: www.byu.edu
The minimum age is 55, and they must be a State resident. The tuition is $10.00 per class and they can take any course but not for credit.

Utah State University
Registrar
Logan, UT 84322-1600
Call: 797-1128 (Summer program for seniors)
!-800- 606-4878
Web site: www.usu.edu
The minimum age is 62 and a resident of the State. The tuition is $10.00 per class, and no credit is given.

Vermont
Castleton State College
Business Office
Castleton, VT 05735
Call: 1-800-639-8521
Web site: www.csc.vsc.edu
Any senior 62 or older receiving retirement benefits can take any course for credit for $78.00 for 3 credits.

Virginia
Clinch Valley College of the University of Virginia
Admissions
College Ave.
Wise, VA 24293
Call: 1-888-282-9324
Web site: www.clinch.edu
Seniors age 60 plus, residents of Virginia (if taxable income does not exceed $10,000) can take courses for free. Any senior can audit or take non-credit courses for free.

College of William and Mary
Registrars Office
PO Box 8795
Williamsburg , VA 23187
Call: 257-221-2800
Web site: www.wm.edu
Any senior 60 years or older and a State resident can audit classes for non credit free. If they want to take classes for credit, the tuition will be waived for them according to their income.

Washington
University of Washington
Access Program
5001 25th Ave., NE
Seattle, WA 98195
Call:206-543-2320
Web site: www.wsu.edu
The minimium age for seniors is 60 and you must be a state resident. You can audit 1 or 2 classes, space permitting. You pay only a small registration fee and a small technology fee.

West Virginia
West Virginia State College
PO Box 1000
Institute, WV 25112
 Call: 304-766-3221
Web site:
www.wvsc.wvnet.edu.wvsc.html
Seniors aged 60 or older can audit classes for non-credit for free tuition, providing space is available in the class.

Wisconsin
University of Wisconsin-Milwaukee
PO Box 413
Milwaukee, WI 53201
Call: 414-229-4481
Web site: www.uwm.edu
Anyone is able to audit classes for reduced tuition. Call for more information.

Wyoming
University of Wyoming
PO Box 3314, Old Main 321
Laramie, WY 82071
Call:307-766-5160
The minimum age for seniors is 65, and you must be a state resident. Courses can be taken for credit or non-credit and the tuition is free. There is a fee for books, supplies and computers.

Nursing Home Complaints

In each state there's someone with the strange sounding title of 'Long-Term Care Ombudsman' to investigate your nursing home complaints. This person acts on behalf of nursing home residents, and mediates disputes between nursing homes and residents or their families. Ombudsman are also ready to help if you need information on the nursing homes in your state, or if you have a complaint about a particular nursing home.

Alabama .... (334) 242-5743
Alaska .... (907) 334-4480
Arizona .... (602) 542-4446
Arkansas .... (501) 682-2441
California .... (916) 323-6681
Colorado .... (303) 722-0300
Connecticut .... (860) 424-5200
Delaware..(302) 453-3820 ext 46
Dist. of Columbia .... (202) 434-2140
Florida.. (850) 488-6190
Georgia .... (404) 657-5319
Hawaii... (808) 586-0100
Idaho .... (208) 334-3833
Iowa .... (515) 242-8643
Illinois... (217) 785-3143
Indiana .... (317) 232-1750
Kansas... (785) 296-3017
Kentucky.. (502) 564-6930
Louisiana .... (504) 342-7100
Maine .... (207) 621-1079

Maryland .... (410) 767-1074
Massachusetts .... (617) 727-7750
Michigan .... (517) 886-6797
Minnesota .... (651) 296-0382
Mississippi .... (601) 359-4929
Missouri .... (573) 526-0729
Montana .... (406) 444-4077
Nebraska .... (402) 471-2306
Nevada .... (702) 486-3545
New Hampshire .... (603) 271-4375
New Jersey .... (609) 588-3614
New Mexico .... (505) 827-7640
New York .... (518) 474-7329
North Carolina .... (919) 733-8395
North Dakota .... (701) 328-8910
Ohio .... (614) 466-7922
Oklahoma .... (405) 521-6734
Oregon .... (503) 378-6533
Pennsylvania .... (717) 733-7247
Rhode Island .... (401) 785-3340
South Carolina .... (803) 253-6177
South Dakota .... (605) 773-3656
Tennessee .... (615) 741-2056
Texas .... (515) 424-6840
Utah .... (801) 538-3910
Vermont .... (802) 863-5620
Virginia .... (804) 644-2923
Washington .... (253) 838-6810
West Virginia .... (304) 558 -3317
Wisconsin .... (608) 266-8945
Wyoming .... (307) 322-5553
Puerto Rico .... (787) 725-1515

free Help from Your State Government

The state governments of 49 of the 50 states have a phone number you can call if you are having problems or need the assistance of a state agency. For example, let's say you have a housing problem or a consumer complaint and don't know where to turn. By calling the phone number listed for your state, you will be referred directly to the state agency in your area that can help you solve the problem you are having.

Alabama	334-242-8000
Alaska	907-465-2111
Arizona	602-542-4900
Arkansas	501-682-3000
California .... Northern	916-322-9900
Southern	213-620-3030
Colorado	303-866-5000
In Colorado, call	800-332-1716
Connecticut	860-566-2211
Delaware	302-856-5011
In DE Only	800-273-9500
Florida	850-488-1234
Georgia	404-656-2000
Hawaii	808-586-0222
Outer Islands Only	800-468-4644
Idaho	208-334-2411
Illinois	217-782-2000
Indiana	317-233-0800
In Indiana call	800-457-8283
Iowa	515-281-5011
Kansas	785-296-0111
Kentucky	502-564-3130
Louisiana	504-342-6600

Maine 207-582-9500
Maryland ....While state information number no longer exists,
if directory assistance cannot help, call the Governor's office at:...410-974-3901
Massachusetts 617-727-7030
In Massachusetts only, call 800-392-6090
Michigan 517-373-1837
Minnesota 612-296-6013
Mississippi 601-359-1000
Missouri 573-751-2000
Montana 406-444-2511
Nebraska 402-471-2311
Nevada 702-687-5000
New Hampshire 603-271-1110
New Jersey 609-292-2121
New Mexico 505-827-4011
New York 518-474-2121
North Carolina 919-733-1110
North Dakota 701-328-2000
Ohio 614-466-2000
Oklahoma 405-521-2011
Oregon ....State information number no longer exists.
Must know the specific state office.
Pennsylvania 717-787-2121
Rhode Island 401-277-2000
South Carolina 803-734-1000
South Dakota 605-773-3011
Tennessee 615-741-3011
Texas 512-463-4630
Utah 801-538-3000
Vermont 802-828-1110
Virginia 804-786-0000
Washington 360-753-5000
In Washington only call 800-321-2808
West Virginia 304-558-3456
Wisconsin 608-266-2211
Wyoming 307-777-5910

U.S. Government Hotlines

Administration on Aging 202-401-4541

Federal Information Center (for all the U.S.) 800-688-9889

Food and Drug Administration 301-827-4420

Health Care Fraud Hot Line 800-447-8477

IRS – US Department of the Treasury Information Line 800-829-1040

   Forms Line 800-829-3676

   Tele-Tax Line 800-829-4477

Lawyers' Fund for Client Protection 518-474-8438

   New York State Only 800-442-3863

Legal Services Corporation 202-336-8800

Medicare Hot Line 800-638-6833
   TTY-TTD 800-820-1202

Social Security Administration Hot Line 800-772-1213
   TTY 800-325-0778

US Department of Veterans Affairs 800-827-1000

US Department of Housing & Urban Development/
   Public Affairs Offiice 202-708-1420

Nationwide Helplines

Alliance for Aging Research	202-293-2856
Alliance For Retired Americans	202-974-8222
Alzheimer's Association	800-272-3900
Alzheimer's Disease Education and Referral Center	800-438-4380
American Association of Retired Persons (AARP)	800-424-3410
American Assoc. of Homes & Services for the Aging	202-783-2242
For publications call	800-508-9442
American Association of Retired Persons	800-424-3410
American Cancer Society Response Hot Line	800-227-2345
American Council for the Blind	800-424-8666
American Diabetes Association	800-342-2383
American Diabetes Foundation	800-232-3472
American Heart Association	800-242-8721
American Institute For Cancer Research	800-843-8114
American Lung Association	800-586-4872
Arthritis Foundation Information Line	800-283-7800
Asthma and Allergy Foundation	800-7-ASTHMA
Bell Atlantic LifeLine Service	800-555-5000
Bladder Control for Women Hotline	800-891-5388
Brookdale Center on Aging	800-647-8233
Cancer Care	800-813-4673
Cancer Information Service.	800-4-CANCER
Complementary and Alternative Medicine Hotline	888-644-6226
Deafness & Other Communication Disorders Hotline	800-241-1044
Domestic Violence Hotline	800-799-7233
Elder Abuse Hotline	800-252-8966
Eldercare Locator	800-677-1116
Epilepsy Foundation	800-332-1000
Equal Employment Opportunity Commission	800-669-4000
Family Violence Information	800-537-2237

Gray Panthers 800-280-5362

Grief Recovery Institute 800-445-4808

Help for Incontinent People 800-252-3337

Hill-Burton Hot Line (if you need help with hospital costs) . 800-492-0359

Leukemia & Lymphoma Society 800-955-4572

Lighthouse Center for Vision and Aging 800-334-5497

Medicare Hotline 800-638-6833

National AIDS Hot Line 800-342-2437

National Alliance of Breast Cancer Organizations 888-806-2226

National Alliance for the Mentally Ill 800-950-6264

National Breast Cancer Coalition 202-296-7477

National Cancer Institute 800-422-6237

National Caregiving Foundation 800-930-1357

National Center on Elder Abuse 202-898-2586

National Citizens' Coalition for Nursing Home Reform 202-332-2275

National Clearinghouse for Alcohol & Drug Info. 800-729-6686

National Committee to Preserve Social Security & Medicare . 800-729-6686

National Council of Senior Citizens 301-578-8800

National Diabetes Information Clearinghouse 800-860-8747

National Digestive Disease Clearinghouse 301-654-3810

National Eye Care Project Helpline 800-222-3937

National Health Information Center 800-336-4797

National Hospice Organization 800-658-8898

National Institute on Aging 800-222-2225

National Institute of Mental Health 800-421-4211

National Institute of Neurological & Stroke Disorders 800-352-9424

National Insurance Consumer Helpline 800-942-4242

National Kidney & Urological Disease Clearinghouse 301-654-4415

Parkinson's Disease Foundation 800-457-6676

Poison Control Center 800-764-7661

Skin Cancer Foundation 800-SKIN-490

Stuttering Foundation of America 800-992-9392

Sudden Infant Death Syndrome Hotline 800-505-2742

Weight Control Hotline 877-946-4627

Y-ME National Breast Cancer Organization 800-221-2141